They Live by the Wind

They Live by the Wind

The Lore and Romance
of the last Sailing Workboats:
The Grand Banks Schooners,
the Square-Rigged Training Ships,
the Chesapeake Oysterboats,
the Fishing Sloops of the Bahamas by

Wendell P. Bradley

With an Introduction by Howard I. Chapelle
Alfred A. Knopf   New York   1969

PUBLISHER'S NOTE

When Mr. Bradley suffered his untimely fatal accident in July 1967, he had finished three of the four sections of this book and was at work on "The Oystermen of Chesapeake Bay." This portion of the book has been made up of the author's text written specifically for this volume and from articles published in THE WASH-INGTON POST *which he had intended to use in his final draft.*

Contents

Illustrations

following page 46

The start of the tall ships' race from Lisbon to Bermuda
Photograph by Erich Hartmann

The view from aloft
Photograph by the author

The *Statsraad Lehmkuhl*
Photograph by Hans Marx

Second Mate Eric Bernes
Photograph by John Sibley

The *Elcano*
Photograph by John Sibley

The *Libertad* working her way to windward
Photograph by John Sibley; courtesy of The New York Times

The cadets haul in the fore lower topsail brace
Photograph by John Sibley

The *Statsraad Lehmukl* in New York harbor
Photograph by Theodore Donaldson

The *Danmark*
Photograph by the Port of New York Authority

Alfred Bain
Photograph by the author

Dinghy racing
Courtesy of Bahamas News Bureau

Thunderbird tacking
Courtesy of Bahamas News Bureau

Line Drawings

Introduction

The rapid disappearance of commercial sailing craft in all parts of the world has made it imperative that records of their characteristics in design, construction, and particularly in their handling qualities be preserved. Also, it is important that we obtain some picture of the men that sailed them. There is no need to "prove" this, for it is a very important part of maritime history, marine archeology, and technological history too, as is so well shown in this book.

As each type approaches its end, it becomes increasingly important that deliberate efforts be made by yachtsmen to sail an example of a type and to learn how to handle her, as will be apparent here. Then judgments can be formed and, sometimes at least, it might be that the "workboat," highly specialized for her trade and locality, will show herself to be superior to a far more expensive sailing yacht.

In this book there are fine accounts of sailing large, square-rigged training vessels, fishing schooners, Chesapeake Bay oyster dredges, and Bahama sloops. In addition, there are excellent character sketches of men that sailed them and descriptions of the culture that produced them.

It is true that no complete account of the New England or

Canadian fishing schooners can be written without dwelling upon the proclivities of their skippers to carry sail in heavy weather. This in part was the product of the short stories of the great Gloucester writer, James B. Connolly. He glorified the "hard-driving" skippers with the result that not only did the skippers believe their press images but also he could not take a trip on a Gloucesterman without being shown that her skipper was a great sail carrier, and having the wits frightened out of him.

The vessels were built and rigged for hard sailing but, in spite of this, loss of spars and gear was common and a source of heavy expense to the owners of the vessels. Toward the end, the owners would not build a vessel whose model showed that she would stand up under a hard press of sail—that is, would not heel easily—which would produce broken spars, torn sails, and damaged rigging. The emphasis on speed was great, after 1850, but the schooners were not stiff under a press of sail in strong winds until the late 1880's, when increased depth, heavy ballasting, and a suitable model made great stiffness possible. The author has captured the atmosphere of these schooners' hard driving in the descriptions of the International Fishermen's Races.

The chapter on the Chesapeake Bay is a pleasure to read—if you have visited for a long time, or have lived, on the Eastern Shore. Although the distinctive culture and economy of the Shore is rapidly disappearing, you can still find isolated areas where recognizable vestiges remain, producing an independent, sophisticated population—part farmer, part sailor, part fisherman, part boatbuilder or engine mechanic. The house may need paint but the boat—never.

Skipjacks must be good sailers to be good dredges. Not all are—but most have a good turn of speed and will sail very well to windward. They are all over-sparred and over-canvassed so that they can work in light winds. Hence the reef points, three or four rows of them, are for use, not looks. When the wind picks up, the jib comes in and reefing starts. I have seen reefs taken in and let out six times in nine hours—fluky winds, of course. But "progress" will put an end to the sailing "drudges" within a few years, so if you wish to see the last stand of commercial sail in the United States, visit the Eastern Shore soon.

Having lived and sailed in the Bahamas I recommend the author's description of sailing in the Islands. The boats have much of the character of early nineteenth-century craft in model and construction, and many are very smart sailers, handling easily—if you know your boat. An ideal sailing country, with trade winds and much good weather, the Bahamas have rapidly become very popular with tourists. As a result, the sailing workboats of the Islands will soon be replaced by the manufactured, not built, boats of the American waterways. The trouble with this book is that it makes you yearn to again sail the small sailing commercial craft that soon will be gone, if not forgotten.

HOWARD I. CHAPELLE
Senior Historian, Smithsonian Institution
December 1968

They Live by the Wind

Prologue

The streams of air that once drove ships around the earth have been superseded by machinery, and now the balmy and agreeable trades, the Roaring Forties, the easterlies, the westerlies are empty except for flights of birds.

We have sacrificed many things of beauty to the machine—among the most beautiful, the sailing vessel—and with them we have thrown away a relationship to nature and to danger and uncertainty, which made sea life, at least, a dashing and sportive pursuit.

But the conquest is not universal yet. In a few places in the world, sailing men still thrive—the last of those subtle artisans who, down through the centuries, caused their ships to travel through the sea not by pressing buttons on noisy engines but by a delicate conspiracy with the invisible winds. When they disappear, much of the art of seamanship will go with them, for it does not take much art to start an engine or plot a course with radar. The men who go to sea in today's electronic marvels have lost the keen eye, the quick sixth sense, the feeling for wind and water that the sailing men possess.

They have lost also the sailing men's delight in their calling. The wind has an ability, almost like alcohol or drugs, to intoxicate. The wind freshens, the boat becomes lively, the people on board feel excitement—a little fear perhaps, if it really blows hard, but if so, elation with the fear. Every time the wind blows harder this happens—in any sailing vessel, large or small, which is why, I think, sailing men are enamored of their occupation. Once I was out with a friend, Dave Faulkner of Tilghman Island, Maryland, on his skipjack in a squally northwester, with the wind gusting to forty and forty-five miles an hour—a wind that kept all the other oysterboats of Tilghman ashore—and as he brought the skipjack about to make another run across an oyster bed, he turned to me and yelled above the sound of the wind, "Man, I love this. I love this."

I remember hearing an old sea captain from Maine say two or three years ago that he had commanded eight of Maine's big Down East schooners and after that, eight freighters. He said that every time he left one of the schooners he stood at the gangplank, looked back at the ship, patted her rail, and wished her luck. He said when he left one of the freighters he packed his bag and walked up the pier without looking back. Floating warehouses, he called them.

Erik Bernes, of Farsund, Norway, owned and captained the last three-masted cargo schooner in the Baltic. When at last he was forced to give her up in 1962, he applied for a job on the barque *Statsraad Lehmkuhl,* a Norwegian school ship. He was told there were no openings for a captain or a first mate. The only available berth was the second mate's. "Yah, I take that," Bernes said. "Oh no, not you, a captain," the secretary of the school-ship association protested. "Yah, I take it," Bernes said, preferring a second mate's berth on a square-rigger to a captain's berth in steam.

My aim with this book is to make a record, while it is still possible, of the lives, thoughts, and feelings of this species of man, the working sailor, who watches the weather and lives by the wind, a species that has become almost extinct. I would claim for this record as much importance as an anthropologist's research concerning a primitive society, because this material deals with one of the most beautiful creations of man, the sailing vessel; because it deals with a significant activity in the history of mankind down almost to the present moment; and because if the story isn't captured now it may be lost forever.

It is correct, I think, to consider these sailing men members of a distinct culture, significant both in its impact on the civilizations of the world and in the number of people it comprised. Taking the United States alone, the beautiful coastal towns of Maine would not be in the same form if it had not been for the age of sail, nor would Chestnut Street in Salem, Massachusetts— which has been called the most beautiful street, architecturally, in America—exist, nor would the character of the Eastern Shore of Maryland be distinguishable from other areas. This culture created enclaves of people around the edges of all the continents whose lives and livelihoods depended on nothing more substantial than the winds. These people made up most or a major part of the populations of New England, Norway, the Malay States, Polynesia, large sections of Japan, and almost every other country with a coastline.

Their role in history can scarcely be overestimated. Sailing men were responsible for almost all of Western man's discoveries beyond his own borders. They are responsible for the incredible spread of the Polynesian race from Asia across the Pacific almost to South America. They transported the world's goods, caught its fish and whales, and fought its naval wars from the beginning of civilization down to three or four generations ago.

The culture was and, to the extent it survives, is international. Taking a boat from A to B is exactly the same in the Indian Ocean as it is in Long Island Sound. A seaman from Chesapeake Bay would be at home in a Chinese junk, just as the Nigger of the Narcissus, a West Indian, was at home in a British square-rigger, and Queequeg, a Pacific islander, was at home in a New England whaler. The large Portuguese population of the Providence–New Bedford area is there because American whalers recruited Azoreans—skilled members of the same culture—to help them sail their ships; the Italian population of Gloucester and the Greek population around Tampa came to those places not to learn a new way of life but as members of the culture that existed there—a culture they shared with the people of Gloucester and Tampa that was in many ways of more importance than the differences of religion, language, background.

A sailor from Chesapeake Bay, besides being able to sail a Chinese junk, would find in the village life, tools, folklore, prejudices, and ideals of a Chinese coastal community similarities to the village life, tools, folklore, prejudices, and ideals of a Chesapeake Bay coastal community.

This universality of the culture means, I believe, that when you describe one branch, you are throwing light on the culture as a whole. This book describes four important branches of the sailing culture, and in so doing, it seems to me, makes four approaches to the same thing—an understanding of a single people scattered all around the earth. They might be lumped together as a people who watch the weather and live by the wind.

In this book I will tell you of the last fleet of sailing workboats in the United States, the skipjacks of Chesapeake Bay, of the men who sail them, and of the racing they engage in. I will tell you what it is like to race a modern square-rigged ship across the Atlantic. I will tell you of the Bahamians, a gifted race of sailors, one of the most gifted, who travel the thousands of square miles of ocean of their country without charts and often without compasses as well, and of their fiercely contested encounters in the annual three-day Out Island Regatta. I will describe the Grand Banks fishery and a famous series of races between the Canadian schooner *Bluenose* and her opponents from Gloucester, Massachusetts.

I think that when you have read of these four branches you will know the culture. I am not saying you will know the Vikings or Sir Francis Drake or Captain Cook. I am saying that the people in this book have bonds with them that we have lost. Drake's "The winds command, I must sail," is related to what an old oysterman of Chesapeake Bay, Millard Price, said to me on his skipjack one day, "I've seen the time I'd rather sail than eat."

I thought it worthwhile to study their culture to find out if what we gained is worth what we lost when we gave up our old relationship to nature in favor of technology. No one can argue that taking one of Standard Oil's super tankers from one port to another is not more comfortable, pleasanter in terms of lack of hardship, than beating a square-rigger across the Atlantic was a hundred years ago. We have the advantage there all right, but the only tankerman I know told me the distinguishing attribute of life aboard a tanker is boredom.

The most noticeable attributes of the culture I studied are the love of the men in it for what they are doing, the pride and delight they feel in their skills and in the excellencies of their vessels, the combining in their lives of vocation and avocation. They are engaged in an activity that requires self-reliance, courage, independence, stubbornness. It is an activity that preserves for them a comprehensible and comfortable relation with their environment. They can feel an identification with their work that has been largely lost, I judge, in the urban culture that is spreading rapidly around the world.

This is not a book about the sea, nor about boats or ships, but about people. The great works of imaginative research, such as, preeminently, Howard I. Chapelle's *The History of American Sailing Ships,* and his *The Search for Speed under Sail,* have preserved the lines, the details of construction, the evolution of the sailing vessels, and the beautiful and ingenious technology of the sailing days. I hope I have done the same thing on a smaller scale with the human part of the subject—to preserve a picture of what kind of men the sailing men were, what they thought about, what excited them, what they felt like handling the magnificent vessels Chapelle describes. Other books will tell you how long the main topmast on a square-rigger is; I will tell you what it is like to sail her, how it feels to take her through a gale.

I emphasize the working sailors' love of racing because it is their most spectacular trait. Their passion for sailing, their possessiveness about their vessels, and their absorption in the details of their calling are vividly displayed when they race. Anything that can be done to make the ship go faster is done; all the sails are watched, all are experimented with until everyone with any say about them is sure they are set perfectly; if it is blowing hard, sails that an earlier prudence caused to be taken in are set again, and if the wind is light, old remedies—whistling for a breeze, tossing a coin overboard—are tried, prayers are said, the horizon all around and each cloud in the sky are searched for signs of wind.

Alan Villiers, who sailed in the grain ships thirty years ago when they raced once a year from Australia to England, wrote that "sailing ships always have raced; while two survive, they always will." And this is true, true of two small pleasure boats out on an afternoon who happen to meet sailing home and invariably make a race of it, although no formal race is called; of the oystermen on Chesapeake Bay, or the fishermen of the Bahamas matching their sloops on the run to the market at Nassau; and, at its most dramatic, when two square-rigged ships are in sight of each other headed the same way. "Sail ho!" the man at the masthead cries, and from then until either the sail disappears ahead or is dropped over the horizon astern, the men on board are not Navy men or whaling men or trading men or sealers, are not sailmakers or carpenters or bo's'ns or cooks, they are racers.

All the winds that ever blew into all the sails that were ever made from the beginning of civilization to the present day left no mark at all upon the earth. They blew, they filled a sail, they pushed a boat, but after they had done their work, the earth remained the same.

Perhaps this is the cause of the affection of many landsmen for the art of sailing. Its contrast to our destructive ways ashore

may be the source of its allure: for of all the technological con-
trivances ever made by man, the sailing vessel may be the only
one to play an important part in history without in any way
disturbing the natural environment.

Part One
The Deepwater Sailors
of the Square-Rigged Training Ships

I

Merchant fleets and navies have been as subject to the inroads of automation as any activity on the land, and, one by one, the skills that once made seamanship a challenging kind of work have become obsolete. Yet, instead of throwing away those skills, which took a thousand years of seafaring to perfect, most of the maritime nations of the world still insist on their mastery. The nations that entered their training ships in the Lisbon–Bermuda race in 1964, and a dozen others whose ships were busy elsewhere, think it wise that those who will spend a lifetime on the sea know how winds and waves behave. Their idea is to make seamen first and technicians afterward. On a steamship, the senses are blunted by machinery. On a sailing ship they are sharpened—for one must learn the secrets of the sea's behavior or fail to make a passage.

Henry Adams said in 1862, "Man has mounted science and is now run away with. I firmly believe that before many centuries more, science will become the master of man. The engines he will have invented will be beyond his strength to control." That danger is obviated on the sea, no matter how automated ships become, so long as seamen stay in touch with their heritage. For instance, as long as the sailor knows how to navigate by sun and stars and log line, he will maintain a proper (and dignified) relationship with the electronic devices that have taken over many of the functions of the navigator. He can use these devices, but he is not their slave.

The landsman might ponder, with profit, the sailor's refusal to give over his ancient knowledge of the sea to a machine. We on the land have embraced the new and thrown out the old with such abandon that today many of us, disassociated from our past, face the future with foreboding. Social scientists talk of modern man's loss of identity, of selfhood, in a world dominated by the giant technological apparatus he has created yet finds alien; they find a bored, restless, aggressive, and frustrated public. For those on the land concerned with preventing such a consequence, there may be a lesson in the seaman's deliberate retention of an outmoded form of transport, the square-rigger, as a means of keeping alive his relationship with his past.

Most of the approximately thirty square-rigged training ships in the world are steel vessels between two hundred and three hundred feet long. All but two or three of them were built specifically as school ships, the most recent being the German barque, *Gorch Fock,* built in 1958, the Indonesian barkentine, *Dewarutji,* built in 1952, the Argentine full-rigged ship, *Libertad,* built in 1962, and the British schooner, *Sir Winston Churchill,* built in 1965. Cadets trained aboard the school ships are usually Navy or merchant marine officer candidates or, in the case of the American barque, *Eagle,* Coast Guard officer candidates. But the Germans also train petty officers aboard the *Gorch Fock,* and the Norwegians use their three square-riggers to train future merchant seamen. The British use the *Sir Winston Churchill* to take many boys to sea on short cruises—most of whom do not plan to make the sea a career.

Regular training cruises last from between two and six months a year. Cadets are taught navigation, helmsmanship, marlinspike seamanship, the use of electronic equipment, and engine-room procedures (all square-rigged school ships have auxiliary engines). They are also taught the art of sailing.

When Captain Knud Hansen, considered by many to be the greatest sailing school ship captain in the world, brought his merchant marine training vessel, *Danmark,* to Washington several years ago, reporters asked him why training in sail is of any use to men who will spend their lives in power-driven vessels.

"Because on a sailing ship you have a little taste of emergency every day," Hansen replied. "The sea will handle atomic-powered ships just as it does us. It is not for the ordinary day that this training is, but for bad weather. That is when you need good seamen."

Captain Hansen has trained most of the officers in the Danish merchant marine since he took command of the *Danmark* in 1936, and he has sailed his ship more than half a million miles. He is responsible not only for keeping the art of deep-water sailing in square-riggers alive in Denmark, he is responsible also for reviving that art in the United States. It had become defunct when he arrived in this country in the *Danmark* in the early days of World War II. All during the war, while his country was occupied by the Germans, he trained American Coast Guardsmen in the *Danmark,* and as a result the United States has hundreds of officers and enlisted men who have had experience on square-riggers. After Captain Hansen's departure at the end of the war, the tradition he revived was carried on in the *Eagle,* which the Coast Guard acquired in 1946.

When Captain Hansen visited Washington several years ago in the *Danmark,* he was engaged in a long-distance fight with a committee of influential businessmen in Denmark who were attempting to cut down the length of the *Danmark's* cruises on grounds that they were a waste of government funds.

"They want to take away the fundamentals in favor of more training in modern instruments," Captain Hansen said then. "I tell them that it takes no time to learn the instruments, but a lot of time to build a man. And ships are no better than the men who sail them.

"The funny thing is, when I meet with the committee, all men of substantial reputations on shore, they spend most of the time boasting about their youth in sailing ships.

"They raise their voices and put their chests a little out in front of the big stomachs that have developed and tell about the old days of sail. I tell them, 'Look, gentlemen, you are going to deprive our youngsters of just what you recall so fondly.' "

Captain Hansen believes that the justifications for sail training are overwhelming: in the daily work in a sailing ship, day and night, in fair weather and foul, a cadet is challenged in countless ways; he must learn to rely on himself and on his shipmates; he must do his tasks well; smart handling of the sails requires teamwork, self-discipline, and self-confidence; good helmsmanship requires alertness, concentration, and an understanding of winds and waves.

The same lessons are not learned in a motorship, Captain Hansen believes, because a motorship's performance depends on its engine, not its crew. "A future officer—what do you expect of him? What kind of man? What qualifications?

"What makes a leader nervous? If you look at one of today's big merchant ships and know how many millions of dollars it cost, you wonder about that.

"There are no end of qualifications. Intelligence is one thing. He must be able to use his head and his hands. And he must have a feeling of responsibility for shipmates, ship, passengers, and cargo.

"This man you are going to put in charge of your multi-million-dollar ship—he must be a fireman, a doctor, a judge, and a policeman, and when mental trouble develops, a minister. He must have judgment, and he must have self-confidence. How in the world do you get these qualities without training—and not on the blackboard, but in real life?"

Maldwin Drummond, of the Sail Training Association of England, would justify experience in a square-rigger for precisely the reason sail-training opponents argue that it serves no purpose. "The more automated a Navy or merchant marine becomes," Drummond says, "the more valuable sail training becomes."

The Sail Training Association's purpose is to encourage sail training all over the world. It has sponsored biannual races, such as the Lisbon–Bermuda Race of 1964 and the Plymouth–Copenhagen Race of 1966, since 1956.

"As ships become more automated," Drummond says, "the people in them become more mechanized, more part of a mechanized whole. But people are not mechanized. The advantage of sail training is that sailing is an attempt to conquer a basic element without the aid of artificial powers and to do so in a way that requires the best of everyone, working as a team. The operation of a sailing ship requires skill and intelligence. It requires initiative. It is, therefore, a most valuable antidote to the increasing routinization of life at sea."

Captain Hansen spent fourteen years in cargo-carrying sailing vessels and ten years in steam before assuming command of the *Danmark* in 1936. Like most of the men of the last few generations who lived through the transition from the age of sail to the age of steam, his affection stayed with the sailing ship— even during the ten years he was in steam.

"It is sad, very sad, to see the sailing ship disappear," he said during his visit to Washington. "Future generations will miss something. When you have been bucking head winds for days and making no headway and then it clears and the sun comes out, the wind shifts and soon you are driving along at ten knots —well, in steamships you don't have anything like the feeling that comes over you then."

II

Every two years the square-rigged training ships of the world crowd into some historic port of Europe, and once more drying sails, tall masts, and long bowsprits overhanging ancient cobbled quayside streets reincarnate the days of pageantry of Western man: Ferdinand and Isabella commissioning the Genoese to sail westward to the Orient; Prince Henry the Navigator sending his mariners to the edges of the oceans; the English swashbuckling up and down the Spanish main, along the trade routes, around the globe; merchantmen of England, France, Holland, Portugal, ornately carved, banners flying, bringing to the ports of Europe the aromas of the East. And later, in the magnificent achievement of commercial sail, the long, low, overcanvassed clippers of a century ago, racing home from China filled with tea, a whole nation watching and betting on the outcome—the *Ariel* and *Taiping*, for instance, in 1871, boiling up the English Channel in half a gale, at seventeen or eighteen knots, faster than any steamship then afloat, a few hundred yards apart, almost neck and neck, over fourteen thousand miles from Foochow where they started—and thousands of landsmen cheering from the shore.

In June 1964 the training ships sailed into the broad mouth of the Tagus, with Lisbon unfolding before them—Lisbon, founded by Ulysses, legend says, and known to Phoenicians, Greeks, and Romans, the starting point of the great voyages of discovery in Portugal's heroic age, the center of the spice trade. The visitors lined up at quays two centuries old near the Praça do Commercio with its ornate steps leading down into the Tagus, the Cas des Colunas, where royalty and high officials disembark. The tall masts and yards cast long shadows on the old building of the quays, long shadows of the centuries before them of caravels and galleons, brigs and brigantines. Hundreds of young sailors ganged ashore like Elizabethan seamen just returned from some distant corner of the earth, roustering and boisterous, singing arm in arm, spinning stories of their voyages, admiring the girls in the throngs that came to see the ships, mingling with the landsmen in the narrow streets and taverns, and recalled the city's ancient, sea-faring past.

The training ships stayed a week in Lisbon. Then, in the hesitation of an early morning haze while the day made up its mind which way to go and the white faces of the cliffs opposite Lisbon were blue and gray just topped with gold, the ships let go their moorings and one by one moved slowly down the Tagus to the sea: past the handsome tenements on the heights of Alfama and the Castle of São Jorge above them, past the statue of Christ, 385 feet high, towering above Lisbon's harbor from the highest cliff on the south bank of the Tagus, past the Church of San Jeronimo and the Tower of Belem—marking the place where Vasco da Gama set sail—and finally, rising and falling slightly in the long, slow roll of the Atlantic, they sailed past the headlands at the river's mouth.

A freshening breeze blew the last wisps of haze away and revealed a sight few men now living have ever seen—eight full-rigged ships (with square sails on all three masts) and barques (with square sails only on the first two of three masts) standing off the coast in close formation; last of the world's windships, last of the long line of square-rigged sailing vessels whose role in the history of man, West and East, from the beginning to almost the present day, would be hard to overestimate. The mighty *Libertad* of Argentina, a full-rigged ship, 301 feet long, carrying 24,000 square feet of canvas, was the largest in the race; there was the barque *Sagres* of Portugal, with twenty-two sails, ten of them square, and each of these adorned with a scarlet Cross of the Order of Christ; the Spanish four-master, *Juan Sebastian de Elcano;* the Danish full-rigged ship, *Danmark,* commanded by Knud Hansen; the German barque, *Gorch Fock,* the winner of a number of previous races, and the three Norwegian square-riggers, the *Sorlandet* and the *Christian Radich,* both full-rigged ships, and the *Statsraad Lehmkuhl,* a barque.

They sailed into the broad bay off Cascais, where, in three hours, at one in the afternoon, they would begin the greatest sailing ship race of modern times, down the coast of Portugal to Cape St. Vincent and Prince Henry's famous school at Sagres where he and his sailors and scholars plotted the exploration of the world, past the approaches to Gibraltar, past Madeira, south to the Canaries, around La Palma, with the tall peak of Tenerife in the distance, and then into the broad path of the northeast trades, the winds that carried Columbus and those who came after him to the New World.

Square-rigged ships, like some beloved *grand dame* of the theater, a Jenny Lind, a Sarah Bernhardt, an Ethel Barrymore, have an extraordinary ability to arouse sentimental thoughts in those who see them. They have been exiting from the world's stage amid outpourings of affection and regret for a long time; it was, after all, in 1819 that the first steamship crossed the Atlantic. Thousands of people went to see the ships leave Lisbon and sail along the shore to the starting line off Cascais; and later, when the race ended in Bermuda, almost the whole island population closed up shop to see them in and, again, to watch them sail away to their next port of call, New York; and in New York a million people packed along the shore in Brooklyn, filling the Battery, and stretching along both banks of the Hudson almost to the George Washington Bridge, watched them parade up the harbor and anchor in the river—the biggest event in New York Harbor since the Hudson–Fulton centenary of 1907.

Now in the bright fullness of the day's strength as the square-riggers sailed, white and gleaming, along the coast to Cascais, people on the shore and in spectator boats could see the beauty of the curves of their hulls and their sails and the beauty of their motion—the slow rise-pause-plunge of their bows and the almost imperceptible leaning down to leeward and recovery of their masts.

Their graceful hulls, their clipper bows, their tall masts, and the delicate tracery of their rigging recalled a time when man lived in harmony with nature and with a technology that required a cooperation with it, not a conquest of it. This is the source of part of their allure, but there is also delight in the ships themselves, so comely, so symmetrical, so lightsome as to make even a landsman with no interest in the sea at all draw in his breath and find, forever afterward, that a freighter, a tanker, a liner looks stumpy in comparison.

The sharp, decisive, knife-like bows of the square-riggers, classic curves in profile, spare and clean; the way the diversity of curves of their hulls resolve in consonance and repose at the end of a ship—in a dramatic meeting at the bow, precise and irrevocable, and in a softer, mellower rounding at the stern; how these curves give to any aspect of a ship's hull balance and proportion, each curve in just adaptation to the others in subtle shadings from convex to concave; how, if you were stationary, a ship as it passed would present one continuous flow of harmonious lines, changing but related always; how thinking of the lines of a ship in this way is relevant, because at rest a ship is only possibility —a ship is built for motion, its element; and how, of the twenty-six sails on a full-rigged ship and the twenty-two on a barque, each is different yet each has curves and relationships that are common to the others, and these curves and the curves of the hull, separately and together, compliment each other; and how the curves in the bow and the curves leading to the bow may be duplicated exactly in a sail, one of the jibs above the bowsprit, perhaps; and how, as the curves in the bow change with changes in perspective (as a ship is sailing past) other sails will pick up the new curves and these may be repeated up and down a mast or on all three masts at once; and how the correspondences between the sails and the hull, and among the sails in relation to each other appear and disappear and reappear in almost regular progression in a square-rigged ship under sail: these may be the reasons for the strength of their allure.

One could study with delight a single sail in its relationship to the winds. In the sail loft it is a figure in plane geometry with straight and curving edges, of definite dimension determined by the sailmaker; but filled with wind a sail can assume almost an infinite variety of curves and shapes. On a bright day, the play of light and shadow imposes another set of curves on a sail and these curves advance and retreat with the roll of the ship, in rhythms blending with but independent of the rhythms made by the wind's constant minor modifications of the sail.

Of all the modes of propulsion in the world, a sail is perhaps the most beautiful—the curving of a sail, holding the wind in its curve. A running horse and the wing of an airplane are graceful, but you are aware of the pumping of the heart and the muscles and the nerves of a horse, of its laboring, of its sweat, and of the fierce, hot agitation inside the engines of a plane. A sail performs its function—capturing the wind and converting it into forward motion—with no show of effort, no noise, no moving parts, invisibly, as if exempted by some dispensation from the rules of work.

For the people on the ships, that day, the sparkling air and the breeze, the whitecaps, the clouds, the clean, green land sloping sharply to the sea, the white of the houses on the shore, the feeling of embarking on some great enterprise (using the wind that had taken Prince Henry's men on their voyages of discovery and perhaps the same wind that had brought Ulysses to this shore), the indescribable lift of the ships to the first long swells of the Atlantic and their heel in the freshening breeze, all conspired to produce excitement and delight—in the cadets, many of whom were only fifteen, adolescent exuberance and even childish expectation; in the officers, especially the captains, old square-rig captains, addicts of sailing, a sense of release and fulfillment, and in both cadets and officers self-congratulation, a sustained happiness, a feeling of victory, almost as if martial music were swelling up from behind the hills on the shore and from beyond the horizon. The mood on the ships was honed to an edge by the yells, the commands, the running back and forth on deck, the concentration on the faces of the officers, the stretched necks of men looking upward at the sails, the taut nerves, and the slight small fear in the pit of the stomach because, although the day was fair and the wind only moderate, in all departures the beatings of the wings of death are faintly heard, so on this afternoon as the ships gathered headway for their precisely planned and timed approach to the starting line, the exhilaration of the moment included this universal intuition of the slenderness of bonds, the loneliness of life, the fatality in all separations.

This intuition is both in the departee and in the one who stays behind and is felt most poignantly when a ship leaves the land. For the departing sailor, a cadet on one of the square-riggers perhaps, as it sailed past the Portuguese destroyer anchored on the starting line, it might come as he, standing on the maindeck, turns forward to stare at the empty sky and sea ahead and suddenly a cold, damp whiff of air from off the ocean strikes him in the face. The sailors lined along the rail of the destroyer waving, along with the pride, excitement, longing, and envy they felt, may have caught a glimpse of the beating of death's wings as they watched the long, shapely stern of the square-rigger slowly rising and sinking in the swells as she rounded the bow of the destroyer escort and headed toward her destination thirty-six hundred miles away. Each drop of the stern —of the thousands between there and Bermuda—could, of course, continue down to the bottom, given the right circumstance—a hole in the thin skin of the ship, a boarding sea, a sudden squall. There was an aimless malevolence in the swirling, unstable, breathing, never-quiet sea—hidden just beneath the tranquil beauty and brilliance of its surface that afternoon. The square-rigger was now committed to the deep. As she sailed away, infinitely graceful and lovely, there was about her an intimation of the ultimate departure.

III

The last ship to cross the starting line in the race from Lisbon to Bermuda was the Norwegian barque *Statsraad Lehmkuhl,* the oldest ship in the race, built in Germany in 1915 and used since 1923 by the Bergen Shipowners Association to train merchant seamen. She had 159 cadets on board, the majority of them fifteen and sixteen years old, who, after this voyage, would go directly onto Norwegian merchant ships as deck boys and youngmen, the two lowest ranks in the merchant service. The professional crew of twenty-seven included two captains—one who commanded her in North European waters and another who commanded her on ocean voyages—three mates, doctor, steward, two cooks, bo's'n, sailmaker, carpenter, instructors, quartermasters, able seamen, two engineers for her small, little-used diesel engine, and, for this voyage, Thoralf Gjesdal, the secretary of the Association, who was seventy-two, the oldest man on board, and a kind of grandfather to the cadets. There were also four Americans: Hans Marx, a photographer on an assignment from the *U.S. Naval Institute Proceedings,* John Sibley, a reporter from *The New York Times,* myself on an assignment from *Holiday* magazine, and Michael Kjølsrud, of San Bernardino, California, who was twenty, and returning to the United States after taking a year off from college to see Norway, where he had lived with an uncle and aunt. He wanted to get home without asking his father for passage money, if possible, and at the suggestion of his employer had applied for a berth on Bergen's schoolship. Because he was older than the Norwegian cadets, and because he proved himself a hard worker on the passage from Bergen to Lisbon, he was made assistant to the bo's'n for the rest of the voyage. Instead of standing watch with the other cadets, he replaced most of the rotted ratlines in the rigging of the ship's three masts, spliced innumerable ropes, learned more marlinspike seamanship than many sailors ever learn, and became, perhaps, the only American of his generation to work his passage on a square-rigger.

The *Statsraad Lehmkuhl,* which is named for the Norwegian cabinet member who presented the ship to Bergen, is 258 feet long. She has three masts and twenty-two sails, ten of which are square sails, hanging from ten long horizontal spars called "yards." The sails are lashed to the top of each yard when not in use. To unfurl them, the crew climbs the rigging and out onto the yards, walking along a single footrope hung beneath each one. When sails are taken in, the crew goes aloft again, and, balancing on the footropes, hauls the heavy canvas sails up to the yards and lashes them. In a storm, it is hard, frightening work.

The highest yard, called the main royal yard, is 130 feet above the deck. To get to it, it is necessary to climb up a set of ratlines to the main top, a platform about fifty feet above the deck, up a second set of ratlines to the crosstrees, a platform about 100 feet above the deck, then up a third set of ratlines to a swaying rope ladder hung loosely against the top section of the mast above the ratlines, and finally up the rope ladder to the royal yard.

To get over the two platforms, the maintop and the crosstrees, a crew member must swing himself out around their outer

1 LOWER SHROUDS; HORIZONTAL LINES CALLED RATLINES **2** TOPMAST SHROUDS & RATLINES **3** TOPGALLANT SHROUDS & RATLINES **4** TOPMAST BACKSTAYS **5** TOPGALLANT BACKSTAYS **6** ROYAL BACKSTAY **7** BRACES **8** FORE TOP **9** MAIN TOP **10** CROSSTREES

edges—hanging by his hands with his body nearly parallel to the deck—and pull his feet up after him.

When the lashings are taken off a square sail, it falls below its yard in loose folds but does not fill with wind. It is held in these loose folds by ropes called "clewlines" and "buntlines," which run from the bottom edges of the sail to blocks on its yard and from the yard to the deck, and which must be released from deck before a sail will drop down. (Clewlines and buntlines operate like the rope that lowers a Venetian blind, except that a square sail has two clewlines and two or more buntlines.) Once the clewlines and buntlines of a sail have been released, still another set of ropes, these called "sheets" and "braces," must be adjusted before the sail will begin drawing properly. The braces run from the ends of a yard to the deck. By slacking off on a brace going to one end of the yard, and taking in on the brace going to the other end of the yard, the crew can swing the yard horizontally into whatever position is required by the direction of the wind. The yard pivots on steel trusses attaching it to the mast. The sheets run from the bottom corners on each sail to the deck. They are adjusted after the yards have been braced to the proper angle.

The largest yard on the ship, the main yard, is eighty feet long and weighs several tons. The braces running from it and from some of the other larger yards to the deck are made of chain and wire rope aloft and four-inch manila line from thirty feet above the deck down to the deck. The braces of the smaller, lighter yards higher up on the mast are made entirely of rope.

Each sail and yard has two buntlines, two clewlines, two sheets, and two braces running to the deck—eight lines in all, or eighty for the ten square sails. In addition, four of the yards have halyards. The other twelve sails on the ship—the four jibs (the sails coming down to the bowsprit), the six staysails (the triangular sails set between the masts), and the mizzen and mizzen topsail (the two sails on the aftermast), also have sheets and halyards. Over two hundred lines run from the sails and yards to the deck. This maze of lines must be adjusted in every major maneuver of the ship.

By the time the *Statsraad Lehmkuhl* arrived in Cascais, her jibs, staysails, mizzen, and mizzen topsail had been set, but her square sails, the real driving force of the ship, were still furled on the yards. She was still under power. Captain Odd Fossa, smiling broadly because, he said, this was the best part of any voyage, signaled the engineer, two decks down, to shut off the engine. The noise and the vibration in the deck stopped, the ship's motion took on a liveliness it did not have when it was the creature of its engine rather than the wind, and an excitement ran through the crew. One of the mates, a silver-haired, smooth-skinned man with a pleasant, happy face, broke into a few steps of a sailor's jig. Captain Fossa smiled and nodded at one of the messboys who had stopped to watch the mizzen staysails fill with wind. The mate grabbed the boy's arm, handed him a coffee cup he had found on a hatch cover, and said, with feigned gruffness, "Here, take this below, you pirate." I saw the young first mate slap the bo's'n's back where they stood laughing together in the shadow of the pilothouse.

Captain Eivind Ottesen, who would be in command for the race, climbed three steps to a little circular platform above the halfdeck from which he could view the whole ship. The rest of the crew took their places, because in a moment Captain Ottesen would give the order to set the square sails. The first mate stood below him on the halfdeck with a megaphone and whistle, waiting to transmit his orders to the crew. He was in charge, specifically, of the mainmast, a sort of master of ceremonies for its five square sails and its maze of buntlines, clewlines, sheets, and braces. The second mate, down on the maindeck, was master of ceremonies for the foremast. The other officers, the petty officers, the seamen, and the cadets stood in groups of ten or twenty on the maindeck waiting for the command that would set the whole ship's complement in motion. No one said anything, in a silence like that of the moment of expectation and tension just before the start of a football game or a symphony concert. Captain Ottesen signaled to the first mate; the first mate yelled what sounded like "Op du riggin"; and a hundred cadets swarmed up the rigging, side by side in the lower rigging, in a V-formation higher up where the ratlines narrow—racing each other, the foremast crew against the mainmast crew, up to the main and foretops, up to the main and fore crosstrees, some peeling off at each of the yards, until finally eight boys on each mast reached the highest yards, the fore and main royals and climbed out on those.

I noticed then and every other time the cadets went aloft that there seemed to be great differences in the ease they felt. A few showed by their postures that if they were enjoying what they were doing it was in spite of fear; most looked sure of themselves and at home; and some scrambled about apparently with no thought that a misstep might mean death. On the way out to Cascais Michael Kjølsrud had introduced me to one of the cadets, a sixteen-year-old boy named Terje Berentsen, whose station was on the outboard end of the highest yard, the main royal. I was struck by Terje's nonchalance as he ran up the three sets of ratlines, swung himself out around the maintop and cross-trees platforms, and clambered up the rope ladder to the royal yard. He looked as if nothing at all held him up on the yard as he took the lashings off the sail, now leaning forward over the top of the yard until it seemed he would somersault to deck, now bending down under the yard with only air and the heel of one shoe on a footrope below him.

When he came down on deck, which he accomplished with a deftness that set him apart from the others, he had a look of delight on his face, as if he found something aloft the others did not feel, or perhaps felt but not as keenly. I said to the first mate that Terje looked at ease in the rigging.

"Yah. He is. The first day the cadets were on board this ship, he climbed to the top of the mast and sat on it."

"Did what on it—sat on it?"

"Yah. Sat on it. He heard a cadet from another class climb to the mast top and put his hand on it. So he sat on it."

"He sounds like a nut."

"Yah. But I don't think so. He is just not afraid. If we would let him, he would be in the rigging all the time."

Captain Ottesen called the first mate to the little platform above the halfdeck. I went down to the maindeck, where petty officers, seamen, and cadets were waiting for orders to set the sails, which still hung loosely below their yards, held up by clew-lines and buntlines. Michael Kjølsrud pointed out to me the names and functions of some of these and some of the braces and sheets coming down from aloft to pinrails along the sides of the ship and around the mainmast and foremast.

Michael kept glancing aloft and at the halfdeck, where Captain Ottesen was conferring with his mates. "What the hell is going on," he said. "Why aren't they getting sail on this old bucket? Look at the other ships. They're halfway to the starting line already. Goddam. I'm going to find out what's going on. I'll see you later."

The others on the maindeck kept glancing aloft at the square sails and from the sails to Captain Ottesen, and they would walk around in little circles, swing their arms, gaze at their feet as athletes waiting for the end of a time-out might. Then a rumor raced through the ship that one of the cadets had suddenly refused to go on the voyage and that the doctor, after a talk with him, had decided he should be put ashore. It turned out to be true.

Permission to put the boy on the Portuguese pilot boat in Cascais took an hour to secure, an hour during which everyone on board the *Lehmkuhl* grew tense, gloomy, worried that the ship would miss the start. The Norwegians were dumbfounded. They could not believe their bad luck. Used to a more flexible regime, they found it inconceivable that the skipper of the pilot boat needed authorization from higher officials to take a sick man off a ship. By now the other seven square-riggers were all at the starting line five or six miles away, jockeying back and forth, planning and timing their precise final approaches to the line to cross it with full headway just as the gun went off. There was an hour left before the start and the *Lehmkuhl* was an hour's sail from the line, so every minute of waiting from then on meant another minute late for the start.

Finally the pilot boat left its station, inshore from the *Lehmkuhl,* to come alongside. One of its officers yelled across to begin sailing for the starting line while he radioed the Portuguese Navy for instructions. Ten minutes later he came alongside again and took off the cadet and a quartermaster who would accompany the cadet back to Norway.

Excitement pervaded the ship again at the prospect of getting her moving at last, with all her sails set and filled with wind.

Now everyone had a place, a function, a duty again. Captain Ottesen climbed onto his small platform above the halfdeck. The first mate ran to the mainmast, the second mate to the foremast, the petty officers and cadets to their places by the rows of belaying pins along the rails of the ship and around the masts to which the clewlines and buntlines were made fast. The supernumeraries in this operation—messboys, cooks, engineers, the carpenter, the genial steward, the secretary beaming at all the activity around him as a scoutmaster might, the visiting Americans—hurriedly took places from where they could see yet were out of the way.

Because the wind was coming from ahead instead of behind, the ten yards had to be swung through arcs of forty-five degrees. Gangs of boys in teams of ten or fifteen hauled on the heavy braces that moved the yards. As the boys pulled and strained on deck, the yards aloft swung slowly on their steel trusses, one by one, until hauled around as far as they could go. "Hold fast," the captain yelled, and his order was repeated, first by a mate, and then by a petty officer, and finally by the boys themselves. And now the tricky part began, for it is one thing to haul on a rope, to use the strength of fifteen boys in a straight pull, but it is another to hold the strain on that rope while it is being made fast to a belaying pin. About half of the fifteen boys who had been hauling let go, entrusting the weight of the rope and the yard above it and the tons of force in the sail to the other half of the group. Four or five of the boys who let go, led by the bo's'n, grabbed the rope again close to where it went through a block on the rail. They clenched it against another rope beside it so that the friction of the other rope acted as a brake. The remaining four boys jumped into the air and grabbed the rope above the block as it led aloft to the yard.

They hung suspended with their feet a foot or two above the deck; the four boys with the bo's'n crouched close against the block holding the rope against the one beside it; the seven boys

still holding the free end of the rope waited with anxious looks
for the bo's'n to signal for the precarious moment when they
would let go. He signaled, they dropped the free end of the rope,
and, with a few quick, sure strokes he made the free end fast
around a belaying pin. In the second before he made the free
end fast, the whole strain on the rope was held by the four boys
near the block and the four suspended in the air. If someone did
not hold, the four in the air would go aloft with the zinging rope
and the boys with their hands on the rope near the block would
probably lose their fingers, at the very least.

The radio operator and the second engineer joined in the
bracing in a place where the cadets were not quite experienced
enough to know just what to do. The bo's'n was directing the
hauling in of a brace on the leeward side. He told the cadets to
hold it, then haul it in some more, but by then some of them had
shifted to another brace and they hesitated—not sure what to
do. The second engineer, who had been sitting on a bench under
the ladder leading from the maindeck up to the halfdeck, ran into
the midst of the boys to lead the hauling with all his might. He
grabbed the brace close to its block and urged on the cadets with
great shouts, in loud heaving bursts of pain and intensity. When
that brace was hauled as far as it should be, he and the radio
operator joined the cadets on another brace and speeded up their
work. I also saw the steward's messboys helping with the bracing, although this was not part of their duties.

After the ten yards had been hauled around to the correct
angles to the wind (each one angled slightly differently) and the
sheets that run to the lower corners of the ten square sails had
been hauled in so that the sails were trimmed precisely, and
while mates and petty officers were going around the decks making last-minute adjustments and seeing to it that the boys coiled
up the masses of rope strewn like spaghetti everywhere, the captain mounted his platform again and began staring intently at
the windward edges of the mainmast sails. They began to quiver

a little, then more. He turned and yelled something to the quartermaster at the wheel and waved his arm in a circular motion to tell the quartermaster and the two cadets on the wheel to turn the ship to leeward immediately. As the ship's bow swung away from the eye of the wind, he turned to watch the sails again. Just before they stopped quivering, he used his arm in a circular motion the other way to tell the quartermaster to bring the ship's bow back up to windward a trifle.

The *Lehmkuhl* had missed the start by forty minutes and her crew did not know what maneuverings might have taken place, who took the weather berth, who may have stolen the wind of a competitor, how the newcomer, *Libertad,* performed in her first meeting with the others, whether there had been any duels for position on the line, what tricks the old fox Knud Hansen may have put his *Danmark* through, and who had been first across the line. But the missed start was forgotten now as the *Lehmkuhl* gathered headway, her huge bow plunging ever more powerfully into the building seas, her sails and rigging straining forward. The shr-r-r of the bow wave deepened into shr-r-r-ru-um, the um low and loudest, followed by almost no sound, and then beginning again—the driving bow wave, the sound that has lured men to the sea for thousands of years and which was becoming now, as the *Lehmkuhl's* speed increased, a huge, steady sh-sh-sh, the sound of rapids, of paper ripping. The wind was freshening, the day was beautiful, the spectator boats were all around the ship, and in a moment the *Lehmkuhl* would cross the starting line herself and commence her passage to Bermuda. Two little French schooners that had come out to watch the start sailed by the *Lehmkuhl* back to Lisbon, almost dancing, so light and dainty, so white and gleaming in the sunshine that they looked ethereal, not real.

As the *Lehmkuhl* crossed the line, a British freighter, the *Chinkoa,* that could easily have passed to windward of the *Lehmkuhl,* altered course ninety degrees to pass astern of her, to avoid the possibility that her hull would blanket the wind in the

Lehmkuhl's sails, an excess of politeness because she was too far away to cause any interference—not politeness, really, but a gesture of affection. She signaled, "Good luck. Pleasant voyage." Captain Ottesen went aft and had the cadet on watch at the stern dip the *Lehmkuhl*'s colors. The *Chinkoa* saluted with three blasts of her whistle as she drew away. Every motorship and steamer the *Lehmkuhl* met from Lisbon to Bermuda repeated the *Chinkoa*'s gesture. Even ships on the edges of the horizon, when they saw the *Lehmkuhl*'s sails, changed course immediately to come over to see her. One, a small French liner painted white, probably bound from Africa to some French port in the Mediterranean, came over from the horizon and went by the *Lehmkuhl* two hundred feet away. Instead of resuming her old course, she circled and went by the other side. She circled the *Lehmkuhl* again. Then, her Gallic captain's longing for this incarnation of his inheritance apparently satisfied, she headed again toward the Straits of Gibraltar. About a mile away, she turned around, came back, and made one more circle around the ship.

When the *Lehmkuhl* sailed by the Portuguese destroyer anchored on the starting line, the destroyer's business there was done. Her company prepared to go back to the land. They would spend tonight in Lisbon, perhaps buying books in the open-air stalls of the Avenida da Liberdade or drinking wine in the cafés of the Alfama or, the settled ones, in the warmth of their own living rooms, while the *Lehmkuhl*'s company would spend tonight alone on the dark sea. The crossing of the line was the *Lehmkuhl*'s moment of departure—the sail out had been a period of transition, when remnants of the land, land thoughts, inhabited the mind. Now a slight shiver went through the ship and suddenly the night before in Lisbon seemed very far away. Perhaps it was this moment of separation from the land that the sick cadet saw coming, and declined.

But the shiver was more than a response to leaving man's natural habitat, the land. It was anticipation, too—anticipation of the bringing of a ship across the ocean depending on nothing more substantial than the invisible winds and on the arts perfected in a thousand years of square-rig seamanship; and anticipation of the beauty of the sea and its companions, wind and cloud, moonrise and starlight, sunset and dawn; and, most of all, anticipation of the race of these last survivors of the age of sail.

The history of the square-rigged ship might almost be called a race. The meeting in the gloom of a snowstorm off Cape Horn of two clippers racing to New York from San Francisco, their first since the Golden Gate; the meeting and two-day chase, sometimes so close that shots are fired, of three British men-of-war and a little American privateer until the little privateer outruns one, then a second, and finally just before nightfall of the second day the last one, which takes in its upper sails, reefs its topsails, and gives up the chase in driving rain squalls while the American heaves overside all extra gear and continues to carry all the sail she has: thousands of chance meetings, chases, evasions, and races down through the history of square-rigged ships are summoned up each time in 1964 or 1966 or 1968 that a sail is sighted from the deck of the *Statsraad Lehmkuhl* or the *Danmark* or the *Sagres* or the American barque, *Eagle,* or any of the other sail training ships of the world.

Although the day was bright when the *Lehmkuhl* crossed the starting line, a smoky haze on the water cut visibility to perhaps five miles. Only three of the other ships in the race were still in sight. They were on everyone's mind. I am sure that everyone on board the *Lehmkuhl* made calculations many times—were they gaining on her or she on them?

In Lisbon it was said that the *Lehmkuhl* was slow except in heavy weather and probably the slowest in the race in the kind of sailing she was doing then, to windward. An Englishman, an official of the Sail Training Association, described the *Lehmkuhl* as a rather clumsy performer to windward. But within an hour it was obvious that she was gaining fast. The other three ships were still too far away to decide who they might be, but even if they were not the fastest (which were probably the *Gorch Fock* and *Sagres* and perhaps the *Elcano,* so far seldom tested in a race), even if they were the slowest, the *Lehmkuhl*'s overtaking at this rate astounded her officers. Within an hour and a half, she had gained enough to identify the other ships, which turned out to be the *Sorlandet, Libertad,* and *Elcano.*

This was Captain Ottesen's time of glory and he reveled in it. He walked to the break in the halfdeck where John Sibley and I stood watching the wind in the sails and the bow and quarter waves leaving the hull. "I'm doing a little thinking," he said.

"Thinking. Thinking about what?" John said.

"Thinking about the sails. Thinking about the wind. I'm thinking we'll soon be up to them."

"Those three up there, you mean?"

"All of 'em."

"Ah good," John said, and all three of us laughed, the captain —a tall, dark man who looked more Latin than Scandinavian— with a pleased, ingratiating smile. "Wait and see, as the Yankee says," he said.

He went off, turning his head back once to us and smiling, as though we three shared a secret. "I'm thinking I may do a little trick," he said, and winked.

Half the cadets and three fourths of the officers and petty officers were off watch, but none of them went below or took a nap on deck or did anything but watch the other ships or try to help with the sailing of the *Lehmkuhl.*

The wind kept piping up. "This is what she wants. This is what she wants," the second mate, Erik Bernes, said to no one specifically, or perhaps as much to the ship as to anyone on board. Øyvind Bøe, a nineteen-year-old quartermaster, coming off watch, where his duty was to oversee the two cadets who were steering, said to John Sibley and me, "When you are really sailing like this and the wind is coming from forwards and you have to watch the sails and be up as close to the wind as you can, you have a certain feeling you never have on motorships."

"In a motorship, you know, you have always got the engine running and you haven't to take care of the wind and weather. But this is very fine—with the sails all set and you are hearing the sound of the sea."

He didn't go below. He went to the bow of the ship.

"Ah, it is coming up, coming up, ah ha ha ha," Captain Ottesen said, standing at the rail waving the wind toward him as a man might motion to a child to come, a bit imperiously. "It's going to fresh a little bit. It's going to fresh. And when the sun goes down fresh a little more."

He smiled triumphantly, as though pretending he thought he was responsible for the increased wind. His face lit up and with a flourish he put his arm out. "I call it, I call it," he said, rubbing his fingers with his thumb as though he had the wind caught between them. "Just wait and see. Just wait and see, as the Yankee says."

A messboy invited us to come below for coffee or tea in the saloon, a spacious room in the after part of the ship under the halfdeck which was paneled in a rare yellow wood and contained, besides the main table, which seated twenty, smaller tables and settees around the curving stern of the ship. We found the doctor and the secretary at one of the small tables. After we were seated, Captain Ottesen came down. The doctor started to get up from the captain's chair. "Sit still, sit still," the captain said. He brought another chair over from the dining table, sat down, folded his hands in his lap, and looked around at us, full of good spirits. Before the secretary could pour him a cup of coffee, he got up, put his chair back at the dining table, and went on deck. As he left he said something in Norwegian and indicated with thumb and forefinger coming together, while he squinted at them and then smiled craftily at us, either that we were closing in on the other ships or that he was going on deck to do something to make us close.

None of us stayed below long. When we went back on deck, the *Lehmkuhl* was about a hundred yards astern of the *Elcano*.

The *Libertad* was ahead and to leeward about five hundred yards away and the *Sorlandet* was about an equal distance ahead and to windward.

Captain Ottesen yelled from his platform at the forward end of the halfdeck, waving his arms down to leeward disapprovingly. The helmsmen, who were trying to edge the *Lehmkuhl* closer and closer to the wind in order to go by the *Elcano* on her windward side, had headed too close and the *Lehmkuhl* mainsail was beginning to shake. They headed her bow down to leeward until the mainsail filled with wind. Then, under Captain Ottesen's direction, they tried once more to ease the bow up to windward, but the mainsail began quivering again and the captain called off the attempt. He altered course twenty degrees to go to leeward of the *Elcano*.

The *Lehmkuhl* sailed by her, going much faster, and kept gaining on the other two. As she went by, Second Mate Bernes shook his head wonderingly. "I never been afraid of that feller there," he said, pointing ahead to the *Libertad*. "I been afraid of that feller, that *Elcano*. Twenty-seven thousand square feet of sail and fore and aft rig."

Many people think that fore and aft sails generally are more efficient going to windward than square sails, but this is not always true. The *Elcano* had fore and aft sails on her four masts —foremast, mainmast, mizzenmast and jiggermast—as well as square sails on her foremast. Sailors in Lisbon thought she would walk away from everyone in any part of the race that required windward work.

I suppose we thought we were invincible then. We were sure, at any rate, that we would soon pass the *Sorlandet* and the *Libertad* as we had passed the *Elcano*, the *Libertad* particularly because she was two hundred yards to leeward, which gave the *Lehmkuhl* a considerable advantage. But somehow the *Lehmkuhl* dropped down to leeward or the *Libertad* climbed up to windward, and soon what seemed a foregone conclusion, passing her, became only a slight chance.

In ten or fifteen minutes the two ships were abreast, almost parallel but slightly converging because the *Libertad* seemed able to sail closer to the wind than the *Lehmkuhl*. Captain Ottesen told the helmsmen to turn the bow of the *Lehmkuhl* to windward to stay clear of the *Libertad*. When they did the *Lehmkuhl's* sails began quivering and she slowed down slightly, and in that moment her winning spell snapped. The *Libertad* started gaining steadily and the old *Lehmkuhl*, behaving now as the Englishman had described her—clumsily—fell behind. Captain Ottesen altered course to sail to leeward of the *Libertad*. From then on the *Libertad*, the *Sorlandet*, and, for a while, even the *Elcano*, gained. By nightfall, the *Libertad* was three miles away.

That night the wind blew hard, causing spray to come over the windward rail for the first time, pushing the ship ahead at an average speed of ten knots. In the morning she was alone.

All that day and most of the night the wind blew from the south, and the *Lehmkuhl* beat against it, endlessly it seemed, heading toward New York on one tack and on the other tack back toward Portugal. Early in the morning of the third day, the wind hauled around to the north, and the ship's head was turned at last in the direction we wanted to go, south to the Canaries. But then the wind turned light, the sea became smooth, and the *Lehmkuhl* plodded along at about a fourth of her optimum speed.

On the fourth morning, I met Captain Ottesen taking a turn around the halfdeck before breakfast. "Not quite enough wind," he said. "But I suppose with the sun the wind strongs." He turned toward the wind and motioned it to him with his fingers. "Coming, coming," he said. It did. By ten o'clock the ship's speed had increased two knots to seven and a half and by noon to eight and a half knots.

The wind kept increasing. From four to eight in the afternoon, the ship averaged nine and a half knots. From eight to midnight, she averaged almost ten knots. For one of those hours she went eleven knots. "Everyone is happy now," Øyvind Bøe, the young quartermaster, said. "Everyone is smiling." It was impossible, as the ship boiled through the night, not to think that we were ahead of everyone. We must be. No one could keep up with the *Lehmkuhl* in this.

There was endless speculation about the positions of the other ships. The second mate said that in a wind that pushed the *Lehmkuhl* along at six or seven knots the *Danmark,* the *Christian Radich,* and the *Sorlandet,* all smaller and lighter, would go faster. When the wind blew hard enough to push the *Lehmkuhl* eight or eight and a half knots, those three would start dropping back, he said. Most of the men on the *Lehmkuhl* agreed with estimates in Lisbon that the *Gorch Fock* and the *Sagres,* newer versions of the *Statsraad Lehmkuhl,* probably had the best chance of winning. The outcome depended most, no doubt, on how well the ships were sailed and how well their captains guessed where the best winds would be; but if all of them were sailed equally well, the outcome would depend, most people said, on whether the *passat,* or trade wind, blew a little harder than normal, favoring the five big ships, or a little lighter than usual, favoring the three little ones. In light airs, even the smallest, the *Sorlandet,* might win.

The speculation about the other ships' positions was confined among the cadets almost entirely to the *Christian Radich.* Michael Kjølsrud told John Sibley and me, "They are just interested in beating the Norwegian. They don't care about the others. With the *Radich* it is a terrific rivalry—Bergen and Oslo, different dialects, the two biggest cities, and all that. The boys say the captain on the *Radich* is stuck up."

He said that in Lisbon the *Radich*'s cadets derided the old and, they said, clumsy *Lehmkuhl.* If the *Radich* won the race, he said, the cadets on the *Lehmkuhl* planned to beat up her cadets in retribution for the insults they were sure her cadets would heap on them, on their city, and on their ship.

Roar Nielsen, a cadet who was acting as assistant to the

doctor on this trip, said of Oslo, "They think we think we are too good. They are the best, they think. They are the biggest city in Norway. In other places in Norway they like the Bergens, but not in Oslo. In Oslo they say the Bergens are talking too much and loud. We say what we want to say."

He said he hoped the *Radich* would not win, because if she did, then, "If we meet the boys from the *Radich* in Bermuda, they say, 'oh they are from Bergen and from the *Statsraad Lehmkuhl.*' If they just say, 'We win,'—that's okay. Be fights if they say more. It isn't serious—you mustn't think that. But if *Sorlandet* win, we wouldn't feel in the same way. We would shake hands. But with the *Christian Radich,* we wouldn't."

Later, the ship's doctor, Emil Gjessing, talked to me about the history of Bergen, Norway's second city and in medieval times the greatest city of all Scandinavia. The Bergeners are a bit contemptuous of Oslo, which considers itself, I gathered, more sophisticated and cosmopolitan. Oslo people have a tendency to think of themselves as brighter and wittier, the doctor said. "They think the Bergen people talk too much—especially about Bergen. They have sayings, you know. They say, 'Even though I am from Bergen, I don't like to exaggerate.' And they say, 'No, I am not a Norwegian, I am from Bergen.' Or they say, 'Norway is a part of Bergen,' you know." Secretary Gjesdal said some Oslo men were on a train once going toward the most beautiful part of Norway, the country around Bergen, and trying to decide where they would spend their holiday. Each time one of them proposed a place, the other said, "No, there are too many Bergeners there." Finally a man from Bergen, with his chest swelling and his face getting red, said, before stamping out of the compartment, "Now, gentlemen, I would like to propose a place for you to go. You can go to hell. There are no Bergeners there."

On the second day of the race the *Radich* radioed the *Lehmkuhl* to exchange positions. She was fifteen miles ahead. But after that one exchange, her captain instructed his radio operator not to give the *Lehmkuhl* any more positions. By chance on the fourth day, the *Lehmkuhl*'s radio operator overheard the *Radich* and the *Sorlandet* giving their positions to Norway. The *Radich* was ten miles behind the *Lehmkuhl* and the *Sorlandet* was forty miles behind the *Radich*.

The news that the *Lehmkuhl* had gained twenty-five miles on the *Radich* in two days when the winds were light and moderate —the *Radich*'s best winds and the *Lehmkuhl*'s worst—went through the ship. The cadets said to each other, "We're ahead, we're ahead," thinking only of the Norwegians and not at all of the Germans, Portuguese, Argentines, Spaniards, and Danes.

Among the adults, however, thoughts of the Germans and the Portuguese were uppermost. The *Gorch Fock* and the *Sagres* were the other two barques in the race; they were about the *Lehmkuhl*'s size, and because of almost similar handicaps, they were the ones she would have to stay close to in order to win the race. Once a German tanker came up to the *Lehmkuhl* and reported seeing a barque four hours astern, news that seemed, considering the *Lehmkuhl*'s bad start and the thirty-six hours of head winds after the start, almost too good to be true. Perhaps the German did not know the difference between a barque and a square-topsail schooner, the *Elcano*'s rig, the secretary suggested to the first mate, adding that the *Elcano* would be much more likely to be astern than either the crack *Gorch Fock* or the *Sagres*. The first mate replied that he thought the German would have known a barque. "If he did not know, he would not say barque, he would say sailing ship—don't you think?" the first mate added. The secretary nodded. No one could tell, of course.

On the fifth day, no ships of any kind were seen. In mid-afternoon of the sixth day, the *Lehmkuhl*'s radio operator talked with the radio operators of the *Sorlandet* and the *Radich*. The second mate told me the *Sorlandet* was more than a hundred miles astern. The captain of the *Christian Radich* would not give his position, the second mate said, and smiled. I said I guessed we had widened our lead over the *Radich*, too.

"We have to do it now. Wind not so strong in the *passat*," the second mate said. Øyvind Bøe, who shared the watch with the second mate, nodded. When the second mate went off to the stern to read the taffrail log, Øyvind said the *Lehmkuhl* had traveled ninety miles in the past twelve hours. In the past hour she had done better than eight knots, he said.

"Pretty good, compared to what we were doing yesterday," I said.

"Yes," he said. "If I understand the second mate, this is just the right breeze for this ship."

The second mate and Øyvind had the eight to noon watch. In the noon to four watch, which was the first mate's, the fickle wind dropped the *Lehmkuhl*'s speed to five knots, and, for an hour, only four knots. The first mate and the quartermaster on watch with him were standing around feeling sorry for themselves and trying fruitless experiments with the sails when a yell from a boy working in the rigging stopped all activity on deck. "A ship, a ship, a sailing ship," he shouted. Cadets on the main-deck wheeled around calling to each other in a kind of chorus, "A ship, a ship, a sailing ship," and then rushed to the rail to look. The first mate, stopping only to grab a pair of binoculars—he forgot them at first and came back—shot up the rigging, ran out a footrope to the end of a yard, and, straddling it, looked where the boy pointed. On the halfdeck, the two captains and the chief officer snatched up binoculars and, surrounded by petty officers, the second mate, the doctor, the secretary, the steward, and last, the first engineer, trained the binoculars at the spot the cadet in the rigging still pointed to. A few of the cadets on the maindeck who could think of excuses to climb up to the halfdeck stood at the back of the crowd. Several seamen climbed partway up the foremast rigging.

No one on the deck, even the ones with binoculars, could see the other ship. When the first mate started down, therefore, the crowd went to the foot of the ratlines to wait for him. He shook his head when he jumped on deck. The other ship was too far off, he said, to tell who she was or even what rig she was, a barque or a full-rigged ship. "She's coming this way, though," he said. "We'll converge."

The bo's'n, using binoculars, said he could see the ship. Soon she was visible without binoculars, and when supper was called no one wanted to go. The men shooed the cadets down into their quarters and reluctantly, a few minutes later, went below, too, except for the ones on watch. Before they did, the bo's'n said the other ship was not a barque, but definitely a full-rigged ship, which meant she had to be the *Libertad*, the *Radich*, the *Danmark*, or the *Sorlandet*.

The Norwegians all talked Norwegian at supper instead of English, for the first time since we Americans came on board. Occasionally one would stop to translate. They were talking about what each of the possibilities would mean. If she were a barque, the *Gorch Fock* or the *Sagres*—not all of them accepted the bo's'n's pronouncement that she was a full-rigger—it would be great news. If she were a ship—reactions were mixed—if she were a ship, it depended on what ship she was. The *Libertad* was bigger than the *Lehmkuhl* and, judging by her performance against the *Lehmkuhl* on the first day of the race, a good sailer. And the *Danmark*, people in Lisbon had said, could probably be expected, under the wily Knud Hansen, to stay up with the leaders.

During supper, the other ship sailed from forty-five degrees off the starboard bow to just ahead, perhaps three quarters of a mile away. She was a full-rigged ship (the rigs are hard to tell apart from a distance). She seemed too small and too low in the water to be the *Libertad*. The bo's'n said she was the *Danmark*. The others did not believe he could tell in the fading light. No matter who she was, the scene—two square-riggers racing southward in the last reddish light of the day in a breeze that had begun to freshen again—made exultation rampant through the ship, calmness or serenity or dejection impossible. The Canaries, the end of the first leg of the course, were only thirty miles away.

It would be a race now, boat for boat, to the westernmost large island, La Palma, where the ships would change course almost ninety degrees to west by south, into the ancient track of transatlantic commerce, the path of the northeast trades.

When the other ship bore thirty or forty degrees off the *Lehmkuhl's* port bow, she signaled. First Mate Gronningen, leaning against a lifeboat davit to steady his signal light, which he held in one hand propped in the crook of the elbow of his other arm, acknowledged the signal. The chief officer stood beside him with a pad and pencil. The captains and half a dozen others stood near them peering at the flashes of light from the other ship, and boys on the maindeck crowded around the steps leading up to the halfdeck. As First Mate Gronningen called out the letters D-A-N-M-A-R-K, he smiled each time, in recognition, and I suppose because he was glad she wasn't the *Libertad* or the *Christian Radich*. The *Danmark* signaled, Have you seen any vessels. The first mate replied, No. Have you. The *Danmark* signaled, No. Good voyage. The first mate replied, Thank you. Good voyage. The crowd around the first mate was excited, and down on the maindeck, the cadets ran around elated, passing the word. It wasn't the *Christian Radich*.

The chief officer said to First Mate Gronningen, "Perhaps she's first, we second"—putting a new, surprising, and most optimistic light on it. "We beat her. We beat her," he added. Gronningen shook his head, laughing. "We have to give her eighteen hours." But no one was thinking of handicaps then.

Being up with the *Danmark* meant being up with the best man in the business, who had been sailing the *Danmark* ten or twenty thousand miles a year every year since the 1930's (except in World War II), and who handled her like a dinghy, beating up rivers, through narrow channels, and right up to piers without deigning to use his engine. She was smaller, it was true, and the *Lehmkuhl* would have to get to Bermuda almost a day ahead of her, but Bermuda was still on the other side of the ocean. It would have been better if she had turned out to be the *Gorch*

The tall ships head out to sea at the start of the Lisbon–Bermuda race in 1964. Ahead in the distance, the *Danmark* leads the *Sagres,* followed by the *Gorch Fock* and the *Libertad,* with the *Sorlandet* bringing up the rear.

The view from aloft.

The *Statsraad Lehmkuhl*.

Second Mate Eric Bernes, a
Cape Horner and owner-captain
of the last cargo-carrying
sailing vessel in the North Sea.

The *Elcano* as the *Lehmkuhl* surges past her early in the race.

The *Libertad*, working her way to windward, managed to hold her lead over the *Lehmkuhl*.

On the main deck, the cadets haul in the fore lower topsail brace.

The *Lehmkuhl* in New York harbor.

The *Danmark,* commanded by Captain Knud Hansen. Each yard and sail makes a slightly different angle to the axis of the ship, creating a spiral effect with the wind.

Fock or the *Sagres,* but the *Danmark* was not ignominious company.

She disappeared in the darkness. Two or three hours later, the men on the *Lehmkuhl's* deck picked up the lights of La Palma. As the ship coasted down its eastern flank, groups of men and cadets leaning along her rail watched the lights of a few houses and the high, dark loom of the island above them. They discussed mostly why the *Danmark* had gone off to the east instead of taking the shortest course to La Palma, as we had. Captain Hansen had been this way many times before, and they wondered if he knew something about the wind and current they did not. The first mate said he had been this way a number of times too, but in steamers. "You don't notice anything about the wind in steamers," he said.

The first real blow of the race came early the next morning shortly after the *Lehmkuhl* rounded La Palma. She passed the lighthouse at the southern tip of the island at 1:20 a.m., with a fine northeast breeze, doing thirteen knots, faster than most freighters until the last few years and faster than many today. She sailed like that for an hour—right into a flat place in the ocean where the wind dropped down to nothing. Her sails hung limp and for ninety minutes she sat stock still in the water. Then the wind came in from the west with a whoosh. She staggered, lay over on her side, and the sea poured over her rail. In a minute or two, she shook herself free, and with water cascading from her freeing ports and from the flanks of her bow as it rose from the sea, she zoomed off southward, like a galloping horse or a dog straining hard on a leash. It was squally, black, spooky. Men pounded back and forth across the deck. In the darkness above, the sails shook violently—flam, flam, flam—with reports like cannon fire. Shouts, commands, responses mingled with the whine of the wind in the rigging, creaks and groans from the interior of the ship, and the surge of the hull foaming through the still flat sea. Now, because the wind had changed direction, the huge steel yards on the mainmast and foremast had to be braced. Mates and petty officers took their stations. Then to the commands of the captain looking down from the halfdeck—his voice magnified by an electric megaphone but, even so, snatched away by the wind almost before he could be understood—boys and petty officers and seamen strained on the slanting deck in nocturnal tugs of war with the heavy braces that moved the yards: pulling, gripping, fighting the braces until tears started, and until aloft the huge steel yards swung slowly into their new positions.

When the five yards on the foremast and the five on the mainmast had been hauled around as far as they could go, and the shouting, confusion, and straining on the deck had diminished a little, the captain mounted the little platform on the halfdeck and trained a flashlight on the windward edges of the mainmast sails. He yelled down to the quartermaster behind him at the wheel for the course. A minute later he turned fast, waving his arm in a circular motion, and yelled to the quartermaster to head the ship leeward. The sails, which had stopped their flam, flam, flam as soon as the yards were braced, were beginning to quiver, and before the ship's head could be turned in response to the captain's order, they were all exploding again. The two boys on the helm, with the quartermaster helping them, no longer had the strength to force the ship's head to leeward, so great was the power of the ship now and so great its tendency, backed by hundreds of tons of force in its sails, to want to head closer into the wind. The wheel is six feet in diameter and the two cadets steering stood on platforms called gratings on each side of it. The one on the leeward side pulled spokes toward him as hard as he could, the one on the windward side pushed spokes away from him. Suddenly the ship took charge, and the wheel started spinning. The boy on the leeward side was thrown across the top of the wheel to the windward side. The captain ordered four men on the wheel. Two more cadets jumped into position.

The ship must sail a precise course now. The strong wind

from the west had forced it into a southerly direction and only a
few miles ahead lay another island, the last of the Canaries, and
the last obstacle between the ship and Bermuda. Unless the captain could work the ship five degrees closer to the wind, onto a
course of 185 degrees instead of 180 degrees, he would have to
tack. If he could clear the island without tacking he would save
half an hour—not much in a thirty-six hundred-mile race, but
enough, perhaps, to make a difference.

It was getting light now and soon we saw the island; and
gradually, taking advantage of every slight variation in wind
direction, we worked to windward of it. The seas picked up, the
wind swung back to the northeast, and by breakfast time we
were on the course we would steer for the next fifteen hundred
miles, west by south.

At a time like this, no matter how many times I saw it, I
would be awed by the struggle of the ship and by her magnificence. Imagine this great ship bowling along at thirteen or fourteen knots, her twenty-two sails, the highest 130 feet above the
deck, molded by the wind into beautiful symmetrical shapes, each
one a smaller, slightly different version of the one below it, and
each one hard as a board now because of the strength of the
wind; the ship heeling over so that the portholes on her leeward
side are dipping far down into the blue water and when she rises
skipping along on the surface with slosh and spume washing
them continually; her great arched bow rising, rising, rising, at
first fast, then gradually slowing until, finally, at the peak of the
rise, the whole huge weight of the bow, the forecastle, the tremendous fore part of the ship, seems to hang suspended, abso-
lutely still, as though all motion of the sea and ship have gone,
and then suddenly down, at first slowly, then faster and faster,
until near the bottom of the plunge the powerful head of the
ship once more slows, and with a settling motion like an elephant
or a fat man sitting down, appears ready in the trough it has
made for itself to give up its career of ups and downs; but at the

last moment, there is a sudden parting of the water—flying outward twenty, thirty, forty feet, in arcs of spray on each side of the bow—and the rise begins again.

Further aft, on the maindeck and the halfdeck, the wildness of the fore part of the ship is muted. Here the motion is a gradual roll combined with a slow rise and fall of the deck. A steamer rolls; the roll is a combination of nature and machinery, and it is jerkier, more violent and abrupt. In a storm it is likely to be sickening. The motion of a sailing vessel is entirely the product of natural forces—gravity, the activity of the sea, the pressure of the wind—and it has a symmetry and balance that the intrusion of a foreign element, the engine on a steamship, destroys. If there is a physiological explanation for the elation that manifests itself at a time like this—some peculiarity of the inner ear perhaps—it lies in the dancing motion of a sailing ship in a breeze. Something inside everyone—an excitement, an intensity of experience, a tingling, a fear, an expectancy—feels like bursting out.

Below deck there were bangings and crashings as a bulkhead door slammed shut, dishes on the uphill side of a counter slid to the downhill side, the oil portrait of the ship in the main saloon swung out from its hook too far at last and crashed to the floor. When I went on deck after breakfast, the captain was standing on the little platform on the forward edge of the halfdeck, his hands gripping its brass rail. He was leaning to one side to look up into the big square mainsail just above his head and smiling. The chief officer, Kjeld Nyebak, who had danced a few steps of a jig off Lisbon to signal his pleasure when the engine was turned off, was pacing back and forth across the halfdeck in front of the wheel, smiling too. "Not so bad, not so bad," he said, and his eyes lit up. The young first mate, with a look of triumph on his face, joined the chief and patted out a fast rat-a-tat-tat with his fingers on the rail of a lifeboat they leaned against. The chief steward, stolid, the most practical of men, concerned, one would imagine, with the contents of the freezer or the two hundred loaves of bread that must be baked that morning, stood near the stern nodding with a gourmet's smile of satisfaction. "Aah, excellent, excellent," he said. The cadets on watch, at a more expressive time of life, their hearts beating faster from the exertion of hauling on sheets and braces a few minutes before, stood along the windward rail engaging in quick mock fights, over as soon as they began, or in boisterous conversations, or working off their excitement with aimless little steps, almost dancing, in circles on the deck. Cooks, messboys, boys off watch crowded along the rail because they could not sleep at a time like this. Michael Kjølsrud, at the wheel with another boy, leaning down from the helmsmen's platform, said, "Jeese, this is great. You should 'a seen 'em a couple of minutes ago, the captain and the chief, jumping around here. They were just like little kids. The chief was down on the maindeck trying to get in more on the yards. When he came up he told the captain, 'We got this much.' It was about a foot. He showed him with his hands. The captain said, 'Yah, yah. With this wind we soon go by the others. We win if we keep this wind,' the chief said."

The bo's'n, a man who, with perhaps two score other square-rig bo's'ns, holds a thousand years of marlinspike seamanship in his head (the few knots and splices that the steamship bo's'n or the average yachtsman knows are a pale one tenth of the art) took the carpenter into the charthouse to show him our position. The second mate, like the first off watch but on deck nevertheless, said, "This is what she wants."

And the *Danmark*—we last saw her when she crossed our bow the night before heading not toward La Palma, which she would eventually have to round as we did, but on a course forty or forty-five degrees to the east of ours. "I think he is afraid of the current around La Palma and wants to stand off," Captain Ottesen said. He met me as he came out of the chartroom. "Come, I'll tell you something. We are going by La Palma close by, and then, and then, we cut off Captain Hansen.

"I plan this this afternoon. We will come by close to the land

and then brace all the yards and go west, west by south, with all sails set—you understand me?"

He laughed. "Yes, and tomorrow we look back and see the peak of Tenerife and the *Danmark* astern." He winked so that I thought he wasn't taking himself entirely seriously. "Just wait and see, as the Yankee says," he said.

At two in the morning, John Sibley and I met him coming out of the chartroom. "At one o'clock I had the *Danmark* twelve miles astern," he said. "I told you I would."

But such is the role of luck (or perhaps I should give Captain Hansen credit for superior sagacity) that our strategy of the past eight hours in the end, at the moment of apparent success, betrayed us. During the ninety frustrating minutes that we sat stock still, and when the squall from the west hit us, we did not know where the *Danmark* was, but in the pale, cold light of the morning we saw a sail. She crossed our bow four or five miles away on a more northerly course than ours. Captain Ottesen shook his head. "I made a mistake. I did not know the local winds and I rounded the lighthouse too close. We had northeast wind and we had thirteen knots and then, suddenly, calm. No wind at all. I say to the chief officer: 'What the hell is this?' I think we in the shelter of the island. And then, suddenly, the wind come very strong from right ahead and we have to head south, east of south, and we want to go west.

"But that was tough, gosh. I had Captain Hansen twelve miles astern, but he knew the local situation. He knew everything about the Canaries. I went west and he went east.

"But that will never happen to me again. What bad news when we saw that ship ahead and at first did not believe it could be *Danmark*. We named it *Sagres* or *Gorch Fock*. Ach."

For the rest of the morning and all afternoon the wind stayed fresh and the *Lehmkuhl* romped along at nine and ten knots.

A boy and a petty officer were sent aloft at sundown to wrap canvas around a chain on the main lower topsail yard to prevent chafe. The boy straddled the yard at its outboard end and as it swung down toward the ocean a hundred feet below and then back up toward the sky, he stayed aloft only by balancing his body in time with the seas; he was using both hands to wrap the canvas. The petty officer stood on the footrope under the yard balancing his body, too, to the roll of the ship, and using his hands to lash the canvas. They looked at home, easy, joyful— doing, it struck me, what Norwegians have done for centuries. When they came down the ratlines and jumped on deck, each had the look of someone who is proud of himself but does not want to show it.

I saw that the boy was Terje Berentsen, the one who sat on top of the mainmast the day he came aboard the ship. I had noticed in the six days we had been at sea that his daring in the rigging contrasted with his manner on the deck, where he was quiet and serious, even-tempered, unassuming. He was quick in the work of the ship, especially the sailorly tasks, hauling on braces and sheets and helping the bo's'n, but also in the boring work—scraping varnish, chipping paint, holystoning the deck. He seemed well liked and apparently enjoyed taking part in the wrestling and invented games in the cadets' off watches, but he was not a member of any of the cliques of boys who stayed together as much as possible on watch and were always together off watch. I never saw him indulge in the almost continuous and often childish horseplay that occupied the free time of some of the cadets, and in which there was, I am sure, an element of rebellion against the routine of the ship.

The first mate had told me on the first day of the race that Terje was a cheerful boy, interested in learning all he could, willing to do more than his share of the tasks of shipboard life, earnest about his career, and, all in all, one of the most level-headed sixteen-year-olds he had ever worked with. Except perhaps for his mania for heights, the first mate said.

I had looked up at the mainmast a number of times in the last few days and tried to imagine Terje sitting on top of it. Shinnying up the last fifteen feet of bare pole seemed feasible enough for a sixteen-year-old boy, but I did not see how, with nothing to hold on to, he was able to pull his weight up over the top of the mast, a flat surface the size of a butter plate, and then sit on it. From 160 feet in the air, the ship must have looked not much bigger than a canoe.

I had decided to ask Terje when I had a chance to tell me what it was he found so alluring in the rigging. His English was limited and my Norwegian nonexistent, so I found Michael Kjøls-rud to translate for us. On the trip from Bergen to Lisbon, he said, the ship sailed through a storm in the Bay of Biscay, and he was one of a number of volunteers sent aloft to take in the royals. The masts swayed quite a bit then. But there could have been more swaying, if he had had a choice, he said.

Before the cadets were assigned to permanent stations on the yards, Terje had been on the royal yard once and on the upper topsail yard once. The upper topsail yard is two down from the royal. "That wasn't high enough," he said. "I had to be on the highest."

I asked why. "It is more thrilling, there is more swaying, and when you are on the top, you are on the top of all," he said.

The first mate, who had witnessed Terje's climb to the top of the mast before the ship left port, felt that on a lower yard he would be less likely to fool around and fall off. He assigned him permanently to the upper topsail yard. No one is forced to go aloft, and Terje told the first mate, "If you don't put me on the top, I won't go up at all." The first mate enjoys going aloft him-self. He relented and assigned Terje to the royal—with the ad-monition that he pay attention to his work and stifle any urge he might have up there to play.

Terje said that it was a fine feeling sitting on top of the mast. "Nothing unusual about it," he said. "Just like sitting on a chair, only higher."

He said he had always liked climbing high. "Some people do it to show off, but I think that is not completely the case with me," he said. "I just like to be up there."

Terje's attitude seemed the exact opposite of braggadocio. I felt, and Mike agreed, that he was not boasting. Mike said he thought Terje was one of the most modest cadets on board. He maintained this opinion even when the mast-top exploit came up again and Terje said, "If I had a guitar, I would have played it."

I decided that perhaps, just as the Mohawk Indians, descendants of the bravest warriors in this country, thrive on high construction jobs, some Norwegians inherit from a line of seafarers that goes back before the Vikings an at-homeness in the rigging that makes such stunts as his a natural activity.

Terje was an attractive looking boy, about five feet nine, lightly built, with smooth, clear skin, gray eyes, and light brown wavy hair. His expression was pleasant, a bit wistful, unexceptional, I thought, except when he smiled. Then his face had a look, surprising in one so young, of gentleness, wisdom, and concern for whomever he was talking to. Terje's father is a ship's carpenter and his three older brothers are merchant seamen. His father sent him on this trip to decide his future. "If you don't like the sea life, never go to sea again," he said. "If you do like the sea life, become a captain." Terje decided on the latter course before the ship reached Lisbon. "It's a fresh life, you get around and see things, and the money's good," he said. He pointed out that captains are paid according to the tonnage of their ships and ships are getting bigger all the time.

When the *Statsraad Lehmkuhl* reached New York, Terje signed off and crossed the country to San Francisco to take a job on a Norwegian freighter plying between the United States and Asia. When he left the *Lehmkuhl*, looking, as do many Norwegian boys, a year or two younger than he is, alone in a strange country, the distance between his situation then and the command of a ship seemed staggering. He looked as if he should be at home playing ball for four or five more years.

His starting salary was fifty or seventy-five dollars a month. At his father's suggestion, he had arranged with a bank in Norway to put half of it each month for the next three years in a savings account. This left him with little to buy curios with in the ports he would visit, or, when he grew old enough, the liquor and sprees ashore that seamen are supposed to enjoy. His plan was to go to sea until nineteen and then to mate's school in Norway for a year, supporting himself ashore with the money he saved. After mate's school he would go to sea again for two years, then to school for another year, then to sea for three more years, and, finally, after six months at skipper's school, to sea again with his captain's ticket. If he succeeded, his accomplishment, it seemed to me, would make working one's way through college seem like child's play.

The *Lehmkuhl* kept the wind she picked up off La Palma for four days, during which she travelled 811 nautical miles to a lonely point in the ocean, where almost no ships go any more, 1,350 miles east by south of Bermuda. If she could have maintained that speed, she would have been in Bermuda seven days later. Instead she took sixteen days. Her best day's run in those four fast days was 228 miles. A week later, her day's run was only 102 miles. Day after day, the wind blew gently, steadily, pushing her along at between four and seven knots, occasionally, in a squall, boosting her speed up to ten or twelve knots; occasionally dropping her speed down to almost zero.

During this long, slow, middle part of the voyage, I became acquainted with the second mate, Erik Bernes, who went to sea forty-five years ago at the age of twelve. He stood the eight to noon and eight to midnight watches, and usually every night before I went to bed I would find him at a place on the windward rail of the poop deck where he could keep one eye on the helmsmen and one on the sails. He told me about ocean currents and the trade winds, the streams of air that once drove ships about the earth but are now deserted, their secrets forgotten. He talked about old cargo-carrying sailing ships whose careers he had watched with devotion as they sailed about the oceans in their last doomed years. He knew their histories, their abilities, their best passages. A few remain as hulks or storage barges in scattered ports of the world, or as museums. I suppose he knows the location of each one.

He spoke close to idiomatic English, but when he departed from it, his phrases were unusually apt. The beautiful angling of the yards—so that when you stand at the foot of a mast and look up you see a spiraling effect, each yard and sail making a slightly different angle to the axis of the ship—he explained by saying, "The old captains did it that way. You want the wind to hit the top one and come diving, diving, diving down." An Englishman in Bermuda explained the same idea with such terms as screw effect, optimal angle, and maximum drive. I thought the second mate understood it better. When the *Danmark* sailed across our bow and disappeared to leeward at sundown after we passed La Palma, and then at dawn sailed across our bow again back up to windward, I asked the second mate what the captain of the *Danmark* was up to. "The old man, I guess he is snuffing around to see where the wind is, north or south," he said.

Once I came on deck after a brief rain squall had pushed us along for an exhilarating fifteen minutes at over twelve knots and the wind was moderating and we were slowing down. "Adam was not long in paradise," Bernes said, when he saw me.

Most of all he talked about the speed of the *Statsraad Lehmkuhl*. Her speed was his compulsion. I would see him at the stern where he had just read our distance for the hour on the taffrail log. "Ach," he would say at the log, "Only four miles." In the most exasperating calm of the voyage, when we were sitting almost still in a high-pressure area, he came into the chartroom and thumped the barometer with his knuckle almost hard enough to break the glass. "I wish that blasted thing would drop," he said—as if the barometer were to blame for the high pressure. Almost every time I came on deck on the eight to midnight watch, I found him studying the wind: the wind in the sails—was it hitting them at the right angle? The wind in the clouds—if there were any—would it come to us? The wind blowing over our starboard quarter—would it veer at any moment toward the stern and slow us down if we were not quick to alter course?

For most of the trip the weather was superb—balmy, cool, and clear. When we met, I would say, "Nice night," and he, "Yah, yah. But we should have more wind."

Once, after the clouds had separated and the moon was flooding the sky, the sea, and the ship with its strange light and lighting the clouds so they looked softer than cotton, softer than down, and making the gray-tan sails a pale, ghostly white and turning the steel ventilators and the heavy wooden lifeboats on the deck into matter without substance, exact duplicates of their daytime selves you could walk through if you cared to; and was causing the captain to break out his accordion and play it softly, sitting on a hatch cover in the shadow of a sail, as the shadow slid back and forth across the deck with each slow, stately roll of the ship, and making the sailmaker, the cook, and the second engineer stay up way past their bedtimes; and was silencing all the adults on deck, so that one, halfway through a story, broke off in mid-sentence, and the few who kept talking lowered their voices almost to a whisper; and was gradually subduing even the boys, on watch down on the maindeck, until their usual loud roughhousing and laughing stopped and they stood silently looking up at the sky or the sails or out at the white moonpath on the sea—I wondered if the night, which had done this to the rest of the ship, might have seduced the second mate away from his vigil. "It's a nice-looking moon," I said. "Yah, yah," he said. "I only wish it had brought some wind with it. He had some wind in a pack on his back."

Second Mate Bernes was a man of about five feet seven or eight who looked as if he had settled down into that height some time before from five feet ten or eleven. He had a longish, strong face, a good-sized nose, and a large mouth that might have imparted sensuousness if many decades before he had not given up the rest of life in his dedication to the sea. His face looked as if it had not changed much since his late thirties but had settled early—like his frame, after a brief, probably attractive youth—into a serviceable mold never thought of by its owner except insofar as it functioned—the nose for smelling, the mouth for eating and talking, and perhaps occasionally for kissing, the ears for hearing, the eyes for seeing. He could have been any age, from forty-five to seventy. On the few occasions he was on deck without a hat one long wisp of hair that originated above his left ear sometimes was blown by the wind straight out to leeward instead of lying flat across the bald top of his head. Perhaps this wisp of hair, not nearly big enough to do the job intended for it, was his one concession to vanity, or perhaps habit only made him brush it across the top of his head as he did when he had all his hair. His clothes and slouch—which actually was not a slouch but a sign of his complete at-homeness on the sea, an easy shuffle adapted to walking rolling decks—were such that for the first three days of the voyage I thought he was a petty officer, not a mate. Instead of directing the work of the cadets, he worked with them, scraping more varnish on the rail or chipping more paint than any of them did. When you came upon him in those first days in the midst of a group of cadets at some difficult and undesirable task you thought, Who is that old man doing boy's work—is he being punished, perhaps? You only learned later that he was in charge of the boys and, in fact, during his four-hour morning watch, in charge of the ship. Bernes was the only man on board who had served on sailing cargo vessels—North Sea schooners and, in the late 1920's, a big Cape Horner hauling cargoes from the west coast of South America to Europe. For several years before 1962, Bernes, in defiance of the laws of progress, had skippered his own three-masted cargo schooner. She was eighty-nine feet long and the last cargo-carrying sailing vessel in the North Sea. Of the three watch officers—the chief officer, the first mate, and himself—Bernes was the strictest with the cadets, hoping, I suppose, to duplicate for them his own apprenticeship on sailing ships in the days when twenty men and boys did the work that on this ship was divided among the 159 cadets.

He said something to me once, near the end of the voyage, when I knew him better, that marked him—although I had guessed his secret earlier—as one of that minority of seamen who are only completely comfortable and at ease when on the ocean and for whom the shore is always somewhat alien. In many cases they may even find that if they go ashore and take a land job they become physically sick after a few months—with an undefinable ailment that soon leaves them when they ship out again. Other men, the ones not so affected, can love the sea and feel an exuberance when the wind blows hard and the ship is going well. Captain Odd Fosså, the second in command, would say, and his eyes would light up, that the best time for him is when they have set all sail and he can signal the engineer to stop the engine. He would laugh and joke and his face and lightness of movement would express his happiness when, after a calm, the ship began to move again until at last she was flying along at near top speed. But you would feel, nevertheless, that his identification was with the land, with his wife and two small children, his garden, perhaps, and the lake at his front door where he went fishing in a small boat like any city burgher. The chief steward had been at sea as long as Second Mate Bernes, been torpedoed twice, and had a third ship sunk under him by bombers; he had been everywhere—"Well, I have never been to the North Pole," he told me—and he said he loved the sea life—"I should just as well die at sea," he said. Yet with the steward you saw this same allegiance to the shore—for instance, when he spoke of his leave-taking. His young wife and their two small children came down to the dockside along with much of the population of Bergen to see the ship off on her four-month cruise. "Ah, but that's no good, no good," the steward said about a leave-taking on the ship. He said he showed his family through the ship a last time and then, instead of saying goodbye on board as he had planned, drove them home, to say goodbye there. When the ship sailed out of the harbor past the steep hillside where the steward lives, his wife was waving a white tablecloth out a second-story window. He ran down to the pantry off the main saloon and got one of the ship's tablecloths and waved it back to his wife from the half-deck—so the last they saw of each other was not their faces but their tablecloths. With a man like that the sea may have a hold, but not a grip.

But the second mate: he told me late at night as we leaned on the rail looking at the bright, tropic moonpath on the water and the stately clouds passing us (which he was gauging for the amount of wind they might bring) that he didn't care if we never came into port. "For my part," he said, "I would like to be at sea—because when you get to port, well well well well—that begins another life." It is a hard thing to explain, this distinction between two men who may go to sea side by side all their lives—yet one looks toward the land and the other toward the sea. Bernes has a wife, too, like the steward, and in his cabin at the end of the voyage I saw a thick envelope addressed to her in his careful hand. It may have been the longest letter that anyone on board wrote home. The best one can say, perhaps, is that for the steward, a voyage is a trip between two points, and, hopefully (and, probably, because he is of an optimistic turn of mind) the second point will be interesting and diverting. For the second mate, the voyage is the end in itself. He is one of those wedded to the sea, not by love, exactly, or perhaps even at all, but by familiarity.

The steward went ashore almost every night during the week the ship was in Bermuda. Bernes, I believe, went ashore only once, for an afternoon bus tour of the islands arranged for the cadets—which struck me as a sufficiently limited kind of contact for even the most dubious visitor.

On the fifteenth day of the race, the *Lehmkuhl* was still 840 miles from Bermuda. She had averaged for five days less than 115 miles a day, compared to the more than 200 miles a day she averaged after the rounding of La Palma. Her officers were disappointed, because the old sea captains they consulted in Norway who used to travel this way reported the trade winds blew harder than we were finding them. Some people on board said nuclear testing has upset the trades. They pointed out that another trade wind, the "Portugees," which has been used since time immemorial, also acted strangely. In the first two days of the race, the "Portugees," which blows from the North, should have given us fair winds for the first leg of the race, the run to La Palma. Instead we had southerly winds. But who was to say if the trades had changed? No one watches them any more.

One night I came on deck after sunset and saw the moon in the east, behind us, and in the west, ahead, red and yellow clouds in stripes and swirls turning to very light blue, and above the blue, a band of pink, and in the band of pink, a row of little ice flows of purple cloud drifting slowly southward. And in one place, a long dark bank of cloud hung along the horizon, like a mythical continent, and above it in a wisp of red there floated a small blue cloud with a thread of gold fluctuating along its top edge. And then the colors began to drain away through a hole in the west, following the sun, as though the sun were a ship and they a great silken fan it towed behind it in its circumnavigation of the earth.

In this light, the steel, rope, and canvas aloft lost their separate identities and merged in one substance; and the sails in their sequence up the masts were silhouettes, moving gently across an arc of the sky as the bow rose and at the top of a rise stood still for a moment, a second of suspension, and then dropped down. And looking toward the stern, I saw the moon over the main yard, disappearing behind a sail with each slow, stately roll of the ship. I thought a person would have to be made of cogs and wheels and springs not to be moved, fairly rapturous, at a time like this; and I wondered why man had ever given up such a way to travel for the mere saving of time. And if someone asked why you could not see the same sunset from the deck of a steamship, I knew the answer. We on this ship were part of the forces that created the sunset in a way the people on a steamship were not. The wind that made those clouds was our intimate companion. We might have to fight it, in a storm, or, at another time, it would bring delight to all on board. It was our friend and sometimes our enemy, but in either case we lived with the wind, we watched it, we knew it. A shift in direction from northwest to northeast or in velocity from fifteen knots to eight could be crucial to us (just as it could be crucial to a cloud). On a steamship, it might not be noticed. Or if it were noticed, it would be noticed only idly, by someone glancing up at the smokestack and seeing the exhaust fumes changing their path. The difference, I thought, is the same as the difference between listening to a symphony orchestra and listening to a record. The latter is sometimes called canned music. In some ways, the people on a steamship are canned people. They are at one remove from the wind and weather. Their allegiance is to the engine in their hold whose vibrations they can feel in the soles of their feet as they walk about the deck in the daytime and on their pillows when they go to bed at night, whose noise they can hear from the moment they leave port until they return, whose fumes they probably can smell. For noise, we had the creaking of the rigging; for smells, the sea air.

I was standing near the bow. When I turned around, I saw two boys sitting on the deck leaning over an instruction book, practicing knots. Not far from them, a third boy was sewing a piece of sailcloth into a bag, I suppose for his toilet articles; Mike Kjølsrud was trying to whittle the head of a narwhale out of a piece of teak. I heard singing coming from the other side of the steel galley house where a white-thatched able seaman was attempting to teach some boys the sea chanteys of his youth, and, once in a while, to their great amusement, doing a jig. A small cadet played an accordion. Light came from one of the doors in the galley house which led into the carpenter's shop, and inside I saw two boys working on a model of the *Statsraad Lehmkuhl,* a surprise present from all the cadets to the chief

officer, which they planned to give him when the ship docked in
Norway at the end of the cruise. The chief steward had secured
a set of plans of the ship for them to work from. Up on the forecastle head, the raised deck in the bow of the ship, the younger
able seamen and petty officers sat consuming a bottle of Norwegian spirits and telling doubtful stories of their exploits
ashore. At the other end of the maindeck, two thirds of the way
to the stern of the ship, eight steps lead up to the halfdeck.
Under a short extension of the halfdeck which makes a kind of
roof over a section of maindeck there is a long bench which is
the off-watch headquarters of the petty officers. Here the sailmaker, some quartermasters, the carpenter, and one of the cooks
were smoking and discussing the progress of the race. The
second engineer was cutting an able seaman's hair in front of the
bench. Another able seaman came by, shook his head regretfully
to indicate it was a horrible job, and moved on. The sailmaker,
Olav Hellesø, who at sixty-one had not been to sea for many
years before this voyage and would not go again after it, showed
me photographs of some of the beautiful ship models, accurate
down to the smallest block, that he makes. He signed on this
voyage, he said, only to live backwards to what he remembers.
"It was exciting and romantic in the old days," he said.
"It wasn't just a job." It is sad, he said, to see a whole age cut off.
He said he understood that of course you could not make a living
with sailing ships in this modern age. "But the excitement of the
old days that is gone now, that is a loss," he said. A boy came up
to him and asked him to tie a complicated knot.

Nearby, half a dozen cadets watched the bo's'n helping a boy
make a rope mat. Two other boys were making rope grommets.
A few minutes later a crowd gathered around them when they
began to play quoits, throwing the grommets at an iron eyebolt
sticking up from the deck. I wondered if they, playing a game
with what was at hand, relaxing between duties, might not be
getting more fun out of it than the passengers on a liner playing

the same game with expensively manufactured quoits, expensive play clothes, expensively bought leisure.

I walked aft to where the first mate, the radio operator, and the doctor were sitting in deck chairs near the stern. The bo's'n, who came aft with the carpenter a few moments later to join them, laughed at the picture of ease they made in the warm last light of the day. "Tourists, tourists," he said.

"Tourissimo," the young first mate said, raising his arms and stretching lazily and then sinking back in his chair with a contented smile.

Captain Fosså came on deck and the bo's'n stood up to give him the deck chair usually used by him or Captain Ottesen. Captain Fosså shook his head, meaning stay there, and sat down on a hatchway cover nearby. (That petty officers felt free occasionally to wander aft to the deck chairs near the stern, an area on most ships reserved to the captain and the mates, was typical of the friendliness on the ship. Perhaps because shipmasters in the Norway merchant marine work their way up from seaman, as they did in the United States in the great days of our merchant marine, pretensions of social superiority do not accompany the necessary superiorities and inferiorities of rank.)

The talk turned to the race. We had learned on the radio that afternoon that the *Danmark* and the *Radich* were north of us. We imagined them being sucked into the Sargasso Sea and going around and around forever. This was too much to hope for, of course, but we thought that being closer to the calm belt than we, they might slow down. Captain Ottesen came on deck and played his accordion for a little while. The talk became desultory and then died out.

Suddenly I realized that I had forgotten I was on a foreign ship, so completely had the Norwegians, without conscious art, made me feel welcome and at home. Norwegian was the language spoken most of the time, of course, but after a few days I found my mind blanked out the Norwegian conversations around me in the same way that on a bus you are only occasionally aware of the voices you hear. And I could be sure, for instance in a gathering like this, that if something funny were said or some point about the race came up, the doctor, Captain Fosså, or one of the others would translate. Usually then all of them would start speaking English, perhaps for as long as I was with them, although this was an inconvenience. I found the Norwegians invariably thoughtful, an attractive, quick-witted, talented people. I was continually charmed by the democracy on board. I would see Captain Fosså and the second cook meet on the maindeck and engage in conversation about the weather. If a cadet had to tell a mate or one of the captains to move from an area he was going to hose down, he did so with no sign of obsequiousness. I believe this social equality is a characteristic of Norway where, I am told, the king is prized for his approachability as well as for other, more usual, kingly qualities.

As I looked at the men around me I was struck with great admiration for their homeland. This little country, with a population of 3.7 million, smaller than sixteen of our states, has a larger merchant marine than any nation on earth except Great Britain, which is thirteen times her size and infinitely richer in resources and capital. Norway is enviable, with her compact and homogeneous population, the continuity of her culture, and the felicity with which she has adapted to modern times her ancient heritage, the sea.

Norwegians, based on their remote plateau, have been ranging the waterways of the globe for more than a thousand years—in the days of the Vikings with unmatched daring; today with unmatched competency. They are the true cosmopolitans. The world is their community and they know Marseilles and Singapore, Mobile and Tenerife, as we know New York or San Francisco. They borrow words from other peoples freely, and a favorite Norwegian seaman's dish, I found on this trip, is not some northern chowder but a Spanish casserole called *baccalat*. They have tremendous knowledge of our country gained not through television or the movies but through familiarity with our ports. They know our slang, our songs, our baseball teams. The chief steward, who would reminisce about the grand shows at the old Singer Theater in New Orleans, where he was in attendance on opening night and many nights thereafter, knew more about the seaboard cities of the United States than I do. He and some other older members of the crew have visited New York more times, I am sure, than most Americans.

Little Norway, with less than a tenth of one per cent of the world's population, owns ten per cent of the world's shipping. It is as if Maryland or Oregon had a whole history, life, and culture of its own, and one or the other of them had a merchant marine of twenty-three hundred ships totaling fourteen million tons. This is enough to carry every man, woman, and child in Norway, with room to spare. It is 3.4 tons of ship per inhabitant. No nation in the world comes close to Norway in her relation to the sea. It is estimated that half of Norway's males have made at least one voyage as merchant seamen. Boys who plan to be lawyers or engineers go to sea to earn tuition, or, if they don't need the money, to see the world. Norway is so adapted to the sea that even though half her ships were sunk by the Germans in World War I and again in World War II, she recovered her preeminence in just a few years.

Perhaps it is natural that Norway's long coastline, which if stretched out would reach halfway around the Equator, should be the most prolific breeding ground of seamen in the world. The sea encloses Norway and its 150,000 islands like a glove, and fjords, like fingers, penetrate deep into the high, precipitous mainland. The Norwegians, inheritors of a great tradition and perhaps the most spectacular landscape on earth, came into the modern world with little else. Of the necessities of modern industrial society, they have few natural resources, only modest wealth, and little farmland—ninety-seven per cent of Norway is either rock or too steep to plow. Thus she must depend on her merchant marine to maintain a standard of living comparable to the rest of northern Europe. That a nation so poorly endowed —as the world counts endowments—and so small is able to maintain one of the largest and most efficient merchant marines in the world (so efficient, for instance, that the United States ships cannot compete without a subsidy) seemed to me an incredible achievement.

Norway's merchant tonnage is so much greater than her own export and import trade that only a few of her ships ever call in Norwegian ports. Instead they sail between the continents carrying more of the world's goods than the countries that produce them. This means that most of her seamen never see home except for infrequent vacations. Captain Fosså, who went to sea at fifteen, did not get back to Norway until he was eighteen. Captain Ottesen, who went to sea at fourteen, was nineteen when he came home for the first time. Some of the men on the ship were away for a decade. Forty boys on this voyage were scheduled to get off in New York to sign on Norwegian tankers and freighters in the United States. They would not see home again for at least eighteen months.

I walked from my deck chair to the rail where Second Mate Bernes, on watch until midnight, was leaning, looking at some clouds. "We may get some sou'west wind," he said. "Those heavy clouds with wisps up there have sou'west wind in them. But with a northeast wind here blowing this way and sou'west there blowing that way, it can't blow sou'west right away. They crash together. May be a while with no wind." After he left the rail to go to the other side of the ship to see that all was well there, the quartermaster on watch with him, Øyvind Bøe, came up to me. "What did the second mate say about the wind?" he asked. I told him he said we may get some southwest wind. "Yes, I think there is wind in those clouds," Øyvind said, and I thought, He is learning from Bernes, a little here, a little there, as Bernes had learned almost half a century ago from some old shellback, and that shellback in turn had learned from an older generation, and so on back in an unbroken line for centuries.

The next night when I went into the saloon for supper I saw that the table was set for a banquet. My table companions—the two captains, the chief mate, the chief steward, the chief engineer, the doctor, the secretary, and the other two Americans— were standing at the far end of the saloon chatting, smoking, and drinking glasses of Norwegian beer. The doctor told me it was Midsummer Night, a holiday that goes back before Odin and Thor, I suppose, to the days when the Norwegians worshipped the sun. We drank aquavit and beer with the meal, and, for the first time since I came on board, the conversation turned to Norway's past. Captain Fosså spoke of the Norwegian place names and even family names in Scotland and the islands north of it dating from the days of the Vikings. Secretary Gjesdal described a voyage to Iceland made by one of the early adventurers.

After supper, Captain Ottesen played Norwegian folk songs in his cabin for the doctor, the chief engineer, and the messboys, and Secretary Gjesdal organized a sing for the cadets in their quarters, a huge room below the maindeck. Mr. Gjesdal had been attempting without much success all during the voyage to teach them sea chanteys. But tonight they sang Norwegian songs with gusto.

Afterward the cadets whooped onto deck, all of them trying to crowd out the two exits at once. They milled around noisily for a few minutes, but the moonlight, or perhaps thoughts of home, soon quieted them. Some were singing near the bow, accompanied by an accordion. I saw a boy I knew named Karl Øby standing at the rail. I had met Karl a few days before when Michael Kjølsrud invited me to eat a meal with his crew in the cadets' quarters instead of aft in the main saloon. The crew Mike and Karl are in consists of nine cadets who are responsible for furling and unfurling the four sails on what we call the bowsprit and they call the clever boom (pronounced cleever). This crew is also responsible for all the work on the raised forward part of the ship, the forecastle head, which they call the *bakk*. Karl, the son of a minister, a handsome, somewhat moody boy who had been in some difficulty at school shortly before the voyage because of a fight, was leaning on the rail now with his chin cupped in one hand, looking down at the sea.

"You have been to Norway?" he said.

"No. I have been to Sweden—for two days," I said.

"I suppose Norway is more beautiful. I think Norway is the most beautiful country I see."

"Because of the mountains?"

"The mountains, yes. And the fjords. The mountains are very —high?" He looked at me to see if that were the right word and if I understood. "And the fjords . . . There is no air."

"No air?"

"You can't *bru*. Do you say *bru*?

"Breathe, maybe."

"Yes. You can't breathe."

"You can't breathe? Why can't you?"

"It is so beautiful." When he saw I understood, he smiled. "The fjords are steep and in the spring the trees are . . . The side of the mountain is all white. I suppose you know what I mean?"

"Yes, I do." When he did not say anything more, I asked him how he liked the trip on the *Statsraad Lehmkuhl*.

"I like it very much. The best thing I like is to tie up the sails on the clever boom. Because we did it so fine before we arrive in Lisbon. I suppose we did the best job of all the ships. You know, I looked over all the other ships on the clever boom and I thought our ship was the finest.

"The flying jib is the worst sail on the whole ship to tie up. I am sure we do it fine now. We get a feeling those sails are ours so we have to do it best. And we are very proud of the *bakk*. We feel it is our place and we have done what we could to make it the best place on the ship.

"And we like to see how fast we can go. We want to strike the record. And you know, we have touched fourteen and a half knots. In the North Sea. You saw smiles everywhere. Some boys were seasick but still they were smiling. We didn't know how fast we were going then. Now we can tell. I suppose I can tell how fast we are going any time. And we thought, oh, just let them come on. We'll beat them. Just let *Radich* come on, we'll just beat them. I'm sure we could beat every one of them if we could get the right wind.

"And I like to be at sea, especially on a windjammer, because you have to leave it up to the wind and weather. It is something, you know. The old Vikings left it up to the wind and weather. When we are at sea we can see what can happen, and we can see how fine sailors the old Vikings were. We are much more sure because we see a plane or a ship and we don't get a feeling we are lonely on the sea.

"But nobody did care for the sailors then and they were frightened of . . . big worm. They thought it was lying around the world and every ship that fall down from the edge—that was it!"

A little cadet, the smallest and youngest on board, I think, came over to the rail. "I see blink," he said, pointing to a small flash of lightning on the horizon that lit up a section of cloud the size of a thumbnail. "Is very nice," he said. He was excited and trying to say something more. "In Norway tonight we have . . . *bol*—you know *bol*?" I looked at Karl. He smiled down at the little cadet in rather a fatherly way and said it meant a fire. He said all over Norway on Midsummer Night people light fires outdoors and in many places row around in boats while the fires burn near the water's edge. The lightning did look remarkably like the reflection of a bonfire when it flashed again. The little boy said: "Is very nice," again, and walked away.

"Do you think he is homesick?" Karl said.

"I think he is."

"Yes." Karl said, in a way that included himself, I thought. He was quiet for a few minutes.

Behind Karl and me about ten boys were taking turns climbing up a line that ran at a forty-five degree angle to a block swinging fifteen or twenty feet above the deck—hand over hand, with their feet dangling. Karl smacked the rail with his open palm and ran to the line. He went up easily to the block and then about a yard beyond it on a wire rope leading aloft. When he came down, I asked him why he didn't keep going. "I could," he said and laughed at himself because obviously he had gone the limit.

Most of the Norwegians I came to know on the ship had fine wits. Captain Fosså, almost every meal, got off two or three comments that made the whole table laugh. I met the first mate on the hottest of the two uncomfortable days of the voyage walking up the deck, weary with the heat. "I guess you miss Norway weather," I said. "Miss Norway wind," he said. When I was describing my fourteen-foot sailboat to him, he asked straight-faced if my boat was square-rigged. "She was," I said, "but I changed her over to a modern rig." "Couldn't get crews for her, I guess," he said. Øyvind Bøe showed me his wrist watch once. I asked him if it were waterproof, and mistakenly thinking he did not know the word, added, "Can you wear it under water?" "Yes, I can," he said. "But it will stop." Karl once told me about his eleven-year-old brother, who, he said, would probably grow up to be a professor or something like that. "What about you?" I said. "I don't know," he said, then thinking a minute, he added, "Probably I will attain a high position—like airline pilot. That is a high position, don't you think? Forty thousand feet." He had two cigarettes, lit one and gave me the other. I protested that it was his last one. "No, it's your last one," he said, crumpling the pack and throwing it overboard.

The day before, I had gone aloft to take some pictures of an able seaman named Nils Strøther, Mike, and two cadets installing a new royal stay, a wire rope running from almost the top of the mainmast to a point halfway down on the foremast. Nils— twenty-eight, a bo's'n on deepwater tankers and a captain of Norwegian coastal craft, on this voyage as a seaman at a considerable cut in pay, because he loves to sail—had one leg thrust over a rung of the rope ladder leading to the royal yard and was leaning over four feet of nothing to direct the operation. Mike and one of the cadets were standing on the upper topgallant yard reaching up and attempting to loop the end of the wire stay around the mast. The other cadet had one foot on the bottom rung of the ladder and the other foot on a cable leading to the topgallant yard. All four of them together were able to loop the end of the wire stay around the mast. But it took them a long time to twist the loop enough to allow them to fasten it with U-bolts. When they finally did, they had to pound the U-bolts home with wrenches before they could screw nuts onto them. There was much banter and, on Nils' and Mike's part, much swearing. Someone dropped a U-bolt. They argued, laughing, about who was going down to get another one. One of the nuts did not fit. Nils told Mike it was made in America. They blamed the bo's'n for not sending aloft the right equipment and complained they would miss supper. They were talking, it seemed to me, out of sheer exuberance. After a half hour of exertion, the job was done and the four dropped down to deck. On deck or ashore, it would have been a mundane job—merely the making of an eye in a wire cable around a pole. In the rigging, for those thirty minutes, it was touch and go whether they would succeed. When they did, they were triumphant. "It was great," Mike said. "The whoosh, whoosh of the masts back and forth. The eyes of everyone on you and all that. Looking down at the sails with the sun on them. The colors in the water. The waves breaking. The wind in your hair, and the sound of it rolling off the canvas."

The soft tropic nights and days slipped by in orderly procession. In the days, the cadets scraped and sanded teak—rails, hatch covers, grillwork, moldings, and the teak charthouse, a square structure on the halfdeck the size of a small summer cottage containing, besides the chartroom, a radio room, a small cabin, and the stairway to the main saloon. They chipped paint off all the steel parts of the ship except the outside of the hull—stanchions, ventilators, lifeboat davits, skylights, the compan-

ionways to the cadets quarters, the steel house on the maindeck
containing the galley and carpenter shop, and stairs to the quarters of the able seamen and quartermasters. They varnished the
teak, painted the steel, then, on their hands and knees, they
holystoned the deck. They scraped, sanded, and painted the
wooden lifeboats and boarding ladders. They painted the masts
and applied a mixture of grease and white lead to the mile or
more of wire rigging—hanging in bo's'n's chairs from the tops of
the masts. The ship began to look new again, not a time-banged
fifty years old. The first mate and some of the petty officers grew
beards and a number of the cadets followed suit with peach fuzz.
The doctor, explaining the beginnings of a mustache, said that
growing a mustache is supposed to bring wind.

No other ships showed up except the *Danmark* once. On the
sixth day after the rounding of La Palma, she appeared ahead,
heading on a course that took her across the *Lehmkuhl's* bow.
She disappeared to the south and west of the *Lehmkuhl*, but
when heard of again, in a radio report, she was back to the north
once more.

The radio report—a conversation overheard by chance between the *Christian Radich* and a British yacht—put the *Radich*
and the *Danmark*, which was in sight of her, slightly ahead of
the *Lehmkuhl*. From then until the end of the race, we would
frequently hear of the position of the other two. One day they
would be eighty miles ahead, two days later, thirty-two miles, a
day later, forty or forty-five miles.

The second mate, who believed that a sailing ship should
never run directly before the wind, was always uncomfortable
when he came on deck and found the *Lehmkuhl* doing so. After
he learned I subscribed to his theory, he would talk about it,
although with no disrespect for Captain Ottesen. "If I had this
ship, we would be laying right that way," he would say, indicating a course thirty degrees off to one side. "Look at the staysails.
They doing nothing. The foremast ain't working. Only the
mainmast is working. I would be laying off there. Then the wind

come in all the sails. Zigzag, we call it. We should be zigzagging since La Palma.

"Well, well. I don't get mixed up in it," he said once. "I don't care if we win or not. I get paid anyway." But the next time I saw him at the place by the windward rail where we usually talked, he said: "Those other four fellers, I'd give anything to know where they are. I just wonder what surprises for us when we stick our nose into that harbor."

The first mate, like the second, favored zigzagging, or what American and English sailors call tacking downwind. He experimented and found that by sailing twenty degrees off the downwind course he could increase the speed of the *Lehmkuhl* 1.5 knots. To make up the extra distance covered by zigzagging required, he figured out, an increase of only .35 knots. I think Captain Fosså and Chief Officer Nyebak believed in zigzagging too. The problem was Captain Ottesen—a strange, attractive, at times melancholy man who was incapacitated by a vague illness for much of the voyage. He said to me once, "Have you heard of King Saul? He was asking David, Won't you please play something for me. Because he was . . ." (he looked at me, patting his heart) ". . . sad. David played him a little song. Saul, he freshened up, freshened up a little bit. That's the way with me. But I have no one to play for me." He had been a hero in Norway's torpedo boats in World War II. He was undoubtedly a fine seaman. (He took the *Lehmkuhl* through a gale in a record nineteen-day passage from Boston to Bergen in 1952 in which the seas floated her lifeboats, hung in davits above the halfdeck, and in which a workbench bolted to the steel floor of the engine room was ripped from the floor and flung against a bulkhead, pinning four cadets. He tied and held the injured cadets on the dining table in the main saloon so they would not be thrown while the doctor patched them up, and then the dining table, also bolted down, was uprooted from the floor and hurled across the saloon.) He was kind-hearted, generous, fair with cadets and crew, and witty. I remember a mimicked contrast he did of Boston and

New York—in Boston, a dowager holding her teacup with little finger extended delicately saying, "Come, please, dear captain, won't you come with me to my garden to see the roses?" and in New York, a burly man saying, "Hey, Cap, follow me. We'll go around the conrer and get a Tom Collins." John Sibley and I found him charming and surprising and as the voyage went on more and more charming and more and more surprising. He loved to play an accordion—Norwegian folk songs, some Grieg, and most of all, American songs like "Carry Me Back to Ole Virginia" and "My Old Kentucky Home," which he would sing as he played, looking up at the paneling above him, or out a porthole. Once he said, "When I am playing music I forget all about the sailing," and he did, as far as John and I could see. Sometimes he would not appear on deck for days. There were four other men quite capable of taking command of the ship—Captain Fosså, of course, and Chief Officer Nyebak, and the first and second mates. I was told the bo's'n, Alf Skårnes, whom the first mate said was the best bo's'n in the world, could also command a square-rigged ship. Captain Ottesen's absences made the sailing of the ship and the working out of a consistent strategy difficult, but he was never ill enough to relinquish his command.

Every day after the mates had taken their noon sights of the sun, First Mate Gronningen would plot the *Lehmkuhl*'s position on a special racing chart he kept. On this chart he also plotted the positions of any of the other ships we had news of—usually the *Christian Radich* and *Danmark,* together some miles ahead, and the *Sorlandet,* way behind, but sometimes a vague report of some other barque or ship. He calculated distances to Bermuda, theirs and ours, sailing various courses, and estimated probable winds in various sections of the trade wind belt. Usually, some time later in the day, he would take his friend, the bo's'n, into the chartroom to show him our progress and to discuss strategy. The first mate would also plot the new positions on a chart in the cadets' quarters, while they crowded around asking questions.

Some of the crew were for continuing to sail west until almost south of Bermuda (which lay almost six hundred miles north of the parallel we were on), and then head north to the finish line, believing that the better winds found south of Bermuda would more than compensate in speed for the greater distance required to get to them. Others were for heading northeast now, straight for Bermuda.

One day the radio operator, Bjørn Garnes, heard from a Norwegian freighter fifty miles southwest of the *Lehmkuhl* that he had twenty- to thirty-knot winds and rain. "It must be local," he said. Every man became a weatherman.

Wishful rumors went through the ship. Once she gained thirteen miles in a noon-to-noon run on the *Christian Radich.* A few minutes after this news came over the radio, the first mate went forward to direct the bracing of the yards on the foremast. He heard one cadet tell another we had gained thirty miles.

Eventually it became obvious to even the most hopeful that the *Lehmkuhl* had only the slightest chance of catching the *Danmark* and the *Radich,* and no chance at all, even if she caught them, of making up her handicap. Then many of the cadets said they hoped the *Danmark* would win, not the *Christian Radich.* I heard a cadet ask Captain Fosså whom he hoped would win. Captain Fosså gravely explained to the cadet the reasons why he thought he should hope the *Radich* would win. The secretary took the matter up in one of his frequent evening assemblies in the boys' quarters, saying that Bergeners and people from Oslo are all Norwegians.

Sometimes a rainstorm would approach the ship—riches of clouds piled into spirals and folds of deep purple and blue with rain slanting down from their flat bottom edges and slices of rainbow bridging the spaces between them. Then the crew of the ship would stand along its almost windless windward rail and watch, guess, and hope. Rain, which we in the cities usually see only as miserable wetness coming down from a dirty yellow sky and smelling, as likely as not, of exhaust and diesel fumes, at sea is often a stately spectacle—a drama in the sky with a beginning, development, and climax—which one can look at from far away and guess its future and watch to see if the guess was right, and use later, perhaps, to take a shower in. If the watchers were lucky, the rain, preceded by wind ruffling the water into quick crowded whitecaps underneath it, would reach the ship, and she would be reprieved from her slow four or five knots and take wing, her big foresail lifting her bow, and her other sails bending her down to leeward and ahead. Then, as she drove ahead, the people on her slanting deck would be gripped by a most unreasonable optimism, imagining that she could keep this wind, and (because wasn't it true that all the old *Lehmkuhl* needed was a breeze to show what she could do?) go by all the others. The bo's'n, who speaks no English, might, laughing, make a circle on the deck, indicate the *Lehmkuhl* in the center of it, and by gestures make clear that in his opinion we might keep the wind while the ships to the north of us, out of the circle, would miss it. The first mate, instead of reading the ship's distance from the taffrail log at the stern once an hour, would look at the log every ten minutes and convert the distance run and the time into speed gleefully as her speed climbed from eight to ten to twelve knots. The two cadets at the wheel, who may have been daydreaming, somewhat listless, before the new wind came, would become excited, a little scared, on edge, proud to be at the helm in this storm. The cook would emerge from the galley and stand leaning into the wind, his apron flying out behind him. The carpenter and sailmaker might come out of their shops, and even the first engineer, tinkering with his diesel down in the bowels of the ship, might decide, after feeling the new surge and excitement in the motion of the ship, to climb up the flights of steel steps to the maindeck.

After one rainstorm I was talking with Karl Øby when Øyvind Bøe came off watch and walked over to tell me that the radio operator of the *Christian Radich* had told our radio operator of a Washington weather report predicting winds increasing to thirty knots in this section of the ocean. Because Øyvind and I were talking English faster than Karl could understand, he stopped us to protest. Øyvind repeated the weather report in Norwegian. Karl broke into a smile. "Hi, hi, oo-la-la," he said, and hit his thigh with his fist. He and Øyvind talked excitedly and then, coming back into English, he said, "Marvelous—a storm. She goes in a storm."

"And she does not need to take in sail," Øyvind said. "And the *Radich*—" he shook his head deprecatingly. "She won't go. She has to shorten sail."

"This ship will sail into a hurricane, I think," Karl said. "In Biscay, we had a big storm. *Radich* took down her sails."

"Not all of them. You don't mean that, do you?"

"Many of them. She just lay against the wind and her engine running. Her engine running!

"She was before us until the storm. And after, we were. Well, we beat her by two days to Cascais."

Øyvind nodded. "Yes, and there was some talk afterward that her captain was afraid to carry sail."

He and Karl, reverting to Norwegian, decided the broadcast came from too far away to be accurate and that the smoothness of the sea indicated there was no storm anywhere in our neighborhood. They were right.

These passing rainstorms were too insignificant to do much good. One would miss the ship, and another, a cloud and its accoutrements, towering over the ship, dwarfing it, drawing near with well-formed thunderheads and sure indications of wind and rain, twenty minutes later would be lifeless and indistinct, still perhaps in the shape of a rainstorm but now an apparition—its rain, wind, and motion gone. Then it would dissolve into the haze of the horizon.

At noon on the eighteenth day of the race, which was June 23, we were six hundred miles from Bermuda in a straight line, and about seven hundred miles on the course the captain intended to follow to take advantage of expected better wind. Our day's run from noon on the twenty-second to noon on the twenty-third was one hundred nineteen miles, not much for a ship that with a good wind could sail three hundred miles. "It's a funny wind," the first mate said, meaning, it is a disappointment, it is lighter than expected, it seems to be becoming sporadic. A sailing ship is a thing of moods, and during the next few days, as the wind became weaker and sometimes left us altogether, a tenseness came on board that I had not seen before. There was a tendency for the officers, having done all they could when we had a decent wind, to go off somewhere with glum looks, to mope, I suppose. Everyone wore an exasperated, embarrassed look, like people on a New York subway on a hot day. Yet all that was needed to give us boundless happiness was a good wind, or news that slow as we were moving, we had gained on the other ships.

On the twenty-seventh our day's run was fifty-seven miles and on the twenty-eighth, fifty-three miles. By breakfast time on the twenty-eighth, even the little breaths of air the mate had chased the night before disappeared and all motion stopped. The clouds stood still. An empty flour barrel thrown overboard at eight o'clock floated a few hundred yards from the ship at noon —ahead, not behind her. "It will probably beat us to Bermuda," someone said.

With all chance of filling the sails gone and no choice but to sit and wait for the wind, the second mate's mood changed too. When I saw him during his morning watch at the rail looking out at the lifeless clouds, I said: "Where's the wind?" "The wind?" he said. "The wind? Well, the ocean is wide and he can't be every place . . . He is going around collecting all the ships and putting them together."

This turned out to be exactly the case. The wind blew for the Argentine, Spanish, and Portuguese ships, and the third Norwegian ship, the *Sorlandet*, and they all caught up.

We sat still until late at night on the twenty-eighth, and, just as we had forgotten all the way from Lisbon that the *Sratsraad*

Lehmkuhl could stop dead in the water, now we forgot that she could move. That night the first faint stirrings of movement—fits and starts—pleased us. But we had forgotten what it was like to sail in a breeze, what it had been like to sail thirteen knots around La Palma.

A few wisps of air played about the ship from time to time at sundown but always left us before the ship could even begin to set its ponderous bulk in motion (what had been so light, dainty, frisky with the wind was now clumsy dead weight). Finally, at 11:30, near the end of the second mate's night watch, they came again, and, instead of disappearing, began to turn into a breeze. The second mate, sniffing the air, feeling at first afraid to move for fear perhaps it would become scared and go away, finally concluded that it might stay. He waited a few minutes more, determined in what quarter it was settling, and then, with a mighty voice, triumphantly, yelled for manpower to brace the yards.

Three days later we crossed the finish line to find that the *Gorch Fock* had been first across. On corrected time, however, she was beaten by the *Christian Radich* from Oslo and the *Danmark* under Captain Knud Hansen. The *Libertad* was fourth, the *Sorlandet* fifth and we were sixth, beating the *Juan Sebastian de Elcano*. The *Sagres*, hopelessly behind as the deadline for the race drew near, gave up and finished under power.

But as we sighted Bermuda at dawn the wind was strong, we were moving at a fast clip, and the disappointment of losing was forgotten. I noticed again, as I had at La Palma and every time the wind freshened since then, a sustained lifting of the spirits in which it seemed almost, at times, as if you became the ship and the ship became you: You, if you were the mate on watch who had been keeping the ship at top speed and on course, edging her higher into the wind each time you could and causing her to fall off when necessary; you, if you were the quartermaster standing by the two boys at the wheel and keeping them from swinging the ship too far one way or the other when the mate called for a change in course; you, if you were the two cadets with your hands on the spokes of the wheel, feeling the ship respond to your commands, but not your commands alone, for it was also obeying the commands of the wind and the sea; you, if you were the fourteen boys who had just hauled in the sheet of the mainsail and given the ship an extra ounce of speed; you, if you were the sailmaker who stayed up all night to sew up the tattered flying jib after it had blown out in a squall; you, even, if you were the second cook, whose accomplishment may have been cooking a fish chowder for two hundred men the night before, while standing on your ear. It was your ship now. And I saw people bang her on the rail affectionately, or nod their heads at each other as proud relatives might, or say, warmly, "Feel her go. She's a good ship," or "This is what she wants."

"When I was a deck boy on motorships, I never get a feeling like this," Øyvind Bøe said to me when he came off watch. "When you are sailing hard, with the railings almost under, and you have to watch the sails every minute, you have a feeling you are really in the sea. And you have a try of your skill and your intelligence.

"If they scrap this ship and the other two and only have motorships and shore schools for training, they will never get so many boys who want to be cadets. And they will not be such good seamen because the wind and the weather and the sea have more to say on a sailing ship than on a motorship.

"But now, even if we spend all our lives on a motorship, we have come to know the sea. And afterwards, we will like it very much to think of this trip.

"Did you notice every time a motorship saw us, even if they were far away on the horizon, they came over to look? And that French liner near the Canaries that went around us three times. Don't you think the men on those ships were happy to see us? So, if you take these ships away, those men will be sorry too. They will miss them too.

"And this ship gets letters from Norwegian captains and chief mates and chief stewards and chief engineers who say their training on our ship was the best school they ever had in their life."

I watched Øyvind and the others on his watch, after a last look aloft at the wind in the sails, go below. Sail training, I thought, is no longer necessary if human beings are no longer necessary. And this of course may be the case; human beings may not be needed any more. Ships may soon operate with a push of a button in New York and nothing more to be done until the captain walks down the gangplank in Liverpool. But the Norwegians have so far held to the idea that a thorough grounding in the fundamentals of seamanship is still important. In so doing, it seemed to me, they are providing for all the needs of man for glory, excitement, and a chance to test his mettle, and for an increasingly apparent necessity today, his need to establish an understandable relationship with his environment, in this case, the ancient sea.

This is an idea, I thought, that we on the land might consider in the task of reconciling our technology to our needs as human beings. We have been made comfortable as objects. But where is the advantage of our abundance if the technology that provided it has robbed the lives of many of us, our work lives, at least, of variety, challenge, and the opportunity to demonstrate skill?

Part Two

The Fishermen
of the Grand Banks

I

Before the internal combustion engine had taken most of the glamour out of following the sea, there lived on the northeastern coast of North America a breed of seamen whose hardihood and skill have never been surpassed. They were the fishermen of Gloucester, Massachusetts, and Lunenburg, Nova Scotia, who sailed to the Grand Banks in some of the most beautiful vessels ever designed—powerful, seaworthy, and incredibly fast. These vessels reached such a degree of perfection that yacht design was influenced by them in the early days of this century and still is even today.

There are distinctions that must be made between the Lunenburg end and the Gloucester end of this society. Gloucester considered herself the queen of the North Atlantic fishery. Her schooners ranged the farthest. *They* whitened the waters and used the harbors of Nova Scotia and Newfoundland, not vice versa. She was the great innovator: innovations in hull design, in rig, in technique found their way from Gloucester to Lunenburg, and from Lunenburg to Newfoundland, not the other way.

In the late nineteenth century Gloucester developed a fresh-fishing market, which centered around the old T wharf in Boston. The fresh-fishing schooners had to race to market to beat rivals for the highest price and to keep their fish from spoiling. Schooners became lower, more heavily canvassed, faster. In Lunenburg there was no economic reason for extreme speed, because in Lunenburg's salt-fishing trade it made no difference whether a vessel arrived today or next week. Lunenburg schooners, therefore, had to have a large cargo capacity. They were usually longer, higher, wider, and bulkier than the Gloucestermen.

Angus Walters, captain of the famous Lunenburg schooner *Bluenose*, remembers when he was young the large fleets of Lunenburg and Gloucester schooners that met frequently on the banks or in coves in Newfoundland or the Magdalen Islands, where they went for bait. "They used to build a much neater-looking vessel and they were down low in the water. Their vessels was always low-cut vessels. If we see an American come along—they look to us loaded down.

"They wanted them only for fishing, you see. We wanted them for two things, to fish and carry freight. That was why, when they caught us out fishing, they had fun with us. As a rule, when it came to haul by the wind, naturally they would beat us.

"They called us just a bunch of Dutchmen. Oh, hell yes, great fun in those days. We had these clam arks, they called them. It was the crews, you know—not the masters.

"They always used to crow. I remember when I went with Father. They used to crow crow crow. Spruce junks they used to call us. Pick a chew of gum off our vessels anytime.

"The Americans were brought up on racing. When they left the Banks they carried sail like all hell. They lost many men that way. Yes, they were used to racing [formal racing]. We never raced, only unless we met each other. Never fit out for racing. If we met and raced, one might be in trim, the other not."

But if in the days before the *Bluenose* the Yankees were faster, this should be pointed out: just as Donald McKay, America's greatest clipper ship designer, was a Nova Scotian, so, too, were many of Gloucester's best skippers. Marty Welch and Ben Pine, the two most famous Gloucester racing skippers in the 1920's and 1930's, were from Nova Scotia and Newfoundland. "We called them white-wash Yankees," Angus Walters recalled. Seventy-five percent of the Gloucestermen's crews, he said, came from Nova Scotia.

The Gloucester schooners and their Canadian counterparts reached their highest development in the first twenty years of this century. Just as the American clipper ship—probably man's greatest achievement in the art of square-rigged ship building—was a product of the 1840's and 1850's, when the steamship was already smudging the horizon, so, too, the Grand Banks fishing schooner reached its zenith at the very moment of its extinction. The most famous of them were launched between 1920 and 1930 —ironically, after they had become doomed as a species by the squat, tubby deisel trawlers that now scoop up the fish of the Grand Banks with robot-like efficiency. By 1930 the schooners were clearly obsolete. By 1940 there was not a schooner left that had not had its masts cut down and been converted into an engine-driven, lifeless machine.

The lone survivor in Gloucester of the old style of fishing gave up in 1953. The last survivor in Lunenburg gave up in 1963. (Both of these schooners were motorized, but their method of fishing, trawling from dories, was the same as that in the heyday of the fishing fleets.) Only a few old captains are left. When you see these old captains thirty years after their world began its swift decline, there is a haughtiness about them, a sense of su-periority—perhaps like old Indian chiefs who made names for themselves in ancient battles. They have a manner which seems to imply that they, having looked the whirlpool in the eye and not flinched, know something that the rest of us outside their small circle do not know, about the limits of endurance, about life. It does not seem to be arrogance, but an opinion, that you —clerk or tourist—deal in irrelevancies.

It is no disparagement of the Chesapeake Bay oystermen, the

Bahamians, and the deepwater sailors of the square-rigged training ships to single out the Grand Banks fishermen for their skills,
the perfection of their vessels, the flair and style in their sailing.
They were of a special mold, partly because the circumstances of
their occupation put a premium on daring, hard sailing, speed at
all costs: enroute from the Banks they might not see the lee rail
of their vessels for three days, and, like the clipper ship captains
of a century ago, it did not often occur to them to take in sail.
The economic reasons for this kind of sailing—on the edge of
disaster—worked less in some fisheries than in others, but even
when speed was not essential to beat rivals to market, the
fishermen were addicted to hard sailing. Often fog, snow, dories
straying from the schooner, sudden appearances of shallow
ledge, sudden storms—elements beyond their control—taxed
their seamanship and nerve. When these elements were absent,
they taxed themselves, just for the hell of it, apparently, and
because they were captivated by the power and beauty of their
schooners in a breeze, and because they lived to see them pushed
to the extreme, spray flying, green water washing down their
decks, masts and rigging straining to the breaking point.

During the off season, they took their vessels, loaded with
salt codfish, to the West Indies, Spain, or the Mediterranean—
racing all the way. A skipper bound for Turk Island in the
Bahamas, for instance, would wait a day or two if by so doing he
could start off with another Lunenburger and thus make a race
of it. Sailing alone, he tried for a fast passage; if the record was
thirty days round trip, including unloading fish at Puerto Rico
and loading salt for the return trip at Turk Island, he tried to do
it in twenty-nine. I know a man who was a passenger on a transatlantic steamer in the 1920's and saw a Lunenburg schooner
come out of the fog astern, gradually overtake the steamer, and
disappear in the fog ahead. They could sail fifteen knots in a
good breeze, faster, until the last few years, than most steamers.

After some goading, Angus Walters told me the wild story of
a race he was in when he was a little over twenty and in com-

mand of his first schooner. It was a race from Lunenburg to the West Indies and back, and the wind blew hard all the way down and all the way home. Walters broke his main boom, which almost stove a hole in his boat as it lay like a huge battering ram in the water before it was cut away; he was forced out to sea by a sudden storm while anchored at a Bahamian island waiting to take on cargo; he was delayed twenty-four hours longer than his rival at another island because of loading difficulties; but even so, after almost a record run back to Lunenburg, he won the race by seven hours, seven hours in a race that had taken thirty days, including unloading and loading in the West Indies. A record run—in those days everyone was trying for a record—meant driving a schooner to the limit, carrying more sail than was prudent, driving, driving, driving, day and night. In any kind of blow, it was seven days of exhilaration, or nine days, or however many days it took to get to port. Coming home the time the boom broke, the wind was behind them blowing half a gale for five straight days. "By the Lord, did she go, did she go," Walters said. "By the Lord, did she go." He brought his hands together in a V and then spread them out. "She spread the waves forward, I can tell you."

Walters' usual reticence about the sailing days is common among old Banks fishermen. One, whom I know better than Walters, told me it stirred him up too much to talk about the old days in sail. I got the story of the *Bluenose* from Walters only by constant questions and partly, I think, because I read everything there was about the boat before I met him, and because I knew a fair amount about the fishing industry. He often gave the impression of half wanting to tell me to leave and half wanting very much to talk.

I made a trip on a fishing vessel a few years ago (which I shall recount in the next chapter) and the oldest crew member, Johnson Cook, was on the *Haligonian,* one of the fastest schooners of the 1920's, when it made a record passage from Sable Island to Newfoundland at an average speed of close to fifteen knots. The captain, George Himmelman, had gone below leaving instructions to be awakened if the wind increased. The wind increased all night but the crew, enthralled by the speed she was making as she charged along, her decks awash, ignored the instructions, let the captain sleep, and kept whole sail on her until the morning. "Word went from watch to watch, 'Let her go. Let her go,'" Cook said. "The man at the wheel had water in his hip boots. You poured the water out when you come off watch."

Many years before that, Cook was on a Lunenburg schooner returning from the West Indies when it ran into bad weather. The captain, who had made a fast passage up to then and thought he had a good chance of breaking the record for the run, kept all sail on. The masts were bending, the booms and gaffs groaning, the bow plunging deeper and climbing higher each hour of the day. There was another Lunenburg captain aboard, who had been stranded in the West Indies when his schooner burned. The other captain, Cook said, stood by the halyards all afternoon, scared to death, waiting for the word to lower the mainsail. "But our captain wouldn't. He kept her right to it."

Ralph Hemphill told me about his father, who carried coal on his fishing schooner from Nova Scotia to Newfoundland when fishing was slack. He was notorious for losing deckloads of coal because he loved to see his schooner sailing hard. He hated to shorten sail—which would have saved the coal but slowed his schooner down. "Many a time I've seen him standing there in a good breeze ignoring the coal washing off to looward and yelling, 'Now she's driving, boy. Now she's driving.' He loved to sail. Gloried in it."

The exuberance of Captain Hemphill, of Johnson Cook's skipper in the West Indies run, of the crew of the *Haligonian,* of Angus Walters would be incredible on a modern fishing trawler. It is, among the world's seamen, a distinguishing characteristic of sailing men alone.

The schooners were a delight and a source of pride to those who sailed them. Today that culture no longer exists. The schooners are gone, the dories are gone, the relationship to nature is changed. That culture—and who can even catch a glimpse of its understanding of sea, weather, habits of different species of fish, techniques of catching fish, techniques of sailing —had evolved through three centuries.

At first the fishermen hand-lined from the decks of their vessels. In the nineteenth century the schooners began carrying nests of dories—eight, ten, or twelve of them, which were stacked like saucers one inside the other in two nests on the deck. The Grand Banks dory, fourteen or sixteen feet long, is flat-bottomed with high flaring bow and narrow stern. The dories would be lowered into the water early each morning and the crews would row or sail out from the schooner to fish. Instead of individual hand lines they used trawls—long lengths of twine a mile or more in length, from which, every six feet, a hook was hung on the end of three feet of smaller twine. Each end of the trawl would be anchored. The dorymen would go from end to end hauling in the trawl and plopping the cod into the bottom of the dory.

They often worked out of sight of the schooner and of each other, and in a snowstorm or thick fog they frequently became lost. Many times they were never seen again, or not seen again until they had rowed four or five hundred miles to shore.

The schooners carried crews of twenty or thirty men. Their captains invariably were former dorymen; there was almost no other way to achieve command. A boy would go to sea at twelve or fourteen as a "throater" or "cutter," his duties to clean fish and help sail the schooner. He would graduate in two or three years to a dory paired with a more experienced fisherman. A small minority of them would in the next five or ten years prove so outstanding as dorymen and seamen as to be considered for command. If they were, in addition, tough, ambitious, and intelligent, and could command the respect of their colleagues, they would have their own schooners by the time they were twenty-five or thirty. Captains usually owned part or all of their schooners. Most of them sailed several schooners in a career—losing one or two on a ledge or in a gale, replacing others because they thought they could build better ones. Invariably each wanted the fastest schooner in the fleet. Their mania for speed led them to extremes. Howard Chapelle, in his monumental study, *The History of American Sailing Ships*, writes that in the 1870's and 1880's the fishermen developed a speedy schooner with such a large sail area that it had a fatal tendency to capsize.[1] They developed a safer schooner in the 1880's, but it was also very fast. Few yachts ever built could beat the fishing schooners of the nineteenth century and the early twentieth century.

The captains earned reputations as sail carriers, or as great fish killers—with an instinct for guessing where in all the vast area of their domain the fish might be—or as bullies, or as Christians. In Gloucester and Lunenburg they were demigods, whose quirks, mannerisms, exploits, and characters were discussed by ordinary seamen, by landsmen in those towns where prosperity depended on the catches of the fishing schooners, by women, by children. When one of them walked down a street people stood aside or nodded deferentially. They were in continuous competition with each other—to be the first to fill their holds on the Banks, to land the largest catch, to make the fastest passage. And their records, trip by trip, were known to everyone at home, in all the fishing settlements up and down the coast, at the Boston Fish Pier, at Fulton Market in New York, if they landed there.

They ranged the thousands of square miles of the Banks, into Newfoundland, along Labrador, north to Greenland—ranchers of fish, students of wind and sea, intimate companions of waves, lordly, independent, sovereign—each voyage an accomplishment, each encounter with storm a victory, each passage home a contest. Their occupation gave a gloss to life, a glamour, an allure, an aura of excitement and suspense. It made of life a series of scenes, a performance.

[1] Howard I. Chapelle: *The History of The American Sailing Ships* (New York: W. W. Norton; 1935), p. 254.

But the mechanization of the fishing industry has wiped out this immense know-how of the fishermen of Nova Scotia and New England, this art of sailing which they had brought to near perfection, both in the design of their vessels and in the use of them. Making a vessel go fast today is a matter of revving up the motor; finding fish is done by turning on the fishscope, which enables the captain to see if fish are in the area; finding your position is done with electronic equipment—radar and loran. Storms are foretold not by the way clouds are making up to the north'ard, not by the wisdom inherited from generations of Grand Banks fishermen, but by the Coast Guard weather reports.

The last time I visited Walters, we walked from his home down to the Smith & Rhuland shipyard where the *Bluenose* was built, and where, on that day, there were three deisel trawlers waiting to be repaired. We looked in the steam-heated pilot-house of one of them. It was a mass of electronic screens. I asked Walters about the difference between commanding these vessels and the ones he went on. "In those days you had to know something," he said. "Today you could put an old woman into 'em."

Today tubby-looking, wall-sided draggers pull huge nets over the bottom scooping up everything—marketable fish, unmarketable fish, baby fish. We have been warned by the Food and Agriculture Organization of the UN that we face the depletion of many stocks of fish. In increasing our efficiency we may not destroy our fish, or we may. We have certainly wiped out beauty, a relationship to nature that was not just depredation—that included reverence, or at least awe, and respect—and a love of his tools that characterized man in earlier technologies than ours and in no occupation more than in that of the seaman. Life on the fishing banks today is boring, for there are no jobs on a dragger that require the judgment, the poise, and the courage of a doryman, or the complex of skills, knowledge, intuition, and sensitivity of a schooner captain.

II

Several years before the last Lunenburg dory schooner gave up in 1963, I made a trip to the fishing grounds along the New-foundland coast aboard one of the other schooners in the dory fleet, the *Arthur J. Lynn*. The *Lynn* was built after engines had replaced sails, but even so her hull recalled in corrupted form the graceful lines of a sailing vessel. She was halfway between —a curious combination of the clumsier lines of a modern trawler and those of a schooner, as though the fishermen's re-luctance to leave the old life was personified in her lines. She had the comely overhanging bow of a schooner and the boxy-looking stern of a motor vessel. She had two masts, shorter than a schooner's but taller than a motor vessel's. She had no mainsail or jibs, but she had a foresail, which was used to steady her— and which her captain told me he would hate to go to sea with-out. When the wind was not strong enough to counteract the power of her diesel engines, the *Lynn*'s foresail slatted about, and that forlornly flapping sail seemed to me a vestige of a former epoch, like the legs on a whale or the wings on an ostrich.

The *Lynn* carried twelve dories and a crew of twenty-eight— two men for each dory, a captain, a cook, an engineer, and deck hand. All the dorymen except one were Newfoundlanders. That one doryman, and the captain, the mate, the cook, the engineer, and the deck hand, were from Lunenburg. The captain, George Himmelman, who was sixty-six, had commanded some famous sailing vessels in the 1920's and 1930's. He was the last captain of that era still active.

Except for the substitution of a diesel for sails, her procedures were the same as those of a hundred years ago. Although no one knew it then, she and the other ten motorized schooners in the Lunenburg fleet were acting out the last scene before the end.

As we plowed toward Cape St. Mary's on Newfoundland's southwest coast in a driving rainstorm, the *Lynn*'s thin, white masthead light and the port and starboard lights on her foremast shrouds were sometimes obliterated from view. In the main cabin, the engineer, the mate, and four dorymen sat on a bench and talked sporadically or stared at the floor. The captain kept himself apart in his tiny stateroom off the main cabin, except for brief, uncommunicative trips into the cabin to check his position on loran or listen to a weather report.

At the other end of the schooner, under the foredeck, in their wedge-shaped, airless home—snug, warm, and blue with smoke —the rest of the crew sat one above the other in two tiers of bunks or on benches on either side of a table, wedge-shaped too, that filled most of the floor space. The ones at the table, heads close together, told stories to each other in their fast, animated, earnest, and incomprehensible accent. They talked of close calls in dories, dirty weather, fishing for salmon in little rivers near their homes, deer hunting, and disasters—which in Newfoundland meant ships lost. Three played cards at the after end of the table, where just above their heads their yellow oilskins and sou'westers swayed slowly back and forth. Another, a short, lithe youngster named Sammy McDonald, with an impish, friendly face, who smiled every time he spoke and every time someone spoke to him, sat a little apart nailing together a cheap metal suitcase.

Two of the dorymen from the main cabin, coming forward for a mug of tea, climbed down the companionway ladder in oilskins. The first, long-necked, long-faced, long-nosed, said, "Rain, rain, Jesus Christ, if it ain't rain, it's fog." The second, a little fellow named Studley, fifty or fifty-five years old, came down the ladder singing, "What a friend we have in Jesus," and at the bottom stood dripping, to smile at everyone in the fore-castle, even the dour Lunenburg cook sitting alone and silent on the bench below his bunk. He took off his sou'wester, smiled at it, shook it gently, and hung it and his oilskins on the foremast. He poured himself a mug of tea. "Fine, fine weather, ay cocky?" he said to Sammy, squeezing Sammy's shoulder and sitting down beside him. "They was two dorymen lost from their schooner. One feller says to the other, If only our wives know'd where we are. Our wives go to hell, said the other feller, if only we know'd, by Jesus." Voices grew louder. "Ay, ay, by the Lord you are right," he would say to whoever was talking and crowd him out with another of his stories. "Sheared right in two at the foremast, by Jesus. We got in the dories. Belgian steamer took us to Brook-lyn . . . During the war (he pronounced it 'wire'), during the war, two American warships heading for Argentina ran on the rocks. The women left their little ones to home to let down ropes down the cliffs. Saved a lot of lives. One old lady kept washing this nigger to get the oil off. Finally she said, 'I'm sorry sir, I can't get any more of it off.' After the war, the Americans built a hospital for all the people there."

The long-nosed doryman, talking at the other end of the table, said, "You know why we ain't getting fish? Bad bait. You know where that bait come from? Trinity Bay . . . washed up on the shore. They picked it up off the shore. Yes, sir. Feller told me that outside the plant. Dead when it came in."

"Hi? Hi? Hi Tom! What's that?" Little Studley yelled with a show of ferocity. "Ye've no call for saying that. Bad bait ye say Tom. What's your explanation for them big plump cod Reggie and the dories at his end caught yistadey? Maybe them cod likes spoiled squid, do ye say? It ain't bad bait. Tom, it ain't bad bait. It's no fish.

"Birds! Birds!" he said, his voice rising. "Did ye see any birds? They was there before. The fish's gone. The birds is gone." He glared at Tom, scrappy, angry and friendly at once. Mugs of tea were poured. The talk grew louder. "I'll tell you where there's fish. Lamb's Rock. Get one on every hook . . . There's fish right where we was today. We was too far out. Fifteen fathom is too deep for the fish . . . Ye're right by the Lord Jesus. Ye got to get right in on the rocks . . . If I had this schooner, I'd fill every freeze plant on Newfoundland. Have to build more . . . Ay, sure, chummy . . . Hey, Cecil, pass down the sugar . . . Ay, honey, glad to . . . Next trip we'll go to Canso . . . Ay? Ay? What have ye got—a special line to the Captain?"

"I can't understand a word they say," the cook said to the only other Lunenburger in the forecastle, the old deck hand who lay in his bunk, almost asleep. "They can't understand themselves half the jeesly time what they say to each other. They don't know what they're saying. Ach.

"They eat all the time. It can't all be from hunger. Part of it is habit. They eat to pass the time of day, I think."

The cook was stripped to the waist, and the skin of his fat stomach, powerful chest, and enormous biceps gleamed with the dull sheen of enamelware. A son of a cook, and his son a cook, a doryman ten years, once mate on three-masters trading to the West Indies, reputed killer of a Trinidad Negro, white-haired, jowly, grumpy at sea, drunk ashore, bilious and bullying to the happy Newfoundlanders in both places, he had the look and the voice of a man perpetually wronged. He eyed the back of Sammy's head resentfully as Sammy wolfed down biscuits and handed some to Studley, who stopped talking to eat one and thank Sammy with a squeeze of his neck. "It can't all be hunger," the cook said. "At least I don't think it can."

But the conviviality in the forecastle at last made him unbend a little. He decided to have a mug of tea. When he hiked himself to his feet to go to the stove, he said to a doryman named Baker, "Yah, I'm not much goot any more. Can't get goot headway any more. Underpinnings are going, y'know," speaking, like most Lunenburgers of his generation, Angus Walters, Captain Himmelman, with a German accent, even though they cannot speak German—an accent inherited from the people who settled Lunenburg in the 1750's.

At the stove, he said to Studley and anyone around him who might listen, "If I go till next March it will be forty-five years and I don't know if I have anything to show for it. A little maybe. I got a little."

Studley squinted up at him. "I don't know about you. You have some stored away. But a doryman, if he starts out with two sharts, he'll end up with only one. He'll only have one when he gets through."

Two men sitting in the most forward bunk in the very bow of the schooner began humming. Baker called to them, "Sing 'Auld Lang Syne.' Let's have 'Auld Lang Syne.'" "Or 'Charlotte Brown.' On the deck of the old *Charlotte Brown*," Sammy said.

This roused a man called Coxy, who wore a piece of cod line loosely around his waist as an amulet for a weak back and who, if the Newfoundlanders are primitives, as the cook believed, was the most primitive of them all. Coxy's face, encircled by a mass of tight ringlets of brilliant, golden hair, looked like a satyr's perhaps, or a coarsened and aged copy of a young Greek god. He was thirty or thirty-five. His face seemed to reflect every passing process in his interior—thoughts, feelings, maybe even the digestion of his food. When he smiled, he smiled with his whole face and with his body too. When someone talked to him or he talked to someone, his whole being seemed engaged, every nook and cranny of him, his arms and legs and ears and jaw as well as his mind.

Sammy's calling out "On the decks of the old *Charlotte Brown*" caused Coxy, who was lying in his bunk awake but silent to sit bolt upright. "Don't sing that. Don't sing that. Don't sing that," he said. "Don't sing that or we'll go down like they did."

Sammy looked at Studley, Studley at Sammy, and they smiled. The hummers began "Auld Lang Syne." *"Charlotte Brown"* was never sung—not, I think, because the others put much stock in Coxy's old superstition, but because of the invariable kindliness of the Newfoundlanders to each other, crowded for almost ten months of the year in quarters the size of two small rooms.

Just above the dorymen's heads, separated from them by two-inch deck planking but in another world, a shivering lookout, occasionally ducking sheets of spray, kept his hour's watch. In the pilothouse near the stern of the schooner, the oldest and the youngest dorymen, sixty-two and twenty-two, stood on either side of the wheel staring at the rain on the pilothouse windows and down at the compass. The oldest, Johnson Cook, was at the wheel. The youngest, Tom Skinner, had come to the pilothouse to ask Johnson's advice, as he did on every occasion. They were dorymates, sharing long hours alone together, hours of small triumph when the catch on their trawl lines was good, hours of disappointment when their trawl lines came into the dory empty—disappointment combined with the uselessness, ennui, and disgust with oneself that a commercial fisherman feels, however unjustified, when his efforts go for naught. They—one at the beginning, one at the end of a career—were completely dependent on each other, because a doryman's effectiveness, and in a sudden storm or in fog, his safety, depends on his partner. The captain had paired them, no doubt, to complement Johnson's declining powers with Tom's young strength, to complement Tom's rashness with Johnson's wisdom, the wisdom of half a century on the Banks. Tom was impatient, excitable, sometimes ridiculous, prone to accident, thoughtless, but very protective of his dorymate, always trying to take all the heaviest tasks they shared and jealous of any slights or criticisms the other dorymen might essay toward Johnson (although in this he had no reason, for the other dorymen liked Johnson and were proud of him).

Johnson, patient, calm, was deliberate in his talk, in sharpening a knife, baiting a hook, filling his pipe, deliberate in thought, in judgment, tolerant of short-sightedness, short-temperedness, foolishness—acutely aware of foolishness, recognizing it quickly from his vast store of experience, but not upset by it. He had survived. Not very many dorymen survived forty-five years on the Banks. He seemed aware of the hardness of the life he had led, of its small reward, of what it had sucked out of him, but he had an air, all the same, not of resignation but of pride in his capacity to bear the life, withstand its rigors, pass its tests.

The dim light from the compass in front of Johnson outlined his face, the flat planes from his high cheekbones to his jawbone, the squared hook of his nose, the straight line of his lips. Tom's face was in shadow.

As Johnson's hour at the wheel progressed, the seas grew bigger. One, towering over its neighbors, caught the schooner precisely right, flinging spray from the bow more than a hundred feet aft to the windows of the pilothouse. "Hey, dorymate, that there was some big sea," Tom said. Johnson looked toward him and smiled. "I saw a sea come aboard a schooner and pick up all the dories on the windward side and throw 'em off to leeward," he said, offhandedly—not to impress Tom, one would guess, but as a workman describing working conditions. He said it in the tone of a man who had seen waves sweep over vessels an incalculable number of times. After a pause he added, "Two hours later we had them all back."

"Was that the worse you ever saw?" Tom said.

"I saw a sea bash in the side of a motor vessel once. We got her patched using the bunks. Got her headed off before the wind. Engine dead. Pumps clogged. We went a day and a night after that. Finally we flagged down a steamer. The crew refused to lower." Johnson took the pipe out of his mouth and turned to Tom. "The crew refused to lower. The captain was going to send the boats over, but the crew wouldn't man them. He said he'd take us off in the morning. If we're still afloat, we said."

"Was you running rum, dorymate?"

"Yah. When we left her go, we had a thousand cases of whisky aboard. We'd thrown two thousand over. We'd kept a thousand."

Johnson smuggled whisky to the United States for two years at seventy-five dollars a month and a bonus if the trip was successful. One vessel he was on had been machine-gunned by the Coast Guard. He had seen others machine-gunned outside the three-mile limit. Once the vessel he was on anchored off Long Island in a fog, and while he was ashore making contact, the Coast Guard came by and towed the vessel away. He went back to Canada by land. "I wish I was alive then, dorymate," Tom told him.

"The times for a young feller was in the schooners," Johnson said. "Great sport for a young feller then. Racing to Spain. We did it in eighteen days one trip and it's been done quicker than that. Those old captains let 'em go. Talk about go. Seven days from Turk Island to Lunenburg. We'd 'a done it quicker if the gaff jaws hadn't broke. That was the *Lloyd George*. She was one of the best vessels out of Lunenburg. Always making a record down south. Every trip.

"David Himmelman was master. He wouldn't take sail in. Before the wind he'd take no sail in no matter how it blew. Just let her go, by God.

"The *Lloyd George*. She was a nice vessel. Small. A hundred feet—smaller than this one. Her sails were light. Light sails. I used to go aloft to take in the topsails just for the fun of it."

"How 'bout in the old *Bluenose* days. You was never in her."

"Never in her. But in the *Haligonian*."

"Ay, dorymate. The *Bluenose* beat the hell out of her. She was no good."

"You don't know nothing about it," Johnson said. "When she raced the *Bluenose*, she'd just come in from fishing. She wasn't trimmed right. Her masts was too far forward. There was a lot of things wrong. There was a lot of things they could a done to make her go faster. Her owners weren't interested and her skipper was scared of her. He was all right fishing, but scared of her.

"If this Old Man here, Cap'n Himmelman, had been in her she'd have beat the *Bluenose*. Yes sir. Beat her or given her a good run. He was interested in sailing.

"He had her ten years later. There was a lot wrong with her then. She needed fixing up. But he sailed her hard. He never raced the *Bluenose*; it was too late for that. But if he'd had a chance earlier he'd a given her a good run.

"I was with this Old Man on the *Haligonian* off Labrador. Go into a little harbor every night to dress fish. There was five vessels there. We sailed circles around all of them. In the morning we'd start out last and go past every one of them. In the evening, be the last to start in, but beat 'em all in.

"He'd give it to her, I can tell you. He's a lot different now."

Not thirty feet from Johnson the captain lay in the bunk of his small compartment off the main cabin, perhaps sleeping, perhaps brooding—last of the old Grand Banks schooner captains, last of Kipling's Captains Courageous—a poetic, sometimes gloomy man, who saw himself, the fish he chased, the sea and winds he lived with, the famous vessels his town once built that had all disappeared or been cut down into motor vessels, saw the life he had outlasted as a romance—a drama whose significance somehow had eluded him. What was the meaning of that life— was there any reason to continue—was his skill gone—had he lost his nerve?

That afternoon two dorymen, standing around the corner of the pilothouse, had discussed the day's poor catch.—We were too far out—Ay. Ye got to be closer. Right in on the rocks—Last year he'd'a took her right in in the fog—Ay. He don't have the courage he did—Dorymen's talk, dorymen's talk. Was he too old? Should he quit?

In Sydney, where he had landed his last catch instead of Halifax, his regular port, he had finished his business with the fish plant manager and gone ashore. We had walked together through several narrow streets. He stopped frequently, as though not sure of his way, until we came to a dilapidated store front built into the first floor of an old wooden house. The street was deserted, the store front was dark, and the house it was part of, like its neighbors, seemed unoccupied. He had knocked, stepped back from the door, and stood, humming tunelessly under his breath and rocking lightly on the balls of his feet. An inch or two over six feet, straight, well-built, with little excess weight, he moved with the elasticity of a much younger man. In the shadowings thrown by a street lamp halfway up the block, his long, good-looking face—with a large ski-jump nose and humorous, wide mouth— had looked almost youthful. He had listened intently, scowling a little, his face bent close to the door. He knocked again. This time, a light went on in the back of the building. A slight, dark-skinned woman opened the door and looked at him a minute. She said, "Yes? Yes?" and then cried, "Captain George! Captain George!" He had taken her thin hands, smothering them in his. She had said, Captain George. Who would have thought? Come back to the kitchen.

In the light of the kitchen, they had stood smiling at each other and it seemed they found it hard to think of what to say—how to put into words the memories flooding back to them. In the days when the Lunenburg fleet numbered a hundred schooners and Sydney was a frequent stop for them—coming in from the Banks or, some of them, a quick trip south with whisky—the store front had been a restaurant, run by a Syrian. He had four beautiful daughters and a very strict wife watching over them. The captains made the restaurant their gathering place, headquarters, master mariners' clubrooms. They came there to learn the news of each other, of new schooners building, of new records; to tell of their trips, to enjoy the company of their peers, to sing, to drink (those who did). They danced and sang—but nothing more—with the four beautiful daughters.

Standing in the little kitchen, thinking back, he remembered the bright black eyes that used to laugh in delight at the captains' stories, and the long shiny hair, still black; but he couldn't for the life of him figure out which of the four daughters she was. He had said, The name I don't remember, but the face I remember so well. Rosa, Captain George, Rosa. Rosa, of course. How are you, Rosa? You haven't changed a bit. Sit down, sit down, yah. How is your sisters, Rosa? It does me good to see you. It must be twenty-five years.

Two of the other daughters had come into the kitchen, smiling with disbelief. He had said, We had some great times here.

The daughters talked about his older brothers, Long Albert Himmelman, helmsman for Angus Walters on the *Bluenose* in some of the International Fishermen's Races, and the others, all top skippers in the Lunenburg fleet, all dead. (There were eight boys—all became captains except one, who went West.) They talked about their favorites among the captains, who for them in those near-forgotten years were daredevils, knights in armor. They had asked where the captains were, what they had done since they stopped sailing into Sydney. What about this one, what about that one? Ah! he had cried, he ended up a drunk! It gets a lot of good men. He lost his money. Finally he had nothing. The last heard of him, he went off in a little boat with some Americans for Bermooda. Never seen since, though there was some talk he was seen later in Bermooda. No one knows.

The youngest one had brought in her fifteen-year-old daughter and told her, This is Captain George, one of the highliners of the Lunenburg skippers. He had looked down at the girl, at the same beautiful time of life as the old Syrian's daughters when he used to sail into Sydney. She wasn't even thought of then, he had said with a musing smile. Yah. A fine girl. Wonderful.

Rosa had said, You keep going. He replied, Yah, I keep going. I'm scared of retirement. Well, you see, you get up in the morning. Come into the kitchen. Well, I guess I'll have a little breakfast. Then after breakfast you can take a walk. But Lunenburg is only a small town. See the whole thing in five minutes. Well, then, it's time to go home for dinner. So you walk back—and have dinner. Then what to do in the afternoon? You can take a little nap. Or take a drive in the country with your wife. I do that now. You'd soon get sick of it. It might be all right for the first week. But how about after that?

Yes, it is a problem, he had said. I don't want to be condemned. No, I don't want to be condemned like an old vessel.

A year before, his daughter had come across a photograph in a magazine of one of his schooners—heeled over in a fresh breeze coming right at the camera. Look! Daddy's schooner, she had said. His teenaged grandson, who never saw Lunenburg's harbor crowded with masts, never saw its streets crowded with sailors, had said, What's so much about that? What, indeed? what had any of it meant—the five schooners he had had built, the others he had commanded, the big catches, the storms, the fast passages with the lee rail buried and the wind in the rigging, and the power of the schooner, surging through the seas, enough to spellbind anyone? What had any of it meant? What did it matter now? He had gone to sea when he was fourteen, become a captain at twenty-five, had his first schooner built for him at twenty-eight. Four years later he had a second one built, the *Margotte,* better than the first one. He was sick one winter and his nephew took her south and lost her. Dismasted in a gale and then broke up just after a steamer picked off her crew. She was a lovely vessel. Oh, she was a dandy. Noted to be one of the best, quite the best, in the Provinces. A fast vessel. Exceptionally fast. A moneymaker.

He had lost the next one, the *Canusa,* himself. Foundered with a load of salt in a gale down south. They had rowed two hundred miles in four days and four nights, part of it in a hurricane. Taking sights. Imagine taking sights and pulling the books out and figuring your position in a bloody old dory with the water washing over her. They had landed on San Salvador— come out of the sea right in front of the Christopher Columbus monument.

You get all worn out and about to say the hell with it. Then you say, I'm not going to give up till I have to. I'm going to see how long I can stay on top of the sea. Eight men in three dories. They had stayed together till the last night, when they got separated in the dark. Eight men and a dog and a cat. You say I'm going to see how long I can stay on top of the sea and I'll court-martial any man who doesn't try.

Then he had taken command of the *Haligonian,* built with much fanfare seven years before to beat the *Bluenose.* She had failed at that, and the days of formal racing were over and she was in sad shape; they had called her a bust. He had nurtured her back. Changed the rake of her masts. Trimmed her different in every way and found her in every way a champion sailor. They had called her a bust, but he wondered what she might have done. She might not have beaten the *Bluenose* but she would have given her a damn good race.

She had finer lines than the *Bluenose.* More on the Yankee type. Sneakier up forward. But that of course may not count. It's not the forward end that makes the difference. It's the after end. If you take a log and tow it by the thick end it will go faster than the thin end . . .

He had been interested in sailing. When he went to the sail-maker to have a sail made, you could bet there'd be a row. They were the best of friends but they'd fight over those sails until he thought they were right. And before a sail was worn out, you could be sure he'd be ashore twenty-five times to get it recut.

What did it matter? What had it meant? When he was young there had been a man in Lunenburg who was tops in the profession. Competent. Successful. He'd said to himself, I pray to God I will be like him when I reach my prime. He had been.

And then power had come in and modern instruments like loran, until any fool could take command. And he'd kept on. Forty-one years in command. Never been seen in history before —a man with forty-one years in command. He had said to the Syrian's daughters, My class of men is all dead, buried. Three or four around ashore, but not active. The life of a deep-sea fishing captain is short. He had told them, In the ring the one that stays the longest is the winner. I'm not saying that there weren't others better than I. There were. But none of 'em went forty-one years.

Anyone else but a fisherman would have something. A fisherman hasn't got nothing. No pension. No stripes. Nothing. He could have rooted in alleys all his life and nothing to tell he didn't. Anyone else but a fisherman would have a pension as big as the President of the United States, and a monument when he dies.

When we left the Syrian's, his head pained him. It felt clogged, and the atmosphere in the kitchen—of his futile memories, of his futile tirade against time—seemed to cling to him like a cloud as we had walked down the narrow streets to his schooner. He was quiet until the wharf where the schooner lay came into sight. Then he turned to me. "If I would get a good vessel, I might think of going on. An old feller should have the best. He shouldn't have to struggle like a young man. A schooner with better accommodations and good equipment. I don't know. I might be tempted to go on then. Do something then."

But the next morning, which was the morning of departure, the cloud was gone. "We'll make a trip if we have the weather," he had said. "Yes, we'll have a good trip this time.

"I feel it. This will be a good one. We're starting out right. The start's very important."

His decisions had all been made: whether to take on herring bait in Sydney or wait until he received word from Long Harbor, Newfoundland, about squid for bait; whether to go to St. Pierre Bank, halfway between Sydney and Newfoundland, where the cod liked herring, or Cape St. Mary's, where they were used to squid from the other dory schooners and would spurn herring; whether to wait for a new foresail to be trucked to Sydney from Lunenburg. He had seen to a score of minor details about outfitting the vessel. He was ready to go. He was confident.

As for the dorymen's talk, it was talk within the family. Now that the schooner was fishing along the shore of Newfoundland close to Cape St. Mary's, the Newfoundlanders might discuss among themselves his failure to get in close to the rocks where they thought (but how did they know?) the fish were. Johnson Cook might contrast his former feats with his present caution. But they liked him, respected him, considered him a good fisherman—still.

Ashore the captain was talkative enough, if somewhat formal, and aloof toward a stranger. But in the five days since the schooner had left North Sydney, the captain kept his own counsel. He seldom spoke to anyone except to give an order or discuss tersely a problem of the fishing. He either skipped meals or ate them after everyone else was through. If someone had started a conversation with him about some ordinary matter he would probably have stared at him in disbelief.

On this fifth night out, Johnson Cook was relieved at the wheel by Little Studley. "Southwest by west half west. Wake the cook at half past one." "Southwest by west a half west." Studley was relieved by Baker, Baker by Coxy, Coxy by Reggie Bungay.

When the cook got up at 1:30 a.m., he was only a half hour ahead of the rest of the crew, who stumbled out of their bunks with closed, reluctant faces. Oblivious to poking elbows or shoulders they clumsily pushed their arms and heads into sweaters of coarse, brightly dyed homemade wool and their legs into trousers. The old ones stomped stiff-jointed, lumpily gathering themselves together. They retrieved rubber boots and oilskins and, crowded together, sat down to pull on the oilskin pants. They stood to pull suspenders over their shoulders, sat to struggle into boots, stood again to work themselves into their oilskin jackets and button up. Studley, standing at the ladder leading to the deck, hit his chest and shook himself vigorously to adjust the layers of clothing underneath. "Not a Christian life, do ye think, boy?" he said to Sammy McDonald behind him. Sammy said, "It don't give you much time for praying," and half shoved Studley up the ladder onto deck. The rest of the crew went up after them.

Hoisting the main.

Below, left to right:
Captain Angus Walters,
Captain Ben Pine,
Captain Clayton Morrissey.

The *Bluenose*.

The *Elsie*, moments after
her foretopmast carried
away in a 27-knot wind
during the 1921 races
for the International
Fishermen's Trophy.

With decks awash, the *Henry Ford* drives to windward.

The *Bluenose* and the *Henry Ford* fighting for the lead during the 1922 series.

The *Thebaud* driving
through heavy seas.

The *Gertrude L. Thebaud*
leading the *Bluenose* during
the 1938 series.

And so the day began in patterns, sequences, and methods related to three hundred and fifty years of Banks fishing before it, and with skills and tools that had evolved through use by generations of fishermen. The day would be divided into four operations—baiting up, making a set, hauling back, and cleaning the catch—each carried out with a precision and economy of effort that is characteristic of men in any nonmechanized repetitive activity and that is invariably rhythmical and graceful.

Studley, Sammy, Banker, and another doryman named Charles Strowbridge, who were the first on deck, jumped into the hold to shovel half-frozen squid bait into large tubs. Other dorymen hoisted the tubs out of the hold and set up two crude cutting tables across the main deck. They hung a string of light bulbs in the rigging over the tables and wedged a few torches on poles along the rail. In the next two hours, twenty-four dorymen, twelve at each table, cut up a thousand pounds of bait and baited almost twenty thousand hooks.

Standing side by side, swinging long-bladed knives so fast they were blurs inches from each other, never pausing from cut-up squid to new squid, they might have been a group of primitive dancers performing with common movements an ancient rite. The blackened ship in the black, starless night did look like the stage for a ritual—its main deck suddenly lit now by naked, swaying light bulbs and smoking torches, and peopled by the strangely dressed dorymen, silent and intent, their faces in shadow under the rims of their sou'westers, their bodies shapeless in the armor of their stiff oilskins, their hands and flailing knives sharply outlined in the light. When they had reduced the squid to bits, the tempo of their motions speeded up. In rhythm and with perfect coordination, they baited hooks on eighteen miles of trawl lines and coiled the lines into thirty-six separate tubs (three tubs, containing a mile and a half of trawl line apiece, for each of the twelve dories). Twenty-four bodies and twenty-four pairs of arms swung almost in unison—bait and coil, bait and coil, bait and coil—one man baiting, at the rate of a

hook every two seconds, while another coiled, in a single operation so well timed between them that there was never any stop.

Suddenly the whir was over. The teams broke up, lit cigarettes, began to talk, and strolled forward away from the tables
like a troupe of players at the end of an act. A few of them,
released from the tempo of their communal performance, lazily
and clumsily took down the tables, stowed them, and moved the
tubs of baited line to the rails of the schooner where they could
be placed aboard the dories when they were launched. Then
those few followed the rest into the forecastle.

In the forecastle, the men stood swaying by the stove or
flopped down on benches around the table. Tea and coffee were
poured; handfuls of doughnuts and biscuits were scooped out of
pans; sou'westers and oilskin jackets were thrown off. The men
around the table gazed silently at each other or leaned back
against the bunks behind them and closed their eyes. At the
stove, Little Studley grinned at the men around him. "Get a deal
of tea and put on my wool socks to my feet. Pretty cold to your
feet down in the hold," he said. Hardly anyone bothered to take
off his oilskin pants or boots. Some did not even take off their
oilskin jackets but unbuttoned them and pushed their sou'westers back on their heads. Johnson Cook could keep up to the
dorymen's pace only by the most careful economy of energy, so
he took off his oilskins and boots and climbed into his bunk. The
captain had not shown himself on deck or made his plans known;
presumably he was in the main cabin figuring out his position
and where, among the canyons and outcroppings of rock below
him, he would be if he were a cod.

A short blast on the schooner's foghorn startled the forecastle.
There was a moment of silence in which someone growled, "No
rest for the weary," but not really in complaint because the dorymen were as anxious as the captain to start fishing, to get overboard to see if there were any fish. They lurched to their feet and
crowded toward the ladder. Charlie Strowbridge leaned over
Johnson. "Johnson, Johnson," he yelled, and sure that Johnson

was awake, he went toward the ladder. He saw that I had watched him and said as he went up the ladder, "He's sixty-two, you know. He's a damn good feller," expressing a pride in the old Lunenburg doryman that seemed general among the New-foundlanders.

On deck the men, with no orders given and with little talk, almost offhandedly began the arrangements that would see them, in a few minutes, go over the side in their small dories into the blackness surrounding the schooner.

The Grand Banks dory is one of the most seaworthy small boats in the world. North Atlantic fishermen have used dories for centuries, ridden out gales in them, survived bitter snowstorms, sleet, icing up, the worst that the stormy corner of the stormy North Atlantic which they inhabit could produce; they have rowed or sailed in them for hundreds of miles in open ocean when lost—not only in the old days when Johnson Cook was young and before, but also in recent years. Charlie Strowbridge, who was twenty-nine, for instance, had within the past year be-come lost from his schooner in a dory, searched for twelve hours, then rowed two hundred miles to shore. His case was not un-usual.

The *Lynn's* dories were nested in two stacks on the maindeck just aft of the foremast, six in each stack, fitted snugly one inside the other. Some of the men stationed themselves at ropes leading aloft that would be used to hoist the dories overside; some began sorting the gear that would go into each dory—a bailer, a bucket, a flagon of water in case the dory became lost, a foghorn, a compass; some lined up in order the numbered tubs of trawl line—three tubs marked Number 1 for Number 1 dory, three marked Number 2 for Number 2 dory, and so on—along the schooner's rail, so that in the rush of dories going overboard the tubs for each would be in proper sequence; some lit torches on the four-foot wooden poles that would be placed in the dories just before they went overboard.

Two young dorymen scrambled up into the dories on the top

of the two nests. The men at the hoisting ropes swung long hooks attached to the ends of the ropes through the air; the men in the dories caught the hooks and secured them. The dories shot up into the air and down to the rail of the schooner, where they hung above the water while two dorymen jumped aboard each. Trawl tubs, oars, sails, a bucket, and the rest of the dory's gear were handed aboard. At a signal from the captain, who had come on deck and stood near the mainmast, one of the dories was dropped to the water with a splash. It banged against the schooner until its dorymen released the ropes holding it, then drifted astern until they stepped the mast and sailed away. The schooner proceeded for another thirty or forty seconds, the captain signaled, and the second dory splashed into the water. Two more dories were hoisted out of the nests, followed by two more, until all twelve were in the water.

The captain told the engineer to turn off the engine, and the schooner, her foresail half filled with wind, glided easily along, silent and mysterious in the indistinguishable blackness of night, fog, and sea. The dark around her was dotted with bobbing torches, which in the distance were just glimmers suspended in nothingness, in a void. In the closer dories, the torches, smoking and eerie, lighted the constantly shifting planes of water—fleeting white patches on the oily blackness of a little circle of sea visible around each dory—and cast grotesque shadows of the dorymen against the sails.

Soon only one torch could be seen. The captain and the engineer stood in the pilothouse talking in low tones as the schooner drifted in sight of that torch. If it grew dimmer, the engineer would go below and give the schooner a boost with the engine for half a minute to bring it close to the dory again. In the dory, one man rowed while one played out trawl line over the stern in a circular motion of his arm, like a sower of seed. The trawl line, anchored and buoyed at one end, hung in such a way that its hooks were suspended close to the bottom. When all of the trawl line was played out, a mile and a half from the first anchor and buoy, the dorymen anchored and buoyed the other end. Then they sailed alongside the schooner, and on the crest of a swell, jumped aboard. The other dories rowed or sailed to the schooner, appearing as if by magic alongside. They were hauled aboard, and the dorymen went below.

While the dorymen ate breakfast, the captain headed the schooner back to the point where the trawl lines were first anchored and buoyed; after breakfast, which he did not take time to eat, he dropped the dories off, one by one, at their buoys, to begin hauling back on the trawl lines.

In the thick fog, dawn came late, bringing a ghostly daylight that extended no more than three lengths of the schooner. The dories faded into it like images on a screen until only the last one overboard was still in sight.

One of the dorymen sat in the stern rowing while the other stood in the bow hauling trawl line aboard. When one of the hooks, which hung every six feet from the trawl line, came aboard with a codfish on it, the one in the bow removed the fish by knocking it against the inside of the dory without a stop in his rhythmic handing in of the trawl line.

The captain and the engineer took up positions on each side of the pilothouse. The captain leaned forward, squinting, with an arm leaning against the frame of the open pilothouse door. He had a puzzled, worried look on his face and occasionally he would say something to himself or loud enough for the engineer to hear. The engineer would respond with assenting noises or a comment of his own. The interchanges were patterned, rhythmic, almost liturgical, separated by long silences and the captain's sighings and mutterings. "I wish the weather to be goot. Yah. I wish the weather to be goot. I am suspicious of it, though," he said.

"Fog ain't lifted any," the engineer said.

They stared at the dory—drained of all color, half transparent, as if it and its occupants were made of fog.

"Damn few fish, it looks like."

"Yah, not so many on their line yet," the engineer said.

The captain took his arm off the pilothouse, walked forward a few steps and returned. "They ain't getting any," he said. "Looks like a bum affair.

"No sense to come this distance for this little fish. No. No sense to come this distance for this little fish."

He gazed off at the fog astern and then up the masts, where sailors invariably look for signs of future winds, future weather, and, in the throes of any decision, inspiration.

"Be fog again tomorrow. Yah. Be fog again tomorrow . . ."

He looked over the stern of the schooner and back at the dory. A new worry struck him.

"Tide! Tide! Lord have mercy, I never thought the tide would go like this, this time of day."

The engineer, who had been using the schooner's rail as a foot rest and leaning with his elbow on his knee, stood straight and stretched. "Look, it's going so fast they lose half their fish," he said. "Going like a steamboat past their dory."

The captain shook his head. "No fish in this year. Dory empty. This place is doomed too, just like the Grand Bank."

The captain and the engineer put the schooner on a course that would take them, they hoped, close to where the first dories overboard would finish hauling in their trawl lines. In the light breeze, the schooner moved slowly under foresail alone. In a few moments Baker's dory appeared.

"Getting much fish?" the captain yelled.

"Not getting a fish," Baker said. "They've shifted. That breeze of wind last night moved 'em."

The captain walked forward to look into Baker's dory. He walked back to his position outside the pilothouse and said, half to himself and half to the engineer, "If there ain't no fish in here, there's none anywhere. It's not much encouragement for another trip.

"Looks like a bum affair," he said under his breath. "No fish— no fish—no fish—no fish."

The engineer came over to the door on the captain's side of the pilothouse. The captain smiled wryly.

"We're stuck like a fish," he said. "Be a poor trip. Won't be half a trip."

Johnson Cook and Tom Skinner rowed out of the fog to the side of the schooner. The captain and the engineer ran forward to hold their bow and stern lines while Tom pitchforked their few fish over his head into bins on the maindeck. After they helped Johnson and Tom hoist the dory aboard, Johnson went forward to act as a lookout. Tom started aft. The captain shouted, "Better get forward there to look out for dories, because they're there some place."

In the distance, the foghorn of a dory ready to unload sounded faintly. The schooner responded with a blast of its horn. The distant dory replied. The dories in between remained silent while schooner and dory answered back and forth.

The captain nodded to the engineer, who started the engine and took the wheel. The captain gave him a course to steer— which could only be an estimate—to take the schooner to the dory. He stepped outside the pilothouse and peered ahead, filled with the immediate task—finding the dory in the nothingness around him. If he saw a dark place in the fog, which might be a dory or might be a trick of light, his brow would furrow, the squint wrinkles around his eyes would deepen, his upper lip would tighten over his teeth. He would stare ahead a few minutes, then break the stare impatiently to pull himself erect, take his arm off the pilothouse door frame, and step inside. He would look across the pilothouse out the opposite door, or walk over to it and back. He would check the compass, lean an arm on the sill of the open window a minute or once more take up his position on deck outside the pilothouse door.

Every few minutes the schooner would stop and drift. A blast from her horn would roll away into the pure silence of the damp gray fog around her. A faint reply, like an echo, would return from the dory. Then nothing—no sound except the slap of water against the hull or a snap of the foresail spilling its wind when the schooner rolled in the long, easy swell. The schooner's horn blasted; the dory's replied. The schooner started, stopped, drifted, started again.

"Tough job to find 'em in this," the engineer said.

"Half impossible," the captain muttered.

Schooner and dory called to each other for twenty minutes. Then Johnson saw the dory, and with arm signals to the captain, relayed by Tom Skinner, standing halfway from bow to pilot-house, pointed the way. "There, there!" Johnson yelled. "Where, where?" the captain yelled.

The dorymen pitchforked their catch onto deck, Johnson and Tom Skinner helped hoist their dory aboard, and the schooner lay drifting to wait until another dory signaled that it was ready to unload. The next one was closer. While it was being hoisted aboard, another dory came out of the fog.

"That ours?" the captain said.

"Yah," said the engineer.

"What's he want?"

"He wants a tow back to his buoy. Line been cut."

"My God, we can't do that in this weather. Oars. What are oars for?"

The captain did tow the dory for half a mile or more until he heard other dories calling to unload. Most of them were easy to find; often the men forward sighted two at a time.

The dorymen went below for dinner, as usual talking all at once, animatedly and fast, about the captain, about last winter at home, about things they had bought in Halifax, and, because I was there, a newcomer among them, about what they thought of the doryman's life. The man I sat next to at dinner, Charlie Strowbridge, said, "To each his own life, ay? And I guess this is about the worst." I asked him if he would take a job ashore. "Doesn't agree with me," he said. "I tried it for six months, but I didn't like it. Construction work. Every time I stay ashore, I lose twenty-five or thirty pounds. It's healthy out here."

"Oh yes, we feel bad ashore," said Sammy McDonald, who was sitting opposite us. "Mostly just eat and lie down. The shore's too still. We have to have it rolling."

Little Studley laughed at Sammy. "It's a hard life, but it's varied, by Jesus," he said. "That's true, ain't it, Johnson?" Johnson, chewing a mouthful of food slowly, nodded. He might have said something then but Studley and Sammy turned to listen to a conversation across the table. "One thing I can't understand is there's no growler at Cape St. Mary's," a young doryman named Ernest Skinner said. "You know that's funny, isn't it? That's an important light."

"Ay, there should be a horn 'a some kind," Reggie Bungay said. "You ha' the Bull, Calf, and Cows, and the Keys and the False Keys. Many a vessel's run into them in the fog." He mentioned two, a schooner lost with all hands twenty years before, and another from Harbor Breton, where many of the *Lynn*'s crew were from, lost more recently but with no one drowned. Everyone knew the details of these wrecks as though they had happened yesterday—and of shipwrecks much older, generations back, which others at the table brought up. Shipwreck was a part of their lives. Reggie told of a close call he had had a few years before. "We were four days under foresail. Water was up to the top of the benches in the cabin. I saw the captain chop away the bulwarks so the water would drain off the deck. So the water wouldn't run down into the cabin and sink her."

"When you going to retire, Johnson?" a sallow-faced young doryman called from the other end of the table, with some impudence, perhaps unintended, in his voice, which caused Reggie to give him a hard, disapproving stare. Johnson ignored the young doryman, but said to Studley, Charlie Strowbridge, and the others at his end of the table, "A fisherman can't retire. Can't get a job ashore. Plant says I'm too old. But I'm not too old to fish for 'em." Stanley nodded and laughed. Johnson chewed up a mouthful of food, then nodded at Studley. "Dory fishing beats them trawlers, I'll say that," he said. "You're nothing but a damn factory worker on a trawler. There's no skill to it. There ain't no seamanship to it. I worked on 'em. I couldn't take it. Roll, Jesus do they roll."

Maurice Walters, the mate of the *Lynn,* looked up from his plate. "Why is there no fish on the Grand Banks?" he said. "Trawlers tore it all up. If it weren't for Cape St. Mary's these dory schooners would be out of business. Trawlers get trash, I call it. Small haddock, flounders. Fill up the freeze plants with that. That's why we get such a poor price.

"They are making money now for a few years. Then they'll be no fish left. The government thinks it knows it all, but it don't." Walters, a tall, usually silent man, with a nose and a chin that drew closer to each other when he smiled or squinted, pointed his fork at Johnson.

"Am I right, Johnson?" he said.

"I think you are, Maurice. Them trawlers catch up everything, spawn, little ones. They're cleaning the bottom. It was tougher in them days, but we didn't kill all the fish."

"Them was good days, Johnson," Walters said. "There was sport to it then. Thirty year ago I took a berth as mate of the old *Dalsatian*—you remember her? I guess you do. She was like the *Bluenose.* Unless she was loaded down by the stern she wouldn't go at all. Get her low aft, my would she go. Yah. Fair breeze with all her sails, my she'd go.

"Down to the West Indies. Down with fish, back with salt. We logged fourteen knots. Yes, fourteen knots."

"You didna' average that?" Reggie said.

"No, but several days we did, I think. Coming back. I think it's sixteen hundred miles. Let's see—we made it in eight days, four hours. Except for one day when the booms was slatting around in the calm, we had fair winds.

"The last leg we traveled! We had a spell of weather close to home. Skipper should have taken in sail. It was dirty weather. Dirty. But he wouldn't do it—she was going then. Going more than fourteen knots then. We sailed with the sails wung out—

wung out in that. She spread the waves forward, I can tell you."

The mate, who usually discouraged talk about the sailing days and seemed concerned only with present problems and a fisherman's hard life, talked with fire in his eye. He used his body and arms to describe how the *Dalsatian* cut the waves forward.

"Racing," the mate said. "Racing, there's where they really carried sail. Only time they took it off is when it tore off. That's right. When it tore off."

Johnson nodded. "There was sport to it then, all right."

On deck a doryman showed me a round wooden plug which is taken out of the bottom of a dory when it is hoisted on deck to allow water to drain out. "My father was nine hours on the bottom of a dory once. Hanging on upside down. See this loop in the plug. That's what that's for. To hang onto. His mate drowned."

The dories were put over for another set.

Fog, blown by a strong, damp, fresh-smelling wind, lay in wisps aboard the schooner. Overhead the cloud was lightening. The sun broke through. Suddenly the massive cliffs of Cape St. Mary's appeared, rounded downward from light green hayfields to sheer faces dropping hundreds of feet to the ocean—a sculptured image that in the pale, washed air of Newfoundland stood desolate and pure. The pastel sky, soft and indistinct, still partly fog, merged into clouds behind the Cape, clouds piled on clouds, rolls of clouds, blue-gray, white, hanging suspended like the painted backdrop of a play. In that whole bold sweep of land, the only sign of life—three tiny horses grazing near the whitewashed Cape St. Mary's Lighthouse—heightened the sense of loneliness. They might have been the only life in all the world, mythological horses, horses of the gods. The sea, which had been oily-black all morning, turned icy-blue, glinting with sunlight. The dories, strung out on both sides of the schooner, advancing toward the Cape under blue, red-orange, and white sails, were dwarfed by the immensities around them, by the swells into which the farther ones would disappear, by the sky, by the barren eminence beyond them, by the roar of surf.

An obelisk of rock rose a hundred feet or more out of the sea a mile away from the schooner, surrounded by thousands of birds, swarms of them that looked like shimmering heat waves rising from the sides and top of the rock.

The vessel, deserted and asleep while her dorymen were out, rolled slowly in the swells. An eerie sound rose from the codfish sliding back and forth in the bins on deck—a doleful sigh, repeated with each roll of the schooner. A mild despondency hung over the schooner and her few people—the captain philosophizing by the pilothouse, abetted by the engineer, and down below, the cook complaining about the outrageous Newfoundlanders to the deck hand, Mike Landrigan. It would continue until the dorymen clambered back aboard and their talk and laughter filled the schooner's empty spaces.

The captain and engineer stood on each side of the pilothouse, talking sporadically.

"They ain't getting many fish in that dory, George," the engineer said.

"No, that dory ain't getting many fish," the captain muttered.

Gannets and hags skimmed by the schooner, the hags chasing over the contours of the sea never more than an inch above it.

"Years gone by the tide running to the south'ard past the Cape would be full of fish. Full of fish . . .

"We're stuck like a fish. Wind and tide against us. Strange." Under his breath, he said, "Inhuman." He straightened up and slapped his stomach with both palms and took a few steps up and down the deck, his back arched, shoulders back, stomach puffed out. "All my life I look for a fish," he said with an amazed look on his face, as though such a pursuit was incomprehensible. The schooner overtook the dory ahead. The captain looked into it. "No fish this year," he said.

But then the man in the bow of the closest dory began pulling in fish one right after the other. The captain stood rapt.

"Plenty of fish just here," the engineer said.

The captain nodded. "Jack, that's nice-looking fish they're bringing in," he said.

"Yah. Good ones," the engineer said.

The mournful cry of a foghorn came across the water from the farthest dory, the signal that it was loaded down with fish and needed to be lightened—even though it was only halfway down its trawl line. The schooner came alongside, the dorymen pitched their fish on deck, and sailed away to finish hauling their trawl line. The captain went forward to look at the fish. When he came back, he said to the engineer, "They're good fish. Good! Yes."

Before the end of the afternoon, all but two of the twelve dories had to be lightened. One had to be lightened twice. The dialogue at the pilothouse changed. The captain hummed in the silences sometimes. He told a joke. He described an encounter with a Hollywood director two years before, when he had been the stand-in for Gregory Peck in "The World in His Arms." For the movie, an old Gloucester schooner was refurbished. Tall masts, topmasts, and bowsprit were put back into her and she was supplied with sails the size of her original sail plan. Captain Himmelman trained a crew of Lunenburg boys to sail her, as the retired sailing fishermen left in Lunenburg were too old. Once the director called for a bow-on shot of the schooner. When Captain Himmelman sailed her by the camera platform on the photo ship, the director called, "Closer, closer." It was blowing quite hard. Captain Himmelman turned the schooner around and came back toward the photo ship, heeled over and moving fast. On he came until the cameramen, assistants, and the director himself took one look and jumped. The director never urged him to get closer again. "We had some fun," the captain said.

When the dories came back to the schooner at the end of the day, the dorymen hauled them aboard, nested them, and lashed them down with a bustle and purposefulness betokening the good afternoon. As the last one was hoisted aboard, the captain turned the bow of the schooner toward Nova Scotia—three hundred miles away.

The day's catch was twenty thousand pounds, which was not at all good. Forty or forty-five thousand would have been good. Nor was the total catch, one hundred and fifty thousand pounds, much to be elated about. Two hundred and forty thousand would be a good catch. One hundred and fifty thousand might bring each man fifty dollars for the eight-day trip. It had been a poor trip and a poor last day. But the poor last day had ended well. Three quarters of the twenty thousand pounds were caught in the afternoon, and the dorymen chose to concentrate on that as they lashed down their dories and set up the tables for the last task of the day, gutting, icing, and stowing the catch. Remarks were made about the good-looking fish. As the first were slit open, they proved to have fine large livers (which were kept separate in barrels)—a bonus for the fishermen. Furthermore, on her way to Nova Scotia the schooner would pass over St. Pierre Bank. If the weather were good, they might make a set there. Who knew, perhaps every hook would come up with a codfish on it. Perhaps they might catch halibut, which brought a better price. The issue was in the lap of the gods—as their lives and their whole livelihood were. Perhaps only two men on board worried—the cook, over some unfairness he thought of, and the captain, weighed down by his sense of the responsibility of command. The dorymen sang and joked and talked about North Sydney as they cleaned the catch. It was a happy ship. They worked in fours. One slit open a fish, the next gutted it, the third washed it, the fourth threw it into the sluice, where it would slide into another bath; all then would be thrown below to be iced and put in a bin.

After the fish were stowed, the men went below to their part of the ship—just forward of the fish. They were separated only by a bulkhead, the fish stowed tightly in one compartment, the dorymen slightly less tightly in another—all essentially sea creatures. The only ones on deck were the two on watch and Reggie Bungay, who in his thrifty way laboriously coiled a mile or more of condemned trawl line he had saved. It was no good at all any more for offshore fishing, and almost no good for anything, but he would take it home and use it trawling around his native rocks during the two months in the winter in which the *Lynn* did not fish. Every time it broke, he would tie it together, after a time-consuming haul back to his trawl buoy. A workman needs good tools. A fisherman needs good rope, but rope costs money, and if Reggie could make this do for a few catches, it might make a difference in what his wife and three little children ate later on.

The watches, a lookout forward and a helmsman aft, changed. The new helmsman's dorymate came up with him to keep him company in the pilothouse. They softly crooned old Newfoundland songs, about shipwreck or love. It was dusk. A few dorymen came on deck for a last look at Newfoundland. They had not been home for six months, except for one brief visit, and, except for a possible visit in six weeks, would not go home again for four more months. Light shone from the light-keeper's house, and Charlie Strowbridge, leaning on the rail with four or five others, said, "In a little while that man will go up-stairs to bed with his wife."

During the night the wind and seas increased, so that by mid-night steering was difficult. At two, the dorymen went on deck to bait up. They worked in raw, dripping blackness.

By dawn, when the schooner arrived on the bank, it was much too rough to fish, and the captain ordered the bait put back in the hold.

The wind veered from northeast to south to northwest and blew harder. The dripping fog lightened, became drier, snaked through the rigging faster. Spray came over the bow. The sun peeped through crevices in the overcast, then took charge of the sky from fleeing clouds, pulled apart and scattered by the wind, crowding pell-mell to the horizon, where they piled up in long, low drifts of cloudbank. The last wisps of fog disappeared. The faded colors of the vessel—the red of the deck, the green of the trim, the red and yellow of the dories—glistened in the sun, changing hue with its coming and going: when a cloud covered it, the red on the trawl tubs turned almost gray. The hard, blue, glinting sheen of the sea made so much light you could not look at it, except away from the sun. Battalions of immense white-maned waves, tossing spindrift before them, swept southward. Under a fine white mist of blown spume, glancing squalls flashed out across the surfaces of the waves like flicked fingers, in little jet spurts, fast and mean. Spray crashed aboard, at first on the foredeck, later on the maindeck, and finally hitting the pilot-house windows with force. Spray came with almost every wave, sometimes in torrents, blotting out the helmsman's view of everything in front of him—the two nests of dories, the foremast, the bow. When the schooner hit a wave a certain way, spray would shoot up almost to the top of the foremast. Occasionally green water came over the bow. The deck was awash. Every time the schooner rolled, water came in through her scuppers amidships. The crew began the heavy-weather method of travel, waiting until a moment when the deck seemed relatively stable and the next big wave some distance off and then running for it—running, as a bicyclist pedals, to stay upright. Trawl buoys began sliding around amidships.

I stayed in the pilothouse all afternoon and toward the end of it saw something Captain Himmelman said he had not seen in twenty years. A large schooner, like ours—only one that had once been a true sailing vessel, with bowsprit, tall masts, and topmasts—came toward us with the wind behind her. Her long tapering bow, the flowing lines of her hull, her low profile and pronounced sheer showed her to have been, before her masts were shortened and her bowsprit chopped off, a fine example of the Grand Banks schooner, a creature like the *Bluenose* or the

Columbia. She had three sails, a forestaysail, a foresail, and a small triangular sail on her mainmast. She could have carried twice as much sail, and in the old days she would have. But even with her cut-down modern rig, she was moving at ten or eleven knots. And her engine was off. For the first time in many years, probably, her engine was off and she was really sailing. She swept by us majestically, lifting powerfully on the crest of a sea, then almost surfing down it, heeling gently so that her lee rail was close to the water, moving rhythmically, easily, elegantly, with a sailing vessel's characteristic harmonizing of hull, sea, and wind. By the coincidence of a chance meeting in half a gale, which happened to be blowing in a direction she could take full advantage of, I witnessed a sight that had vanished many years before—a Grand Banks fishing schooner, one of the finest vessels ever developed, engaged in the activity she was built for. Most of the crew of the captive *Lynn,* pounding doggedly into the wind and seas instead of running free before them, and incapable, anyway, of the other schooner's performance, came on deck and watched the other schooner out of sight, even though it meant donning oilskins and braving continuous drenchings. "Ay," Reggie said, "we'll na see sight like that again."

III

In the years between 1920 and 1936, the America's Cup races off Newport were almost as popular as the World Series. It was the era of Sir Thomas Lipton, Harold Vanderbilt, and T.O.M. Sopwith, and the big and costly J-boats. No one followed the races with more interest than the fishermen of Canada and the United States.

When one of the races of the 1920 Cup series was called off because the New York Yacht Club Race Committee decided a twenty-three-knot breeze was too dangerous for the two contenders, a great hoot of derision went up from the fishermen. They began demanding a series of races between "honest-to-God vessels." The publisher of the *Halifax Herald* took up the demand and sponsored a series that year between a schooner from Lunenburg and one from Gloucester. In each city schooners just in from the fishing banks were hastily scrubbed down and elimination races were held. The fastest schooner from each city then met off Halifax in a series of races, which the Gloucestermen won. They held the International Fishermen's Trophy for one year. Then the *Bluenose* won it and Gloucester never got it back. Built in 1921, she defended the trophy successfully against all challengers until 1938, when the competition was discontinued.

Held off Boston, Gloucester or Halifax, the International Fishermen's Races attracted as much attention as the America's Cup competitions off Newport. Canadian and American wire services and newspapers sent reporters to cover the races, and accounts were carried in newspapers from coast to coast and in magazines. Destroyers from both nations were assigned to escort the schooners, and thousands of spectators gathered on shore and in boats.

The intensity of the old rivalry between Gloucester, capital of the New England fishing industry, and Lunenburg, capital of the Nova Scotia industry, can be judged by the fact that nine new fishing schooners were built to beat the *Bluenose*. Four of them were Canadian, built to win from her the right of defending the trophy. Five were American, built to challenge the trophy. Of course, all of them fished. But the initial push for their building was the racing fever that gripped the fishermen. Indeed, a stranger listening to the talk in Gloucester or Lunenburg in those years might easily have come to believe that racing, not gathering fish, was the principal occupation in those two towns.

The fishermen, cast in an unfamiliar role as leading sporting figures, offered a brand of competition more colorful and less predictable than the orderly, restrained, and gentlemanly sailing done at Newport. There were around thirty men in the crew of a racing schooner and many were skippers off other schooners. Instead of racing by the intricate rules that govern yachting contests and give to them something of the dry, intellectual air of a chess game, the fishermen raced by no rules but the International Rules of the Road governing commercial vessels and sometimes ignored even these.

In a strong breeze, the races were a magnificent sight: the *Bluenose*, 143 feet long with ten thousand square feet of canvas on her two towering masts, her decks awash as she charged along and her bow wave wetting half her foresail; her Gloucester rival, a slightly smaller schooner of the same type.

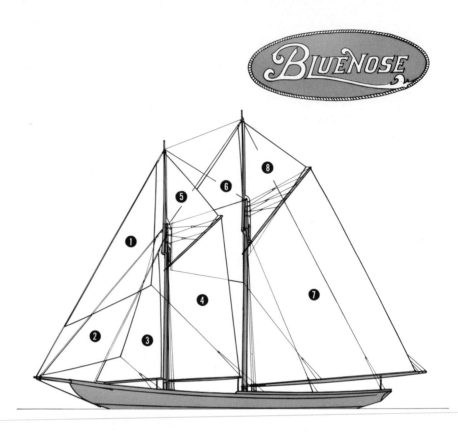

1 JIB TOPSAIL **2** JIB **3** JUMBO **4** FORESAIL **5** FORE GAFF TOPSAIL
6 FISHERMAN'S STAYSAIL **7** MAINSAIL **8** MAIN GAFF TOPSAIL

The races were often close, but the *Bluenose* defeated the
Gloucester schooner *Elsie* in a series of races off Halifax in 1921,
the *Henry Ford* in a series off Gloucester in 1922, the *Columbia*
off Halifax in 1923, the *Gertrude L. Thebaud* off Halifax in 1931,
and the same schooner again in another series off Gloucester and
Boston in 1938.

She also defeated ten Canadian schooners, the *Independence,
J. Duffy, Canadia, Alcala, Ada R. Corkum, Donald J. Cook,
Delawanna, Mahaska, Margaret K. Smith,* and *Haligonian,* in a
series of races in 1921, 1922, and 1926.

Besides her victories in the official International Fishermen's
Races in Canada and the United States, she won all or almost all
the informal brushes she engaged in on the fishing banks. The

only defeat the *Bluenose* ever suffered was in a series of races for the Lipton Trophy against the *Thebaud* in 1930.

It was an America's Cup series in reverse for the British Empire, and the *Bluenose* was very popular in Canada and England. Her likeness is on the back of the Canadian ten-cent piece and on a commemorative stamp. She was a Canadian exhibit at the Chicago World's Fair. The ship that ferries American tourists from the United States to Nova Scotia is named for her. In 1935 the British invited the *Bluenose* to England to help celebrate the Silver Jubilee of King George V. The king gave her a mainsail from the royal yacht *Britannia*.

Captain Angus Walters, who skippered her in all the races, became undoubtedly the best-known fisherman in the world. He was admired by the leading yachtsmen of his era in Canada, the United States, and Britain; by premiers of Canada, by King George, by President Franklin D. Roosevelt. He became one of the great men of his nation, and his fame continued long after the last race in 1938. Clerks in Toronto and Winnepeg, even farmers on the Western plains, who had never seen the ocean, identified with him. Brian Backman, a writer in Halifax, told me in 1963 that he was the closest thing to a national hero Canada has.

I will give one example of his skill, not from his racing days, but from his years of fishing on the North Atlantic banks. Walters was anchored off Nova Scotia's Sable Island, which shares with Cape Hatteras the name "Graveyard of the Atlantic" because of its treacherous and constantly shifting sand bars and its exposed location. He was there because the fishing was good. It had begun to snow in the early morning and by late afternoon was blowing a gale—directly toward the northwest bar of Sable Island. Before the *Bluenose*'s anchor cable parted at six o'clock in the evening, the wind was blowing probably seventy miles an hour and the seas were thirty-five to forty-five feet high.

The waves build up in the shoal water off Sable in a way that is unbelievable to anyone who has not seen it. A friend of mine,

Ralph Hemphill, whose father's fishing schooner was lost at Sable Island in a storm two years before this incident, told me what happens to fishing schooners caught there in a bad gale.

As the wind and waves drive them ashore, they are like corks in water, until finally in the trough of a wave their keels strike bottom. Then these 120-foot to 140-foot vessels, measuring 250 to 270 tons, are rolled by the seas over and over and over up the beach, like logs or driftwood, until they come to rest, often above the normal high-water line. Usually everyone inside is battered to death.

The *Bluenose* was anchored two miles offshore in eleven fathoms, or sixty-six nautical feet, of water, which meant that before the storm there had been more than fifty feet of water under her keel. Now, as she plunged and reared on the end of her anchor cable, her keel was more than ninety feet from the bottom when she was on the crests of the seas and probably less than ten feet from the bottom in the troughs.

The anchor cable parted at six o'clock, and the *Bluenose,* which had been heading into the wind and the seas, fell off sideways and started driving toward shore, her situation being then about like that of a chip of wood caught in a rapids. The problem, if she were to survive, was to turn her seaward again and, against the wind, make her claw her way over the tremendous seas out to deep water.

In these days of radar, radio weather reports, and reliable engines, it is almost unknown for a vessel to come to grief on a lee shore, but in the days of sail it was not uncommon. The outcome depended on the seamanship of captain and crew and, as important, on the sailing qualities of the vessel itself.

Walters raised three small sails and got the *Bluenose* headed not away from the land, because that was directly into the wind, but on a course about parallel to the shore. If the wind veered so that her course converged with the land she was probably doomed. If it veered the other way so she could head more to sea she was probably saved, provided, first, that she did not strike bottom before getting away; second, that she could withstand the battering she was taking from the sea; and third, that she did not sideslip too much to leeward.

When a wind strikes a sail it is converted into two forces, one a forward motion, the other a leeward motion. An inefficient helmsman in an inefficient boat succeeds only in sliding sideways —to leeward. On that night the *Bluenose*'s survival depended on the efficiency of her helmsman and on her own inherent sailing ability, for much sliding to leeward would put her on the shoals.

If one of the three sails had torn, it would have been the end, for with only two sails her forward motion would have virtually stopped and her leeward motion would have been accelerated.

For six hours Walters stood lashed to the wheel, under water as much as he was above it, until finally after midnight the wind hauled—changed direction—and his vessel was saved.

"Just as the cable snapped, the heaviest sea I had ever seen came aboard," Walters said the first time he told me the story. "It carried away the rail and the bulwarks forward, although I didn't know it at the time. We canvassed it up later.

"I tried to go out to the west'ard; it was shorter. But I couldn't. I'd 'a been run ashore. So I had to go out to the east'ard, run the whole length of the island. If I may say so, I never expected to see Lunenburg again.

"I knew the *Bluenose*, that she wouldn't make much leeway. I had great faith in her. But we had eleven miles to go along that shore. If one sail had give way, we were done for. We was lucky. We happened to have good sails that spring—for some reason.

"By staying onto the wheel myself and watching the compass right steady, I could see she wasn't being headed.

"Then I see she was getting to windward a little, getting to windward. If I may say so, I don't think another vessel could have done it."

It was the excellence of the *Bluenose*, but also Walters' helmsmanship, that saw them through that night. The whole forward rail and bulwarks, integral parts of a schooner, were stove in by the seas crashing over her, and the next morning there was sand on her deck, sand churned up by the undertow of the night before.

"I was lashed to the wheel until the wind hauled. I stayed to the wheel because I didn't trust anyone else. They might 'a been as good as I was, but I knew the vessel.

"But I never knew through all that night when we were going to scrape bottom. When they let the lead run and sang out eleven fathom, the shivers ran too, I can tell you.

"You couldn't see the seas coming. Just see the white capping up. Half the time you didn't see the white—it was snowing so damn hard. You could hear 'em coming. Get your feet planted. Get a grip. But not that that did any good. A bucket of water will knock you over if it hits you right. You'd get a grip but the sea would knock it out.

"When the wind hauled after midnight, I was about all in, to be honest with you. It was wet, I can tell you. Sometimes I was all under. Just come up to get my breath."

Walters was born in Lunenburg in 1881, went to sea at thirteen, became a doryman at sixteen and a captain in his early twenties. By the time he was thirty-two or thirty-three he had earned a reputation as one of the most successful skippers on the Grand Banks.

Walters came ashore in 1939 and opened a dairy next door to his house on the edge of Lunenburg harbor. I first saw him in 1956, eighteen years after the last race and thirty-six years after the first one. He talked as if the races had been held the day before. Every detail was indelibly printed in his mind. He did not recount the record; he relived it—his outrage undiminished at some damn fool on the race committee, his admiration for some feat of his old vessel plain on his face and in his voice, a small, quick, quick-tempered bantam rooster of a man, completely single-minded, in dead earnest ("I told him if he ever tried it again, I'd cut him square in two, damn if both our vessels sank"), and so enamored of the schooner he shared his prime of life with that, although he is not by nature eloquent or apt with a phrase, as the Bahamian seamen are, for instance, he defined the relationship of man to sailing vessel better than I had ever heard or read. When he talked of some supposed slight to the *Bluenose,* he talked as a man might of an insult to his wife. "They always said it had to blow, had to blow. It didn't have to blow. She was as lively in light air as those shooflies they were sailing in. They should have been ashamed to say that!"

She was very seldom slow. When she was in trim, nothing could touch her. She was the finest fishing vessel ever built in Lunenburg. "She was faster than American yachts. I know because I raced them over in England. And they told me twelve knots was fast for them. *Bluenose* was clocked at fifteen knots by the cutter off Halifax. And outside Gloucester once, I claim she must have been going almost twenty." She could sail to windward faster than any boat she ever met and could stand up to weather that caused the other fishing schooners to flounder and shorten sail.

"In all the fishermen's races, she'd run off the wind as fast as any other boat, and we never had no competition to windward. The rougher it was, the better it was for *Bluenose* and the worse for the other feller."

Captain Paddy Mack of Lunenburg, Nova Scotia, had a schooner built which he was convinced would beat the *Bluenose.* The more he sailed her, the more convinced he became. When he left Lunenburg for the races at Halifax, he said he would return with a trophy under each arm. After the *Bluenose* shipped him, he set his hard hat—a derby he always wore—down on the deck and jumped on it.

The day before the official race, the *Bluenose* and Paddy Mack's schooner, the *Mahaska,* met by chance. "He was out for a sail when I came up from Lunenburg and we had a little brush. What a crime, what a crime. I could have towed another boat.

"It was the same with all of them, Canadian and American. The Canadian schooners came out of the same yard as *Bluenose.*

And you'd think the Americans could have built a vessel, but none of 'em held a candle to *Bluenose*."

Gradually it dawned on me that the story of the *Bluenose* I had come to Walters to get, the story of a great vessel and a great seaman, was also the story, being told to me by a fiery old man, of a long love. There is a lot of loose talk about the personality of sailing vessels. If there is such a thing, I think vinegary old Angus Walters defined it. Most of his talk was hardheaded, practical, laced with scornful humor and vehement opinions. Then he would put his relationship to the *Bluenose* in a gentle sentence or a phrase: "I watched her. I watched how she sailed." "It was a mystery what made her so fast. Everything in her must have been perfect."

Yacht racing is an intellectual sport. A large literature, covering such subjects as helmsmanship, the aerodynamics of sails, racing tactics, proper trimming of boats under various wind conditions, has grown up over the past fifty years. The theories—often expressed in complicated formulas—of such experts as Uffa Fox, Manfred Curry—the father of scientific sailing, Arthur Knapp, Robert Bavier, and Stuart Walker are part of the equipment a racing skipper brings with him to the starting line. (Under condition x, Curry says do this, Knapp says do that; with this sort of breeze, the aerodynamics of the sails requires such and such a relationship between them, and such and such an angle to the wind—these are the sort of things the racing skipper is thinking of, or has in the back of his mind.) Walters, of course, never heard of Manfred Curry or read a book on racing theory. While the experts and yachtsmen were developing their formulas and refinements in the summer sun of elegant sailing centers, he was out on the fishing banks. Usually wet, cold, and tired, always primarily interested in catching fish, not sailing fast, Walters, nevertheless, as the ornamental capstone of his career, evolved some of the same formulas and refinements that the yachtsmen and their theorists were working out in the laboratory conditions of summer weekend races. This was one of his accomplishments. He was, of necessity, concerned with problems of survival day after day on the open ocean, problems quite different from those of a racing skipper. The aerodynamics of sails, for instance, or racing theory, were extraneous to his business. Yet he became one of the great racing skippers of his generation.

In his conversations with me, Walters now and then has said something that throws light on how this came about.

"Before I was master, I used to stay onto the wheel when I didn't have to, to see if I could beat the other boat. I'd stand there six hours or more if we was in company with other vessels. Lots of fellers used to be crazy for their hour trick at the wheel to get by. To tell you the truth, I liked to steer. If there was other boats around, they didn't get the wheel from me very quick, I'll tell you—before I was master and after." When his relief came, he would say, "I'll take your trick." When the next relief came, he would say the same thing. They thought he was daft.

Another time, Walters and I were discussing what made one schooner fast, another slow. An important element was the trim, how the cargo was placed in the hold. The difference of six inches or a foot in fore and aft trim could markedly affect a schooner's sailing qualities. The schooners stayed out on the Banks two or three months sometimes, gradually filling their holds with codfish. It was a precise matter to load them evenly, and many fishing masters never acquired the know-how or took the care to do the job right. Their schooners would come back to Lunenburg down by the bow or down by the stern, which made them, Walters said, slow in ordinary weather and hard to manage in a gale. "Saddled by one end, I called it," he said.

"Vessels would get a reputation for being slow or cranky. Sometimes it weren't the vessel's fault, it was the master's. They'd want to go fast, but didn't bother.

"Same thing with the sails. They didn't bother to know sails stretch a little and need another pull. Some fellers didn't care if the sails were half up. Other vessels, if the sails needed a pull up, they got it."

Walters said to me once about the *Bluenose*, "I learned exactly the trim of her. She could be slow if I wanted her to be.

"The same with the crew. Why, I used to shift that crew, just a foot, then another foot—in the races, you know."

Shifting the crew forward and aft to improve trim and increase speed is something Olympic sailors become expert at. In a small racing boat, weighing, say, five hundred pounds, the position of a two-hundred-pound crew member is crucial. That Walters, in the 285-ton *Bluenose*, was so particular helps explain his record.

Today sailmakers have advanced the art of sailmaking far beyond what it was before World War II. Knowledge of what is the best-shaped sail for maximum efficiency has become so precise that you can order a sail for winds from zero to six miles an hour, another for six to eighteen miles an hour, another for eighteen to twenty-five, and another for above twenty-five. Some of the more zealous skippers in the top competitive classes have four or five mainsails to choose from depending on wind velocity on the day of a race.

Walters, in 1922, was experimenting with sail changes. Because the size of his regular sails made it impossible to take off one and put on another between races, there was only one he could change, the fishermen's staysail. And that he did: "We always carried two of those with us, in case one of them filled better," he said. If he'd had the money, he probably would have carried more.

A sailboat like the *Bluenose*—or any sailboat, really, but one the size of the *Bluenose* much more than a dinghy—seems to have a motivating force of its own, an independent source of propulsion which you can modify by tinkering (adjusting sails, changing trim, and so forth), but which is in part unrelated to anything you may do. When a boat is going well—modern racing sailors sometimes call it being "in the groove"—this happy condition is the result of expert adjustment of the sails, perfect trim, ideal wind and wave conditions, luck, and a certain mystic capability of the helmsman. But there is also, definitely, an unknown quantity which the vessel itself seems to provide. This is the source of the notion that sailing vessels are alive, that they have minds of their own. This is why they are often called temperamental.

The apparently independent force owned by the boat itself is, I think, what Walters had in mind when he tried to answer my questions about what he did to make the *Bluenose* so fast in the races. It was a matter of understanding her. "When I was fishing, I'd leave the wheel and go all around the vessel watching her," he said.

A friend of mine whose father raced with Walters told me that in the races Walters sometimes would leave the wheel— entrusting it to Captain "Long" Albert Himmelman, the best helmsman in Lunenburg, possibly excepting Walters—and go up by the foresail where he could keep one eye on his competition and one on his sails. He would signal the helmsman with his hands. One finger meant give her one spoke of the wheel. Two fingers meant two spokes. Walters would watch the sails as the *Bluenose*'s course changed imperceptibly. He would listen to the sound of the bow wave. He would feel the slant of the deck. No wonder he had said he could make her slow if he wanted to. It was a case of coming to know her.

At the wheel, when he was steering, the *Bluenose* was send-ing constant messages to him about her performance, perhaps by the shudder, the vibration in the rudder, perhaps by the amount of pressure needed on the helm to keep her on course, perhaps by the little quiver in her mainsail near the mast, or the curve of her jib, or the sounds she made, or the way her bow lifted to a swell—signals that a stranger on the *Bluenose* would neither see nor hear nor feel.

There are two versions of the International Fishermen's Races, the Lunenburg version and the Gloucester version, which bear almost no resemblance to each other. I have the Lunenburg version. It is accurate in specifics, but it is not the entire story. Captain Walters' thoughts about the iniquities of race committees and Gloucestermen, on occasions, could be matched by their thoughts of his. And, in spite of what he says about the Gloucester schooners, even the *Thebaud*, which he sometimes called a toy or a yacht, they were, like the *Bluenose*, able, fast, and well-sailed.

In 1920, when Senator W. H. Dennis, publisher of the *Halifax Herald*, announced that the *Herald* would put up a trophy and prize money for a series of international fishing schooner races, the fastest schooners in Gloucester and Lunenburg were hurriedly scrubbed down, painted, reballasted, and rigged with topmasts. The Gloucester schooners competed in a series of elimination races to determine the fastest American schooner. Eight Nova Scotia schooners, six from Lunenburg and two from LaHave, competed in the Canadian eliminations. The captains who sailed in the eliminations were considered among the best in the fishery. Three were Himmelmans—Albert, Alvin, and Thomas. Angus Walters was one of the youngest and not long before had come in from the Banks in his schooner, the *Gilbert B. Walters*, with the largest catch of the season.

In the elimination race off Halifax, Thomas Himmelman's *Delawanna* and the *Gilbert B. Walters* were about even going around the last mark of the thirty-mile course. Walters ordered his jib topsail set. His foretopmast snapped and it and the topsail went overboard. "I hadn't raced much. When they hoisted the bloody sail, I thought they had it sheeted in. A puff came along and the whole thing went in the water."

He had to head into the wind to clear up the mess. The *Delawanna* surged by the *Walters,* and Himmelman beat her by five minutes. Many observers believed Walters' mishap cost him the race. In any event, he met the *Delawanna* the next summer on the way to the Banks and beat her.

Meanwhile, the schooner *Esperanto,* skippered by Captain Marty Welch, beat her rivals in eliminations off Gloucester. She sailed to Halifax to meet the *Delawanna.* In their first race, the *Esperanto* crossed the finish line nineteen minutes ahead of the *Delawanna.* In their second, she beat the *Delawanna* by seven minutes, and took the International Fishermen's Trophy home. She never had a chance to defend it. She was lost on Sable Island before the next year's series.

After the *Esperanto* went off with the trophy, fishing masters and shipwrights in Lunenburg and other coastal towns talked of building a new schooner fast enough to win the next series. In Shelburne, Nova Scotia, the birthplace of Donald McKay, and long noted for its expert builders, a new schooner was begun. About the same time, a group of businessmen and yachtsmen in Halifax asked a young amateur naval architect, William J. Roue, if he could build a schooner big and burdensome enough to succeed in the salt-fishing trade and fast enough to beat the Gloucesterman. He said he would try. The success of his effort, the *Bluenose,* made him famous.

The group, known as the Halifax Committee, decided to finance the new schooner in the time-honored way in Lunen-burg, by selling one hundred-dollar shares, and to have her built in the Smith & Rhuland Yard there. They also decided they liked the way Angus Walters sailed in the eliminations and what they had heard about his single-mindedness. But Walters wasn't much on committees. "When the idea of building a new schooner for the Fishermen's Races first come up, these fellers from Halifax asked me if I'd take charge of her. I said no, right off. I said, why don't you give her to Tommy Himmelman? I had a vessel then only three years old. I didn't want to get rid of her.

"Supposin' the *Bluenose* had turned out to be no good for racing. The fellers from Halifax would lose interest fast enough, and I'd 'a been without a vessel.

"Then my brother says to me, Why don't you do this? I'll take the *Gilbert* and you take this new one.

"So after a while I said, I'll take her on this condition. They said, We'll finance the vessel and give you what shares you want. I said, Oh no, I'll give you what shares I want. I'll give you a third—that way I'd have control.

"We'll capitalize her at thirty-five thousand dollars, I said. You sell fifteen thousand dollars and I'll sell twenty thousand dollars.

"Then when we were ready someone on the committee said, All the shares ain't sold. I said, What do you mean the shares ain't sold? They hadn't sold their shares. I went out on the street and in less than an hour I'd sold 'em. It ended up they sold twelve thousand dollars. I sold the rest."

Thus, reluctantly on Walters' part at first, the career of the *Bluenose* and her skipper began. Even today, although he thinks of the *Bluenose* as incomparably the greatest fishing schooner ever built, he looks back on his parting from the *Gilbert B. Walters* with regret. For one thing, she had a larger cargo capacity. For another, she too was fast. "The *Bluenose* couldn't beat the *Gilbert B. Walters* by very much," he told me once. Another time, describing the *Gilbert B. Walters*—she had no bowsprit—he said, "With a bowsprit, I think she would have given the *Bluenose* a damn hard time."

His brother took the *Gilbert B. Walters* south in the winter of 1920–1, while Walters stayed at home to watch the building of the *Bluenose*. She was launched March 26, 1921, the one hundred and twenty-first schooner to go down the ways of the Smith & Rhuland Yard. He took her fishing that summer. Besides racing and beating everything she met, she returned home with more fish than any other schooner, reported Andrew Merkel of the Canadian Press, who covered the International Fishermen's

Races and wrote an excellent account of them in *The Schooner Bluenose*.[1]

Eight schooners showed up for the Canadian eliminations off Halifax, including the *Canadia*, a new schooner built in Shelburne. In the first race, after twenty-two miles of the forty-mile course had been sailed, the elapsed time of the three leading schooners, *Bluenose*, *Canadia*, and *Alcala*, showed a difference of less than three minutes, Merkel reported. The *Bluenose* finished four minutes ahead of the *Canadia*, eight minutes ahead of the *Alcala*, and eleven minutes ahead of the *Delawanna*. Part of the reason for the fairly close finish, Merkel reported, was a bad tack Walters made early in the race.

In the second race, the *Delawanna* actually beat the *Bluenose* off the wind. She was clocked at the Sambro Lightship thirty-eight seconds ahead of the *Bluenose*. But in the long thrash to windward, the *Bluenose*, Merkel said, ran away from the *Delawanna*. She finished more than fifteen minutes ahead of her.

After eliminations in Gloucester, the Americans sent the schooner *Elsie* to Halifax accompanied by a destroyer. Captain Marty Welch, who had won the trophy in the *Esperanto* the year before, was at her helm.

Howard Chapelle considers the *Elsie*, designed by Thomas F. McManus, probably the highest development of the New England fishing schooner.[2] She was launched in 1910, lost in 1935. She was only 106 feet long, compared to the 143 feet of the *Bluenose*, which, as Americans point out, put her at a distinct disadvantage.

In the first race, the little *Elsie* stayed up with her bigger and more powerful rival for the first eighteen miles, in spite of winds of twenty-five knots and up. But in the eighteen miles back to the finish line, most of it a long, hard drive to windward, she fell

---

[1] Andrew Merkel: *The Schooner Bluenose* (Toronto: Ryerson Press; 1948).
[2] Howard I. Chapelle: *History of American Sailing Craft* (New York: W. W. Norton; 1935), pp. 255–6.

behind. On the way home Walters put up his ballooner. Welch immediately followed suit, but in the process carried away his foretopmast. Walters responded by taking down his own bal-looner, so that his sail plan corresponded with *Elsie*'s for most of the rest of the race. Merkel believes that the loss of the fore-topmast made little difference in the final outcome. The *Blue-nose* took the race by thirteen minutes. In the second race of the series the *Elsie* led around three of the four legs of the course, but as on the day before, once the two schooners began the windward leg, the *Bluenose* sailed faster. She finished more than three miles ahead. The *Elsie* lost the trophy, but considering her small size, she did amazingly well.

There was great rejoicing in Halifax that night. Aboard the *Bluenose*, the sound of revelry continued way into the night. Merkel reports that some admirer sent down a case of cham-pagne, which was poured out to everyone who came on board, until somebody climbed on top of the cabin table and shouted, "The hell with this apple cider, let's have a drink," and a keg of rum was rolled out.

Only three Canadian schooners showed up the following fall to contest the *Bluenose*'s right to represent Canada in the 1922 International Fishermen's Races. All three were new—the *Ca-nadia,* built in 1921 and a close contender in the 1921 elimina-tions, and the *Mahaska* and the *Margaret K. Smith,* both built in 1922 to beat the *Bluenose.* The *Bluenose* crossed the finish line six minutes ahead of the *Canadia,* twenty minutes ahead of the *Margaret K. Smith.* A second elimination was called off because of light winds, and she was named defender of the trophy.

In Gloucester, a new schooner, the *Henry Ford,* bigger than the *Elsie,* but also designed by Thomas McManus, trounced her opposition. She won the first elimination race with a margin of fifteen minutes, the second with a margin of twenty-five minutes.

The *Bluenose* was escorted to Gloucester for the 1922 series by a Canadian destroyer, and newspapermen, race representa-tives, and government officials followed in a government cable ship. Merkel reports they found Gloucester in a ferment of excitement. The *Ford* had been built specifically with this series in mind. She had walked away from her American competition. A lot of money said she would win back the trophy.

The first race went up in smoke, as any racing official would say it should have, because Walters and Clayton Morrissey, skipper of the *Henry Ford*, completely ignored a postponement signal. Race committees were not held in great esteem by the fishermen, and when the postponement signal flag went up on the Committee boat (the Committee decided a few minutes before the start to signal a half-hour postponement in hopes that the wind would increase) the *Bluenose* and the *Ford* were on the starting line.

"What about it, Clayt?" Walters shouted.

"All right by me," replied Morrissey. The race was on.

The frantic Committee fired a warning shot to draw attention to the postponement signal. Walters and Morrissey ignored it. The Committee sent an escort destroyer after the fishermen to bring them back. Walters and Morrissey ignored the destroyer. They saw no reason to bother with a race committee. The merits of the two vessels had been discussed by fishermen ashore and afloat ever since the *Ford's* launching half a year before. The *Ford* had been built to beat the *Bluenose*. Here she was alongside the *Bluenose*. Why not see if she could?

The *Ford* beat the *Bluenose* across the finish line, but in such light air that the six-hour time limit that governed in official races had run out. When the Race Committee announced that night that the race did not count, the crew of the *Ford* angrily decided to quit racing. They began a party to celebrate their decision, and would have stayed away from the rest of the series except for the emotional appeal of the secretary of the navy, who was prevailed upon to address the crew of the *Ford* and in a fish shed near her berth appealed eloquently to their patriotism. "Never let it be said the men of Clark's Harbor, the Pubnico's and Barrington helped to trail Old Glory in the dust," he ex-

claimed.[3] Although, in fact, most of the crew were Nova Sco-
tians, the appeal worked, pegged as it was to their Canadian
origins, and the *Ford* went out to the starting line the next day.
In the second race, the *Henry Ford* beat the *Bluenose* around the
course by two minutes, twenty seconds in winds almost as light
as in the first race. "Drifting, that's what I call it. She got ahead
of us drifting," Walters said.

The next day there was no race scheduled. It blew hard. The
Bluenose went out for a tune-up sail. She had up her four working sails—main, foresail, jumbo, and jib—but not her topsails.

"Then Clayt comes out with his big, blow-bag crew, their
tops'ls flying," Walters recalled. "It was squally. First thing they
find, they're laying in the water. That took the life out of Clayt
and scared the life out of his crew.

"They'd been better off if they hadn't seen how she was. Or if
they came out, they should 'a had only their lowers and put more
on gradually.

"That night we prayed for wind. During the night, the glass
fell and the next day it was blowing hard. Clayt got sick. If they
hadn't been out the day before, he wouldn't have got sick. Wind
made him sick.

"We got word there'd be no race. I said, 'God a'mighty, isn't
there another skipper in Gloucester who can handle a boat?'
When Pine got sick, they always had a skipper to take his place.

"Next day it was still blowing. Clayt's wife came alongside
and said Clayt was still feeling pretty low and could I wait at the
dock one more day. I said I didn't come here to stay till Christ-
mastime. I told an American feller there, 'I'm going out to the
line and if you're there, fine. If not, I'm going around the course
and to hell with the Committee.'

"I cast off the lines and the funny thing is, the *Ford* followed
us out and Clayt was aboard her all the time.

"It blew like the day before. The *Ford*, she went adrift.

"Before the wind she was all right. Anyone can go before the

3 Merkel, p. 37.

wind. But the last leg was to windward. She fell over and damn near stayed over. Thank God it was the last leg, or they would have called it off.

"Around the last turn, we were no farther apart than from here to the corner. At the finish, they were so far to looward you could hardly see them."

The *Bluenose* won two races in fresh breezes, and took the trophy home.

The year before, in 1921, a group of Boston businessmen, mostly marine outfitters, underwrote the construction of a fishing schooner they named the *Mayflower*. The Boston group, jealous of Gloucester's role as the capital of the New England fishing industry, wanted to draw attention to Boston's increasing importance as a fishing port. The trustees of the International Fishermen's Trophy ruled that the *Mayflower* was ineligible to race because while she could qualify as a fresh fisherman, she did not have the cargo capacity for a salt fisherman. Gloucestermen were delighted by the ruling. They had refused to sail in eliminations in which the *Mayflower* took part; it was only after she was declared ineligible that the *Elsie* was chosen to go to Halifax to defend the trophy.

Walters himself, however, never had any objection to taking on the *Mayflower*. "I'd gone up to Boston one time and looked at her and I said, 'My God, if that goddam thing can beat the *Bluenose,* I don't know nothing about a vessel.'

"Henry Larkin was the *Mayflower*'s skipper. The night of the banquet up to Gloucester after the *Henry Ford* series, he asked me if I'd be satisfied to race. I agreed. The committee from Halifax kicked up a fuss about it. I told them they could go home."

That night Walters' nephew went ashore to celebrate the *Bluenose*'s victory over the *Henry Ford*. His body was found under a wharf the next morning. He had drowned.

"When we beat the *Henry Ford,* they were sorer than hell about it over in Gloucester. He asked me for money to go ashore.

I said no because I knew what it was like. That night, he and one other feller went anyhow. They were the only ones from the vessel that did.

"It has always been my contention that he was shoved off. They seen he had a few drinks in him and shoved him. They had no use for our fellers then."

The *Bluenose* sailed home without racing the *Mayflower*.

The next fall, no Canadian vessels contested the *Bluenose*'s right to defend the trophy. At Gloucester, the *Henry Ford* was decisively beaten by a brand-new schooner, the *Columbia*, in light airs, the kind of weather the *Ford* liked. The *Columbia* had been launched the spring before and in her trials proved fast and able. She fished for a season on the Banks, where, according to Merkel, she caused great excitement and furnished the chief topic of conversation in the fo'c'sles.

When she arrived at Halifax with Captain Ben Pine at the helm for the 1923 International Fishermen's Trophy series, Merkel reported, the *Columbia* received a tremendous ovation. As soon as she was sighted off Chebucto Head, offices and stores were deserted and a huge throng went down to the harbor to greet her.

The Americans had almost disrupted the *Ford–Bluenose* series of 1922. Angus Walters did disrupt the *Columbia–Bluenose* series of 1923—so completely that eight years went by before there was another series of races for the International Fishermen's Trophy.

In the first race he established a lead of two minutes seventeen seconds at the second mark. Then, on the windward leg, he blew it. "We went out instead of tacking and covering the other boat," he said. "Dear God, we stood on. The wind hauled in his favor and that was that."

At the third mark, most of the way around the forty-mile course, the two schooners were exactly even. Then came a furious duel for the weather berth. With everything drawing, and racing neck and neck, Captain Pine kept edging Walters, thirty feet to windward of him, further and further up into the wind, a recognized racing tactic. But just to windward of Walters was a line of jagged rocks. Try as he might, the Lunenburger could not shake his rival. The schooners tore along only a biscuit's throw from the "Three Sisters," one of the most dreaded shoals along the coast. They neared Bell Rock Buoy, marking another shoal, and Pine forced Walters into the green water inside the buoy.

The pilot aboard the *Bluenose*—each schooner carried a Halifax pilot—shouted to *Bluenose*'s helmsman, Albert Himmelman, to bear away.

"Bear away and we strike him," Himmelman yelled back.

"Strike him or strike the rocks," the pilot yelled.

Walters, standing beside Himmelman, yelled across to Pine demanding room, but Pine ignored the yell. The pilot on the *Bluenose* threw up his hands and told Walters that he would no longer be responsible for the safety of the vessel. Walters shouted across to the *Columbia*, "Pine, you can do as you like; I'm swinging and I'm swinging fast."

Swing he did. The *Bluenose*'s main boom hit the *Columbia*'s rigging, swept half of the length of her and caught on a line on the *Columbia*'s bowsprit. The *Bluenose* actually towed the *Columbia* for a minute or so before they separated. She went on to win the race.

The yacht-racing rules and the International Rules of the Road are quite precise in stating that one vessel cannot run another onto the rocks. But the alternative for Pine was to lose all his advantage over Walters by bearing away to give room. The prospect of his opponent surging by him if he did so was more than he could bear, and in the heat of the contest he ignored the danger to *Bluenose*. The danger, really, was almost as great for his own vessel; if the *Bluenose* tore a hole in her bottom on the rocks, it was quite likely that the *Columbia* would too. But these fishermen took their racing seriously.

In the second race, sailed in a twenty-five-knot breeze, the *Bluenose* led the *Columbia* all around the course, never by much, and finished two minutes forty-five seconds ahead. But Walters had passed a navigational buoy—which was not a mark of the course and made no difference in the race—on the wrong side. Walters sailed into Halifax harbor thinking that all he had left to do was collect the prize money and trophy and sail back to Lunenburg. He was informed while attending a hotel banquet with Captain Pine and American and Canadian dignitaries that the Race Committee had disqualified him and awarded the day's race to Pine. The Committee's grounds were that Walters had passed a buoy on the wrong side.

Walters is still mad. "After the race they officially announced the *Bluenose* won. That night they had the banquet to give us the trophy. We were scarcely through with the eats when a feller come to the door and announced, The two skippers are wanted in room so and so.

"The chairman of the International Committee said set still. The feller come in again. I said I think we ought to go and see what this is all about.

"Pine didn't put the protest in. Some smart-aleck Gloucester-man on the Committee did. Pine could have stopped it. If one of our fellers had protested something like that, I'd 'a stopped them. Ben, he's dead now, but he didn't use his head well that time.

"The Committee can't change the rules after the start of the races without the masters being there. They had no right or power to make a change. They sent a letter about the buoys, which I saw in my cabin, but I didn't pay it any attention. After the race I learned about the rule change. I would have ignored it even if I'd knowed about it. If I'd accepted that one thing, they might have made twelve more changes before the next race.

"They called Ben and me into the room and told me I'd done wrong. I said, 'Wait, gentlemen. Don't try to tell me what to do. I've forgotten more about sailing than you fellers will ever know.'

"I said, 'I didn't come up here to sail around every little buoy in Halifax harbor.' This feller from Gloucester—a master, I knew him—started to say 'Black buoys to port and red to starboard.' I stopped him. I said, 'I didn't come up here to take the Board exam either.'

"I said, 'Ben, did I gain or you lose anything by my passing that buoy on the side I did?' I looked right at Ben and he said, 'Oh, I don't know about that.' I said, 'Okay, thank you very much.' I didn't say what I should have said. I should have said, 'Well, if you don't know that, you don't know anything.'

"They claimed they were giving the race to *Columbia*. I said, 'You're going to give the race to the American boat?' 'Oh,' they said, 'You disqualified yourself.' I simply told them to go to hell. I said 'I'm not afraid of *Columbia*. The only thing is I might have a mishap. Then if I give her this race and have a mishap, she'd get the series. What's the sense of that?

"I said, 'We'll throw this race overboard. I'll be sport enough for that. If not, okay then, award it to the boat that finished first.'

"There's where Ben should have said, 'That's pretty square.' He didn't say a word.

"I told them to go straight to hell and we left.

"I wouldn't 'a been so damn small as to accept a race I didn't win. Pine, I never met a better man, personally, but he let the Committee rule him too much. They got hold of him and he consented to it. That was his trouble.

"Many a time, I told him, 'Ben, don't let the Committee rule you. As long as you don't break the rules agreed to before the race, the Committee hasn't got a damn thing to say, unless you or I want to bring something up.' But if anything serious come up, Ben would fade away." (It must be pointed out here that through their differences, Pine and Walters remained good friends. Before Pine's death in 1952, Walters visited him several times in Gloucester to talk about their long rivalry.)

"The next day Murray [the Premier of Nova Scotia] come down. They thought if they sent a premier down it would make a difference. They could send the devil down." The premier said toward the close of their conversation that it's only a sport. Walters said, Yes, but it's damn hard work. He suggested that the premier go along as a member of the crew in the next race, if there was one, to find out.

The dispute made headlines across the continent. While it went on, Walters had his crew put all the *Bluenose's* extra gear back aboard. Halifax ordered all its harbor towboats not to tow him out. There was no wind, so he couldn't sail out.

Walters learned of the embargo when he sent a crew member ashore to look into hiring a tugboat. "They had notified all the towboats not to tow me out," Walters told me. "Then I see the water boat come by. Her name was good for what was to be. Name was *Defiance*. It happened to be the engineer was from Lunenburg. I see him on the afterdeck. I yelled over, 'Where're ya going?' He says, 'Water a boat.' I said, 'Could you give us a tow out later on?' And he says, 'Okay, sure.' He comes by and gets hold of us and never stopped till he got to Sambro. It was all over Halifax, I can tell you."

Sambro Island is twelve miles out of Halifax harbor. The *Bluenose* sat there becalmed all day. But at night a breeze came up, and she got home the next morning. As she left Halifax harbor under tow, the Race Committee, the Halifax Committee (made up of the businessmen and yachtsmen who promoted the race), Canadian and American dignitaries, reporters, and spectators gaped from the shore.

Walters' behavior appears churlish or childish unless it is remembered that the fisherman's relationship to his vessel is different from the yachtsman's to his yacht. Yachts are playthings. On the performance of the fishing vessels depended the lives and incomes of the fishermen. They were jealous of their vessels' reputations with an intensity yachtsmen perhaps would almost never feel.

The North Atlantic fishermen who engaged in those contests were in one of the most dangerous occupations in the world. In an August gale in 1927 eighty men from Lunenburg were lost. Eleven of the thirteen American and Canadian schooners that participated in the International Fishermen's Races or in the preliminary elimination contests between 1922 and 1938 were subsequently lost at sea. The fishermen said there was a jinx against the schooners in the schooner races. Time after time they went missing or broke up on some remote ledge within a year or two, sometimes within a month, of taking part in a race. For the *Columbia,* the end came in a gale one August night in 1927 off Sable Island. She went down with all hands. The next day, the *Bluenose,* which had ridden out the gale some miles away, sailed through debris—trawl tubs, broken dories, and the like—at just about the spot where the *Columbia* was reported to have gone down—an ironic final meeting. The following New Year's Day, a large diesel trawler, of the kind that was already making the schooner obsolete, fouled its big, steel-framed net on something. As its engines strained, the masts of a schooner appeared and her hull followed. She was minus sails and booms, but her appearance otherwise was perfect. The awed crew of the trawler recognized the lithe, flowing lines of the *Columbia.* A moment later the cables broke and she sank once more to the bottom.

After Walters had sailed home from Halifax, Pine could have won the trophy and prize money by sailing around the race course on the appointed day. He sailed out to the starting line, crossed it, and kept on going to Gloucester. The Halifax Committee divided the prize money, sending half to each skipper. When the check came, Walters said, "Send the damn thing back." But, he says, the president of the Bluenose Schooner Company, which built and owned the *Bluenose,* pleaded with him and he gave in and cashed it, even though, as operating manager of the company, he could have sent it back.

Walters has no regrets about his actions. No committee, he says, can tell him what to do. "I went by the rules that were decided beforehand. Then, if I wanted to go out, I went. If I didn't, I stayed and no one told me different."

He does regret, however, never meeting the *Columbia* again. "I think she was the best they had. I'd like to have raced her a second time."

The most ambitious Canadian attempt to beat the *Bluenose* was made by members of the Halifax Committee in 1924, the year after Walters torpedoed the series with the *Columbia*. The Committee had helped to finance the *Bluenose*'s construction, and its members were pleased that she kept winning the trophy, but they had not reckoned on having to deal with such a willful fisherman as Walters was turning out to be. They first took up the fishermen's races in the way a group of North Carolina club-women might establish a mountain center where mountain families could carry on what the club women regarded as quaint handicrafts. There is at least an element of condescension in a situation like that.

"The Committee and I never got along. That's why they built the *Haligonian*," Walters said. "We'd had a couple of set-to's before the *Columbia* series." When Committee members went sailing with him after the *Bluenose*'s launching and made suggestions, Walters' tendency was to tell them to go to hell. "They'd want to sail the boat. They'd suggest this and that. I knew none of 'em knew a damn thing." Once in Gloucester, a group of them came aboard to try to persuade him to let one of their number represent the *Bluenose* as official Canadian observer on the American schooner. Walters replied that one of the men on board the *Bluenose* had said he would go. When one of the Committee members grew insistent, Walters gave all of them five minutes to get up the dock.

"I was always quicker than lightning," Walters said. "If I had a doryman aboard who was slow or not too fussy, he'd get a hell of a yell."

After the 1923 series, the Committee members decided it would be better to have Canada represented by a fisherman more amenable to their direction. They went to the *Bluenose*'s designer, William Roue, and commissioned him to design a fishing schooner that would beat her. Roue thought he could. The result was the *Haligonian,* owned by the Halifax dilettantes, but managed and operated by Lunenburg fishermen. The *Haligonian,* Walters said, was a bust.

"When it got a little rough, she was just like a stone drag. We'd come around in seconds. She be minutes coming around. I used to tack for fun when I was racing her."

Before an official race between the *Bluenose* and the *Haligonian* could be arranged, the two schooners met several times on the fishing banks. These encounters convinced Walters that he had nothing to fear from the new schooner.

He says that once he and the skipper of the *Haligonian* left Lunenburg the same day for the fishing banks. "It was a little rough outside. I waited until he went out because I wanted to race him and I knew he didn't want to race me. If I'd gone out first, he'd 'a waited till I got out of sight.

"The first thing I see when I did go out was his mainsail down. He had took a plunge and filled the fo'c'sle. Chests were floating around on the fo'c'sle floor, they say. I came alongside and asked him why he had his mainsail down. He wouldn't answer me. He was ashamed.

"Roue just overdone it, that's all. When he said he was going to build that boat, I said to him, 'I'll give you back the *Bluenose* plans, and I may be wrong, but I'll tell you where you can make one slight change that might make her a minute faster.' "

Roue turned down Walters' offer, preferring to start from scratch on his second schooner, and this, Walters feels—believing that the *Bluenose* came as close to perfection as is possible —was Roue's mistake. Roue tried to improve on something Walters felt was unimprovable. I asked Walters how the *Haligonian* differed from the *Bluenose*. "She had more spar in her and they were stepped different," Walters said. "*Bluenose* didn't have too much [spar and sail], but she had enough. The other things he did, he cut her up aft too much. That left her with no bearings when she went to tack. We had bearings—the *Bluenose* was full and deep aft, you know. The *Haligonian* had no bearings aft. That's why she was so slow coming around in a breeze.

"She couldn't hold a candle to *Bluenose*. And I told them that up at Halifax when they asked me for a race.

"I didn't want to go to the expense of fitting out *Bluenose* for a race. I told them up at Halifax, 'I'll go as I am.'"

Walters proposed taking on the *Haligonian* immediately after landing his cargo of fish, without hauling his vessel out to have the bottom cleaned or taking any other steps to tune her up. The race, however, did not come off then because of a mishap to the *Haligonian*, and when it was held, almost a year later, the *Bluenose* was tuned up for it.

They raced in October 1926. The *Bluenose* beat the *Haligonian* so badly her owners never asked for a return match. In the first race, the *Bluenose* won by half an hour. In the second, by seven minutes. Merkel reported that the *Haligonian* handled badly and carried a lee helm. She had been ashore the year before and badly damaged. Merkel said that some of her owners believed she had been "hogged," that her bottom had been curved upward in the middle like a hog's back. They believe, he said, that properly tuned up, she could have beaten the *Bluenose*.

This was Johnson Cook's opinion, who told me that under Captain George Himmelman she would have given the *Bluenose* a damn hard time. By accident, I ran into Captain Himmelman in the fall of 1963. After we finished talking about the trip I had made on the *Arthur J. Lynn*, I told him Angus Walters' story about the *Haligonian* taking a plunge and filling her fo'c'sle so that the fishermen's chests floated around. Captain Himmelman had sailed her for four years, from 1934 to 1938. "When I had her, no chests floating around," he said. "She could do anything any of 'em could do. She was a good vessel when I had her. I changed the rigging. There were a lot of things I wanted to do. I could have done better with her if I had the money. Things were bad then, in 1935 and 1936."

I asked him if he raced going to the Banks. "That was in the game," he said. "If you was around other vessels, you didn't want to be behind. She was never behind, always ahead, in any kind of commercial business."

Soon we were talking about the races to the West Indies. "You load with cask fish. If somebody leaving Halifax or here when you are, for sure now you're not going to lay down to sleep. You always had him in mind." He told me about his fastest trip, to Puerto Rico, unloading there, sailing to Turk Island, loading salt there, and back in twenty-nine days. You never knew who won until you got back. "They were great ships—all forgot," he said. "All forgot except the *Bluenose*. And I don't like that," he said. "All the young people hear is *Bluenose*. She was built in 1921 and there was a hundred and thirty schooners around here. Many, many of them were as good as the *Bluenose*."

Many of Gloucester's fastest schooners were lost in the last half of the 1920's, including the *Henry Ford* and the *Columbia*, but in 1929 Gloucester built a new schooner, the *Gertrude L. Thebaud*. In 1930 she issued a challenge to Angus Walters and the *Bluenose* to race, not for the International Fishermen's Trophy, but for a new trophy put up by Sir Thomas Lipton. The *Thebaud* would be skippered by the *Columbia*'s old skipper, Captain Ben Pine.

It is true that in this series of races the *Bluenose* was very slow, but she had been ashore for four days at Placentia Bay, Newfoundland, not long before, on her side, full of water, grinding in the sand—a total loss, they thought at first. She was only brought home in September, and there was no time before the races in October to put her into racing trim. On the way down to Gloucester for the races her new sails had stretched all out of shape. In the first race, Walters said, he could hardly tack her. "I found I didn't have the *Bluenose*. I had some other boat. My God, if I may say so, she was in hard shape," he said. "She should never have been asked to race."

The *Bluenose*, which had always been so quick on her feet—

"I used to tack just for fun. When I wanted to put *Thebaud* to looward of me in a hurry, all I had to do was make a half a dozen tacks"—was now so out of sorts that the crew had to hold the jumbo—what yachtsmen call the forestaysail—to windward to bring the bow around when they tacked. "She'd come around," he said, "But she'd be lazy."

After the race Walters sailed straight to a marine railway at Gloucester. The foreman agreed to haul the *Bluenose* out on the next high tide, which came at midnight. "You can bet morning wasn't long light when I was under her and found out what was wrong. They'd put a piece of keel into her at Newfoundland, put kindling into her. That was taken off at Lunenburg and a new keel put in. The new keel was a half inch or a quarter inch to one side. Wasn't plumbed up right."

Nothing could be done about the keel, but her sails were recut, and her ballast was shifted. The weather was miserable for the second race—rainy and blowing hard. Whatever fine points of tuning were still wrong with her (which would have shown up in a moderate breeze) were counterbalanced by her great power and ability in a blow. She romped away from the *Thebaud,* and at the twelve-mile mark had established a two-mile lead, according to Merkel. Then the race was called off by the Race Committee.

Walters views all committees—race committees, promotion committees, committees of leading citizens—with suspicion. The Gloucester Race Committee, he contends, was not above calling off a race when the Gloucester schooner fell hopelessly behind.

"I'd 'a beat the *Thebaud* by two or three hours that day—she couldn't carry her sail. When we got ashore, I asked the Committee, would they kindly tell me—'Why,' I said, 'did you call off the race, if you please?' 'For the safety of the crews,' they said. 'Safety of the crews!' I said, 'why in God's name did they start us then?' It had been blowing harder when they started it than when they called it off.

"Before the race, they come aboard my boat. They asked me,

What do you think? I said—and I wasn't thinking of our boat, but the other feller. It was all right for my boat. If it was too much for my boat, their boat couldn't race at all. I said I thought it wasn't a very good day for a race. One of their fellers said, 'There's the sun blinking out.' 'All right,' I said, 'If that's the way you feel, let's say no more about it.' Then when they called it off, I had a perfect right to keep on. To tell God's truth, I think they were frightened. Them on the Committee boat, afraid they wouldn't get back."

Walters claims that the *Thebaud* crossed the starting line ahead of the starting gun. He asked the Committee about that. "I said, 'Why didn't you call the *Thebaud* back when she went across too soon?' 'Oh, she didn't, she didn't,' they said. 'Then let's compare stop watches,' I said. They said the *Thebaud* didn't have one. 'Oh, dear God,' I said. 'No wonder. I guess you go by the town clock,' I told 'em. 'I tell you what I'm going to do. I'm going to put one of my crew on board and he will have a watch.' I did and there was never any more trouble."

Walters had a high regard for some of the American schooners in the International Fishermen's Races—the *Esperanto,* the *Elsie,* and the *Columbia,* particularly, but not the *Thebaud,* which, he says, wouldn't have been worth a damn as a salt fisherman.

"We only had her out in one blow and they pretty near turned her over in that. When Pine went to tack her, she wouldn't tack. Twice he tried. She wouldn't come around. The third time, they know they had to do something. Pine had to fill her sails to get headway on her so she'd come around. He'd been scared to—scared to fill his sails. Scared he'd turn that shoofly of his over.

"He filled her away, and dear God, she went over and I thought she wasn't coming back. That's the kind of a toy they had. They pretty near turned her over when they tried to tack. The water on the deck was up around her masts."

The next race was sailed in light airs. The *Bluenose* went

ahead of the *Thebaud*. At the six-mile mark, she was one minute sixteen seconds ahead, and at the eighteen-mile mark she was five minutes ahead.

Then, according to Merkel, Walters pulled the prize boner of his career, an assessment Walters agrees with. Walters went inshore. He says an American on board advised him the wind would favor him. Instead it favored the *Thebaud*, which stayed outside.

The *Thebaud* won the race by eight minutes and with it the Lipton Trophy. For the first and only time in her career, the *Bluenose* lost a series.

On the way into Gloucester harbor, Walters hit a reef. 'I was so mad I wasn't looking at anything. Later they asked the American observer on my boat why he didn't say anything about where I was going. He told 'em, 'I wasn't going to say anything. He was so mad he was ready to throw someone over.'

"Pine was so damn happy he filled up the trophy and all the vessel mugs with rum. It done him a world of good—it was the only thing he ever won."

The next year, Pine brought the *Thebaud* to Halifax to challenge for the International Fishermen's Trophy. In the first race, the *Bluenose* was thirty-five minutes ahead of the *Thebaud* when the time allowance expired and the race was called. In the second, she crossed the finish line thirty-two minutes twenty-six seconds ahead of the *Thebaud*. As the first race hadn't counted, she needed one more victory for the series. She won the third race by twelve minutes. Merkel reports that there was something definitely wrong with the *Thebaud* in the first two races—that she appeared sluggish and her sails did not fit properly, as had been the case with the *Bluenose* in the first race of the 1930 series.

In the last race, he says, the *Thebaud* was greatly improved in trim and handled better. He adds, with perhaps a trace of Canadian bias (although I, an American, would agree with him) that the *Thebaud*'s best was not good enough for the *Bluenose*.

Racing languished in the depression. Then in 1938 Gloucester challenged Lunenburg again. Angus Walters and Ben Pine, who had first faced each other in 1923, readied their schooners and met off Boston for the beginning of the most closely contested series of races they ever engaged in. The races alternated between Boston and Gloucester.

They sailed the first one in a fresh breeze. Pine went across the line first. Walters soon went by him and at the six-mile mark was almost two minutes ahead. Then Pine went by Walters and led by almost two minutes at the twelve-mile mark. Walters cut down Pine's lead and passed him, but stayed ahead only a short time. Pine reached the eighteen-mile mark three minutes ahead of Walters and stayed ahead the rest of the way around the forty-mile course. Walters gained on him at times, then fell back. Near the finish, he lost his foretopmast. According to Merkel, it was too late to change the outcome. Pine beat him by two minutes fifty-six seconds.

Walters led across the line in the second race. He made such good time on the windward leg, Merkel said, that Gloucestermen on the Committee boat who timed him thought that the leg must have been shortened accidentally. They were not aware of what the *Bluenose* could do to windward. She finished twelve minutes ahead of the *Thebaud.* Her elapsed time was four hours thirty-nine minutes, within five minutes of the course record.

Bluenose took the third race. In the fourth, she was ahead when her foretopmast stay parted and she was forced to come into the wind to douse her outer jib. Tom Horgan of the Associated Press reported that her two mastheadmen—who stayed aloft throughout a race to handle topsails, staysail, and outer jib—were momentarily endangered. While the *Bluenose* was headed into the wind, the *Thebaud* surged by. She finished the race five minutes ahead of the *Bluenose,* making the series two all.

The *Bluenose* won the fifth and deciding race by two minutes fifty seconds. Merkel described the finish. "As the great Lunenburger neared the finish line, in what proved to be her last race for international honors, her topsail halyard block gave way. But she was too near to victory to be deterred and the *Thebaud* was too far astern to close the gap. The *Bluenose* slid across the line amid the cheers of her jubilant crew, and blasts from boats at anchor nearby. Tired and old she may have been, but she had kept untarnished her proud record of having never lost an international series for the trophy put up by Canada."[4]

He added that she had unquestionably proved her superiority, on all points of sailing and in all manner of weather conditions, with every schooner that had sought to dispute her claim to the championship of the North Atlantic fishing fleet.

That was a Canadian view. Captain Cecil Moulten, who skippered the *Thebaud* when Ben Pine was too ill to race, said, "*Thebaud* was not beaten by *Bluenose,* but by Captain Charles M. Lyons (United States steamboat inspector and chairman of the Race Committee). He sent us out, day after day, when there wasn't wind enough for a real race and kept us in port when there was a good wind." Pine said, "We took the two races sailed in a good breeze. *Bluenose* got three in weather I don't consider fit for a fishermen's race. I don't want any more of it. You could have paddled a canoe around the course the three days *Bluenose* won." A Boston newspaper described the *Bluenose* as only a fine-weather boat. Walters was beside himself. They were accusing the *Bluenose*, which he believed to be the finest heavy-weather boat in the Atlantic, of being a fair-weather sailor—the *Bluenose,* which had seen him through North Atlantic gales that sank other schooners (including the gale that sank the *Columbia*), which had won every other International Fishermen's Trophy series she was in, which had beaten the Americans in storms that caused sails and spars to be carried away. Pine said that she only won when a canoe could be paddled around the course, but she won one race in enough wind to allow her to almost break the course record—it wasn't light weather then. And she was ahead of the *Thebaud* in the roughest weather of the series when her fore-

4 Merkel, p. 62.

topmast stay parted. "We raced that race without our outer jib. He carried his. If we'd had ours, we'd 'a been halfway to the finish before he went around the lask mark."

Walters disliked the courses the Gloucester Committee set up—twice around a triangle. "The international rule called for a three-angle course of forty miles. Then when I got there, they changed the rule to go twice around a little triangle—a merry-go-round, I called it. Suppose you get out there in a good blow and have to jibe around the mark. That not only put a little dread in me, it did in everyone. You didn't know if that damn boom coming across would take the mast out of her.

"The Committee was always doing things like that. A man who went to sea who knew anything would have to object for the sake of safety. As far as knowing anything, I didn't expect 'em to know anything—my God, when we jibed sometimes, I just shut my eyes, that's all."

The kind of racing these men were used to took them through North Atlantic gales in winter, a thousand or two thousand miles on a leg, with a load of fish going out and a load of salt coming back. When Angus Walters talked about that kind of racing, and pointed out that one reason for trying to make a record passage was that the quicker the trip the fewer days you had to pay wages to your crew and feed them, suddenly I saw why the Race Committee's rules, technicalities, and little buoys seemed to him vastly unimportant.

Every time I talked to Walters about the 1938 series, he would bring up what Pine, Moulten, and the Boston newspaper had said about the *Bluenose*. "All they talked about was *Bluenose* being a fine-weather boat. They should have been ashamed to say that, if I may say so.

"I told 'em, 'Oh, then, we'll have a race around Bermooda to see who's a fine-weather boat.' I told Pine, 'Let's go around Bermooda—either start off Gloucester or Halifax, and finish at the other port.' "

Walters' challenge, which a Canadian businessman backed

with a fifteen thousand-dollar cash price, was never taken up. It would have been a more appropriate finale for the fishermen's races, using an island far at sea for a buoy and a city for a finish line.

In any case, the *Bluenose* was now completely done for, obsolete, her reason for being gone. She and the *Thebaud* in the 1938 series were ghosts, playing roles in a pageant that had ceased to exist. At the time of the 1931 International Fishermen's Races, sails were still in use on the Grand Banks. By 1938 there was not a schooner left in Gloucester that had not been converted to power, and in Lunenburg the last of the sailing schooners were having engines installed. Walters had made the inevitable decision to put auxiliary engines in the *Bluenose* two years before. Cement was poured into her afterhold to make engine beds; fuel tanks were installed; and the sprightly, lively *Bluenose* was gone. You or I couldn't tell it. But Walters, who had felt her response to his touch on the helm before she was weighted down with engines, knew it.

He was a fisherman and a sailor. The fisherman put in the engines. The sailor objected. "I knew damn well I was ruining the *Bluenose*. But what the hell could I do? I didn't see why I should piss around in the fog when the others weren't and not do so well as plenty of 'em who weren't so good fishermen as me.

"We raced again and we won, but we shouldn't have. *Bluenose* wasn't half the boat she had been. We had put all that damn iron and cement into her. It killed her."

Walters took the bowsprit out of the *Bluenose* right after the last race in 1938. Her masts were cut down, her afterdeck disfigured with a pilothouse, and she never sailed again, except with the stumpy little steadying sails with which old schooners were dressed until one by one they died and were replaced by wall-sided, tubby-looking draggers, in the operation of which artistry, excitement, challenge, and daring play almost no part. But even so, Walters clung to the *Bluenose* fiercely. He had no earthly use for her. He had come ashore for good to begin a new career at home with his new wife. His diary took up all his time.

After the 1938 series, Walters had thought that the *Bluenose* should be retired as a monument to the days of sail. "She should have been kept without engines. They should have kept one down there and one here and kept the international races going," he said. There were people all over Canada who agreed with him. Letters appeared in newspapers urging that the nation take her over. In Lunenburg, a citizens meeting was called and it was decided to raise money by selling shares in her throughout Canada at a dollar a share. The war came and the plan died. "I don't know what the hell is wrong with Canada," he said a few years ago, when describing his unsuccessful efforts to interest government officials, businessmen, the provincial and Lunenburg boards of trade—anyone who would listen—in preserving the schooner.

By 1939 the *Bluenose* had ceased to pay for herself. The bottom had fallen out of fishing a few years earlier and what money there was in it was being made by diesel trawlers. Walters put down his life savings in 1938 to save her from the auction block. He saved her, but for what? For most of the next three years she lay idle at her dock—285 tons of fishing equipment that had outlived its usefulness.

In 1942, with the war making it impossible to get crews, he was forced to sell her. A trading company bought her to haul bananas and rum in the Caribbean. When the new owners came to Lunenburg to get her, Walters cast off her lines and watched her leave the dock. It was an overcast day in May. "When she left the dock, if I may say so, there was a lump in my throat. I knew it was goodbye and she was like part of me. To tell you the goddam truth, when I walked home, I felt like coming out of the cemetery."

In the years since he sold the *Bluenose*, Walters has been haunted by visions of what he considered the loveliest thing in the world. Once he wrote the new owners to ask if he could buy the *Bluenose* back after the war, an even more quixotic gesture than his putting down his life savings to keep her from being auctioned off, and then keeping her from 1939 to 1942. But she had changed hands, and he never caught up with the new owners. Then, on a dark night early in 1946, she struck a coral reef off Haiti. Her crew got ashore safely. The next night a storm blew up, and she broke her back on the reef and sank.

Although she had not been in the news since 1938, her loss was, in Canada, a top story—like the death of an old sports figure. When the news was flashed on the radio, Walters' first thought was to fly down to Haiti to try to save her, although reason told him there was nothing left to save. Interviewed by a radio reporter, he said: "It breaks my heart to hear she is gone, but you couldn't expect her to go on forever. She has done remarkably well for a vessel of her age and has more than filled the time expected of her. It is no discredit to *Bluenose,* because she did credit everywhere.

"They still thought plenty of her down there, more than was thought of her here. And she made her owners barrels of money."

In the years after her loss, Walters talked at times of trying to find what was left of the *Bluenose* on the bottom—as if he could put her back together again—and at other times of finding someone to build a new *Bluenose.* An old man is permitted a few vagaries, and I had always considered that kind of talk in that light. But I was wrong. Walters was only ahead of his time. In the fall of 1963, I watched him at the helm of a new *Bluenose,* built from the plans of the old, taking her through her sailing trials in Lunenburg harbor. Sponsored by a Canadian brewery, the new schooner was to be used as a boat carrying people on cruises and for Canadian products' promotions, particularly at the annual Lunenburg Fisheries Exhibition.

Walters, his old mate, Lawrence Allen, and four of his old crew walked around her deck as if something had suddenly materialized they couldn't believe. Jack Pardy, one of his old crew, took the helm when Angus was through. Watching Angus's small form hustling up the deck with his mate behind (where they found lots of things wrong and set them right), Pardy said: "I was seven years with him. He would yell, too." He said, later, "I took her today. I had to get the feel of her. She felt good . . . When I heard the *Bluenose* was gone, I cried. I'm not ashamed of it. I cried."

The new *Bluenose* had a professional captain and crew, and Walters was very conscious of the amenities, of not appearing to take over. Nevertheless, he couldn't contain his interest, and the fact is he and his crew knew a lot more about the little details on board than the professionals—who were good seamen, but not old enough to have ever sailed in anything like the *Bluenose*. He and Allen walked forward and found the jumbo up, not quite tight on its stay, as it should have been. Though at first hesitant lest they appear to interfere, they finally did, with the young crew joining the two old gents sort of reverently. They went aft, and found the mainsail not setting to their satisfaction, and got a gang on that too. Then they came on members of the crew who had never set a topsail before starting to hoist it. They assumed crew member jobs, not as supernumeraries at all, because they were useful. Walters "tailed" the last man on the rope. "Hold it, boys, she's caught, I can see it from here," he yelled. Tacking, he "tailed" on the jib sheet and as they were hauling it in said, "Okay, boys, that's it" and "make fast" at the precise right moment. He could feel it. Someone asked him how to handle the backstay on a tack, and he showed him.

The owners of the *Bluenose* planned to take her south. I asked old Walters if he would go. He said he might, which again I thought was highly unlikely. He was eighty-two. The next I heard of Walters and the *Bluenose* was in July 1964. I sailed into New York for Operation Sail aboard the *Statsraad Lemkuhl*. At the Battery one night I ran into Captain Coggins, the master of the *Bluenose*, and he described sailing her through a hurricane in January 1964. Old Angus did indeed go along. He came aboard carrying his old compass and old barometer from off the first *Bluenose,* apparently not entirely trusting these gadgets on the new one. Then, a year later, when the *Bluenose* left Lunenburg for Operation Sail, he went along. They had a triumphal entry into Gloucester, the old-timers full of nostalgia and talk of the old rivalries. The welcome Gloucester gave her old foes, Angus and the *Bluenose,* was too much for him and he wasn't able to sail on to New York, but went back to Lunenburg. But Captain Coggins said, "Whenever the old man comes aboard, I'll fade away and he'll be the captain."

And so, before he died in 1968, an old man had his grand dream, a new *Bluenose.* And even now the men of Gloucester dream—of building a replica of one of their famous schooners and again racing the *Bluenose.*

But in all this recounting of the details of the races, of elapsed times, strategy and tactics, of feuds, contentions, tuning up, fighting for the weather berth, we are in danger of overlooking the beauty and power of the schooners. Most of Angus Walters' career was sailing, not bickering or racing. Imagine the *Bluenose*'s lovely shape gliding down the moonpath, some land a darkness opposite, and those fine curving lines that few sailing boats have possessed—this is the overriding fact, the beauty, not the races, the contentions. This is the unspoken fact of the story—the beauty and the innocence of our relationship to nature which has now gone forever, traded by man for comfort and efficiency. Can we learn to provide ourselves with what was inescapable before, this innocence, this beauty?

Part Three

*The Oystermen
of Chesapeake Bay*

I

Chesapeake Bay played a leading role in the development of American naval architecture in the seventeenth, eighteenth, and nineteenth centuries. The Bay cuts Maryland almost in two: thus it forced the people of the state to take to the water. This and its mild climate, plentiful supply of moderate winds, and thousands of safe anchorages made it one of the most prolific breeding grounds of watermen in the world. The watermen fished the Bay in winter, spring, and summer and used it to carry the produce of their farms to Annapolis and Baltimore in the fall. Because they did not have to contend with the winter storms that forced New England seamen to give high priority to the stoutness of their vessels, the Bay men could concentrate on speed, and for generations they have had an eye for the "fastness" of their vessels. Local builders who still build by instinct and by what looks good to them rather than by detailed plans, men who can't read a blueprint but have no need to, produce slippery and able hulls, which are, many people believe, as good as anything produced by the naval architects and marine engineers of the yachting centers. The fleet Baltimore clipper, the fastest vessel of the American and French Revolutions and the War of 1812, evolved here, as did many other designs that influenced marine technology in this country and abroad. Their pungies, skipjacks, bugeyes, and sailing log canoes were sleek, fast, and rakish-looking.

Now, of course, most of this sailing culture is gone. The milky-soft gentleness of the Bay is bridged and ringed with superhighways, and the sons and grandsons of watermen are driving trucks or catering to tourists. But along the rivers and coves of the Eastern Shore there still exists a fleet of perhaps sixty sailing skipjacks that are used each winter for dredging oysters. The last fleet of sailing workboats in the country, these vessels, most of them forty to eighty years old, are remarkably fast and seaworthy. Low in the water, with sharp clipper bows and a considerable spread of canvas, they are a graceful sight as they sail back and forth over the oyster beds of the Bay. And when they gather in the coves and creeks at dusk, their long bowsprits and raking masts remind one of their distant cousins, the swift Baltimore clippers that raised havoc with British shipping in the War of 1812 and earned a reputation for speed and weatherliness around the world.

The design of the skipjacks' rigs and hulls is functionally quite efficient; they have changed little since 1890. Centerboard sloops, usually flat-bottomed with shallow draft, they average about 45 feet in length, although the largest, the *Robert L. Webster*, is 60 feet long, 20.3 feet at the beam, with a draft of 5.5 feet, weighing 35 tons and capable of carrying 1,200 bushels of oysters.

The skipjack's large triangular leg o'mutton mainsail and full-cut jib, which are of Dutch origin and were transplanted to England and her colonies in the seventeenth century, provide the pulling power necessary to drag the heavy dredges across the oyster beds. Yet because of their simple rig the sails can easily be adjusted so that the boat does not move too fast to fill the dredges. (An average speed of two to four knots is required to keep the dredges filling; with any more speed they lift off the beds.)

The old-time Chesapeake sailors are called watermen—an old English term that has taken root on the Bay. The watermen of the Eastern Shore have a proud tradition of independence. Until 1952, when the Bay Bridge was built across the lower Chesapeake, the Shore was self-sufficient and considered itself separate and apart from the rest of the state. This is borne home to the visitor to the Maryland Assembly every night after dinner when the delegates from the Shore, wherever they gather, sing: "We don't give a damn for the whole State of Maryland, we're from the Eastern Shore." A delegate from Talbot County once described it as an "island complex." "We like to think we still are self-sustaining," he said, "though the Bay Bridge is bringing in a lot of Western Shoremen who think we're outdated. Eventually they will overcome us and our 'island complex' will be snuffed out. But I don't think it will be in my lifetime."

The traditions of the Eastern Shore are only slowly giving way to the neon-lighted resort culture brought to it by the Bay Bridge across the lower Chesapeake. The Shore's soft accents still retain a trace of seventeenth-century English. The language is richly filled with local idioms. "Why, Lordy go to Hell" means "You don't say." "Oyster" is "orster," "dredge" is "drudge." Everyone, male and female, is referred to as "honey" or "sweetie." Often the opposite of what is said is meant—when a good-looking girl walks by you might hear "Boy, does she look poor!"

Old superstitions still run deep among the watermen. Recently one man painted his boat blue because it was a pretty color. He soon had to repaint it white: some of the older watermen refused to board her because blue was a bad-luck color. In fact, any color at all is considered bad luck, and watermen's boats are almost always white.

On the Eastern Shore everyone is descended from Pocahontas, according to one story. In many parts of the Shore there are so many people with the same name that the only way to tell them apart is by nicknames. Robert Charles Long, an Assembly delegate from Somerset, had his nickname, "Biggy," made part of his legal name because his political opponent wouldn't let him put "Biggy" on the ballot and no one would know him from the other Robert Longs if he didn't. And there is "Hotdog" Simpkins, once Maryland's secretary of state, and his brother "Snap." A lot of people don't know who you mean when you mention Lloyd Simpkins and his brother Fred.

One of the largest fleets of sailing oysterboats on the Bay is found at Tilghman Island. Located on the Eastern Shore between the Choptank River and the Bay, it is less than a hundred miles from Washington and Baltimore, yet it maintains a prosperous economy of its own with methods that have changed little in the past century. When you walk down the main road of Tilghman, you meet people who still use skills that elsewhere died out several generations ago, who still speak the language of the clipper ship era.

For the last few years I have lived on Tilghman Island and I can no more than hint at the pleasantness of life there. Outside my house, which is twenty feet from the water, eleven wild geese swim around. They settled here a couple of winters ago, and no one shoots them; hunters go farther down the road to get the migrating ones during the season. Large flocks of swans come here for the winter. A great blue heron comes almost every afternoon when the tide is right to wade on the flats outside my front window. The disquieting cry of a gull punctures the late afternoon silence. On still days, a duck that seems to live alone in this cove swims around and around it, quacking his comical, at times outraged, at times contented, quack. When the wind blows or it is cold, he stays at home, wherever that is. I can walk a short distance up the road to Black Walnut Point and watch the sun set in the Chesapeake Bay. (It rises outside my window across the cove.) On the walk back from the Point last evening, a deer crashed through the underbrush on my left, crossed the

The dredge, loaded with oysters,
coming aboard. The men on either
side will cull out the legal-size
oysters, adding them to the
bushels of oysters already on deck.

The *J. T. Leonard*—the
last gaff-rigged topsail
sloop on the Bay. Oystermen
are light-hearted about
spelling and this
temporary trailboard
shows her name misspelled.

Skipjacks have elaborately
carved, painted, and gilded
trailboards, which are much
prized by antiquarians.
Occasionally the owner's
name is included—Cook
Todd was the *Leonard*'s
last captain.

The skipjack fleet at Kent Narrows.

Taking a reef in the jib on the *Robert L. Webster*.

Captain Orville Parks, skipper of the *Rosie Parks* and champion skipjack racer on the Bay.

For all their sleek and graceful lines, skipjacks
have a surprisingly broad beam.

The skipjack fleet makes a graceful sight as
it stretches across the Bay during the Chesapeake
Appreciation Day race, in late October.

road sixty feet ahead of me, and loped down a field alongside the Bay to a wood. A little while ago (this is Sunday) a man and his wife and their dog from Cambridge, Maryland, twenty miles away by water, brought their boat to the wharf two hundred feet from my house, coming ashore to work on some crab pots they had stored here for the winter. (I saw them bring the pots last fall, stacked eight feet high on their boat from bow to stern.) Now, as they work on the pots, their dog is playing in the field behind the wharf. My landlord, Andy Bradshaw, is repairing a skiff he uses to commute to the next cove, where the *Reliance*, the beautiful old skipjack of which he is mate, is usually moored. (Those who live along the shore tend to have one or two boats drawn up in a corner of the yard—much like a suburbanite has a barbecue grill.) A little while ago a young fellow returned another of Andy's skiffs he had borrowed to go out to a gill net he set yesterday. He gave Mrs. Bradshaw a few rockfish, the first of the season here. She just asked me if I like rock, and I expect I will have some of the fish she was given.

The people on Tilghman treat each other with great kindness, and their lives are completely pervaded by an attitude of mutual help, because, it seems to me, their environment demands a deeper personal relationship one to the other than can be found in crowded, hustling cities. When I first began to dredge on my skipjack, the *Esther F.*, one man lent me dredges, another taught me to follow behind his boat along the edge of a bed, waving me to where the best oysters were; another took me to a place he had found where he brought up oysters every time. "I can catch 'em up there," he said. "Come with me tomorrow and we'll work together." When my yawl boat sank in a big wind, everyone came down to the dock to help me save the engine.

The playfulness of the Tilghman Islanders is equally as pervasive. Most of the watermen gather at Miss Elsie's, a small restaurant and the only place on the island where alcohol (beer) is served. Miss Elsie, eighty, sharp, fat, hard, runs a tight ship and is the object of much teasing. Young boys come by to ask her to play baseball. And the watermen spend a lot of time trying to convince her daughter, fifty-five, that it's thundering, so she'll be frightened and will, so they say, cuddle up. When the teasing gets out of hand, Miss Elsie has been known to pick up and bodily heave the offender out. Bart Murphy recalls how she recently "smacked me so hard she knocked me sideways."

Fourteen hundred people live on Tilghman, and all but one hundred work on the water. The old term watermen applies not only to the men, but to their families as well, because wives and children are involved in a way that is not possible in today's urban culture. The families often go on the water with the men, particularly in the summertime, and help—preparing bait, setting crab lines, or steering the boat. Or the wives may work in packing houses ashore where their husbands' catches are processed.

Everyone on Tilghman still watches the weather and lives by the wind. When the fire siren blows on a foggy night, it doesn't usually indicate a blaze—it means that a member of the community is still out on the water and his neighbors are concerned about guiding him home. The direction of the wind, its strength, what it did yesterday and what it may do tomorrow are known not only to the men on the water but also to the women in the packing house and to the storekeepers and to the mechanics in the island's two garages, and, probably, to the employees in the banks as well. All are involved in the same rhythms, which are determined not by time clocks but by the sun, and moon, and prevailing winds. A bad blow cuts the activity at Tilghman down to almost zero; a gale arouses anxiety among everyone for the safety of the thousands of dollars worth of boats, for the crab pots in the water. Even the subtlest nuances of wind and weather are known by all: one beautiful late summer day an elderly lady remarked to me "This cool weather is nice but it will be bad for the fishermen." And she explained to me that the northeast wind would tear up the haul-seiners' nets.

Stanley Larrimore, captain of the skipjack *Reliance*—forty-two feet long and one of the most graceful on the Bay—takes his wife, his son, nine, and his daughter, seven, crabbing with him twice a week in summer, getting up before dawn and eating breakfast and lunch on board. On weekends he scrubs the boat down and they go cruising, sleeping aboard Saturday nights. Bartlett Murphy, captain of the *Lena Rose*, remembers going crabbing with his father when he was small enough to sleep in a crab barrel, and he himself took his daughter out before she was even three months old.

Alan Faulkner, who is now twelve, began asking if he could go out with his father, Woodrow Faulkner, when he was four or five. When he was six his father said, "The next good day, I'll take you." He has been going ever since, crabbing and fishing in the summer and tonging for oysters in the winter. "I go tonging with Daddy in the winter a lot of times. It can get right cold. What you do is when you first go out, you put a rope with a chain on it over and drag it and then when it jerks-like, you know you're on top of oysters. Then you'll pull that up and anchor right there and you'll throw your tongs over and start in."[1]

Alan lives on the edge of Black Walnut Cove at the southern end of Tilghman in a house built eighty years ago by his grandfather—with lumber carried from Virginia by skipjack. Very little happens in the cove that Alan doesn't know about: the comings and goings of herons, swans, ducks, and geese, of different kinds of fish. Every afternoon in the summer he walks along the shore looking for "anything like snakes or turtles or real pretty shells." In the fall he stores up an inventory of muskrat holes for hunting later in the winter. In the spring he spends an

---

[1] Tongs are scoops on the end of long poles—eighteen to twenty-four feet long—that operate with a scissors-like action, bringing up a few oysters at a time. Tonging, which accounts for about seventy-two per cent of the oyster catch, is done from small powerboats, called tong boats. Dredging from sailing vessels accounts for about twenty-five per cent, and a third method, cultivation of oysters, which is permitted in certain restricted areas leased to private operators, accounts for the remaining three per cent.

hour or so every afternoon on his father's wharf or out on his skiff, watching the bottom for signs of the first crabs. From then until they leave in the fall, he catches peelers and soft crabs and sells them to a man across the cove. He's a dead-eye with a dipnet. "You have to think where they'll go and put your net over them quick and try to scare them into it."

When Alan was nine, his father gave him a skiff the Coast Guard had found in the Bay. In the next year or so, Alan put a mast in, on one side at first. Then he built a step in the center and cut a triangular sail out of an awning. He would pole the boat upwind and then sail down. After a while he decided it would go a little better if it had a jib, so he recut his mainsail and put it on the headstay. Then he came around looking for an old shower curtain and I gave him an old spread. Within one hour he sailed by with his new mainsail. Now he's planning to make a keel from an old airplane wing and buy a piece of canvas and some large poles and make another, bigger sail. "Well, I'm going to have a little bit of fun," he told me. "When I get older I'm going to buy a larger one. I like sailboats a lot more than any other kind."

Like other watermen, Woody Faulkner, Alan's father, gets up before dawn almost every day and may spend twelve or more hours on the water. For two weeks in August, when he was crab-potting and fishing at the same time, he averaged twenty-one hours a day on the water—taking catnaps between hauls. It is a life that Faulkners have been living on Tilghman Island since before the American Revolution and one that neither he nor Alan would swap for any other.

"I've been away carpentering in the city quite a bit, and, really, you just can't explain how it is to get back here on the water," Woody said recently. "I stood looking out the window one time in Baltimore and I said, you see that block over there —it had Anderson Oldsmobile in it—I wouldn't trade that whole block for my porch."

While he was talking, wind and rain smashed against the

kitchen windows. His wife, Carmelita, and his mother-in-law both said with conviction that they were sure the crew he seines with surely would not go out that afternoon. The telephone rang and one of the crew asked Woody what was holding him up. When he hung up he said, "They're raring to go. Blowing a gale and they're raring to go." He laughed. "A man's got to love it to do it," he added and when he went out the kitchen door he looked like a man anticipating a challenge he would thoroughly enjoy. (A short time later an insurance agent from nearby Easton cancelled an appointment with a client on the island. "It is not a fit day to be out driving," he said.)

When I am asked, "Do these people who make their living sailing like the water?" I can only tell them of Woody Faulkner, or of Captain Nathan T. (Funny) Parks, who owns the skipjack *Dorothy*. He was sixty-nine recently. He said that fall that when he stops dredging, if he ever does, he is going to buy a sailing yacht "with no power fastened to it at all—I want to sail where the wind takes me." He had been sailing for a living every winter since he was twelve, and talked of going right on sailing if he retired.

Captain Orville Parks, the champion skipjack racer on Chesapeake Bay, is a year or two older than Captain Funny Parks. One night the talk turned to retirement and he brought up Captain Bill Bradford, of Cambridge, Maryland, who, when he got up into his seventies, decided to quit. He sold his dredge boat, and then the thought of staying ashore the next season bothered him so much he went out and bought another one. "He couldn't stay ashore. He thought he could, but he couldn't—so I know I can't quit. I couldn't lay home with these boats out in the river. When I quit, I'm going to move away from Cambridge so I can't see the dredge boats."

But the times are changing and it may be soon that oystering, now an art requiring skill and sagacity and creating pride in its practitioners, will be changed to a form of push-button drudgery familiar enough in urban areas but not yet the rule in the country. It is hard to conceive of these watermen showing such exuberance over the kind of equipment—large motorized dredges owned by a few large firms—that would take the place of the skipjacks they now sail with skill and daring and affection.

There is a historic cleavage between townsmen and watermen, not only in Maryland, but perhaps wherever men earn a living from the sea. Before reapportionment upset rural domination of the Maryland legislature, Tilghman Island and the other watermen's communities on the Eastern Shore were strong enough to protect themselves. Now they hardly have a voice. Powerful forces in Maryland, which advocate sweeping changes in the fisheries laws—to permit unrestricted harvesting of clams, power dredging of oysters (limited now to only certain days of the week), and leasing of public oyster grounds to private concerns—hope at last to enact these changes with the help of urban legislators.

Stanley Larrimore, of the skipjack *Reliance*, feels that even if each waterman were leased a piece of ground by the state, within a very few years four or five big concerns probably would have control of the Bay—because of the large amounts of capital required to plant oysters and operate leased ground. As for power dredging for oysters, which is hailed as more businesslike than dredging under sail, the Tilghman Islanders feel it will damage their oyster bars. Captain Nathan "Funny" Parks puts it this way: "Take a lump (a small bar) fifty or one hundred feet square. A power dredger can go around and around till there's not an oyster left and the lump's ruined."

The watermen may be wrong, but there are experts who agree with them. One is Howard Chapelle, an authority on fisheries and fishing-boat design, who modernized the fishing fleet of Turkey and has been a fisheries consultant to Canada and other nations. He is the former curator of transportation of the Smithsonian Institution and a member of the panel of experts advising the director of the Food and Agriculture Organization of the

United Nations. Chapelle doubts the claims that leasing would increase production more than the present public management. He feels that full power dredging might very well be a fatal mistake: a handful of power dredgers could easily clean up all the oysters in the Bay. The ancient beds would be destroyed and it would take years to rebuild them to the point where oysters would again grow in them.

Retention of sailing vessels and hand tonging from small motorboats were originally conservation measures. In recent years the rationale for continuing to prevent changes in the method of gathering oysters has also been—in addition to conservation—that these changes would wipe out the several thousand families of watermen who live along the coves and creeks and rivers of the Bay.

Tilghman Islanders are convinced these changes would mean the end of their island as it now exists. One of them, Captain Dan Murphy, said that the island, which today has a population of fourteen hundred, keeps its young at home in the occupation of their fathers, but would become a ghost town within five years if leasing were permitted. Today, the population of Tilghman is growing; the ambitious stay; the workboat fleet is larger than it has been in fifty years. Bartlett Murphy, thirty-two, who, like many of the other islanders, crabs in a powerboat in the summer and captains a skipjack in the winter, bought his *Lena Rose* five years ago. Since then he has completely rebuilt her, so she is practically a brand new boat. Three years ago his brother Wade Jr., then twenty-four, bought a skipjack and became the youngest captain in the Bay oyster-dredging fleet. Their younger brother, Charley Buck, will take over their father's skipjack, the *Collier*, when Captain Wade Sr. retires—if he ever does.

Tilghman Island has escaped so far the fate of other rural communities whose economics have been destroyed by technology and whose remaining populations have been reduced to a class of menials for the wealthy urban dwellers who have bought up the ancestral acres of the dispossessed. But the situation could change overnight: the watermen may be forced to leave their proud and independent way of life for urban alienation and conformity, and the last link this nation has with its great maritime heritage would disappear.

II

The oyster season begins November 1 and ends March 15. For several years I spent a few days each season out on the oyster grounds abroad the fifty-five-foot dredger *J.T. Leonard*.[1] The last gaff topsail sloop on the Chesapeake Bay, it was built near Cambridge, Maryland, in 1882, and is identical in hull and sail plan to a model developed in New York in the 1840's and once popular up and down the coast. The *Leonard* is an able boat, fast in light airs yet stiff enough to stand up to the sudden storms that descend on the Bay in winter, sometimes without warning. She and the man who owned her for most of her life, Capain Will Jones, of Cambridge, are considered probably the most successful boat and skipper ever engaged in oystering on the Bay. During the depression, when the price of oysters dropped to a few cents a bushel, for instance, Captain Will and one other skipper were the only oystermen in Cambridge able to stay in business. The others found jobs ashore or went on relief.

When Cap'n Will started fishing more than sixty years ago he went out in a Chesapeake log canoe. In those days a man left Cambridge about midnight, and sunrise found him, if the wind

[1] This section was written before the author had bought his own skipjack, the *Esther F.*, and dredged for oysters himself. —ED.

had been good, on the fishing grounds off Castle Haven, five miles northwest of Cambridge, or off Todds Point, three miles further west. Without an engine to help him he laid his crab traps, attached together on a line, and then stood in the bow of his boat and pulled himself hand over hand from one trap to the next, unloading his catch. When the weather was too rough for him to pull himself along that way he had to sail back up the line, often against the wind. And if the weather came off really foul the fight back into harbor took hours.

My first trip aboard the *Leonard* was on a cold February day after a five-inch snowfall that in Washington, where I lived, closed the schools and caused most federal employees to stay at home. The oystermen, however, stay in only when the Bay is blocked by ice or it's blowing a full gale.

No one was aboard the *Leonard* when I parked my car at four a.m. and walked down to the creek that makes its way into the heart of Cambridge, parallel to one of the main streets. The dredge boats, deserted, looked like ghosts, their white hulls shining palely in the darkness, their masts insubstantial shadows against the dark sky.

I climbed aboard the *Leonard* and from my vantage point on deck I could see that I was not quite alone. Light shone from the cabins of a few of the dredge boats tied up lower down along the bank, and I could smell wood smoke coming from their stove pipes. The cooks, apparently, were already aboard getting things shipshape. Soon some of the oystermen began to gather, yelling greetings to each other on the chill night air. Ten minutes after I arrived a man climbed onto the boat alongside the *Leonard* and came over to the rail to see who I was. His name was Charles Todd and he owned and skippered the boat he was on, the dredger *Anna M. Dick*. As I had not yet met Captain Will, who was then eighty-four and the oldest active captain on the Bay, I asked Todd to tell me something about him. It seemed to me that eighty-four was rather old for a man to be spending the four-month winter dredging season on the open deck of an oyster boat.

"It is awful old," Todd said. "Awful old. God knows what keeps the old man coming back each winter. It's not because he has to, that's for sure. He's got considerable real estate around town and money in the bank. Every season is his last he says, but then he spends all summer fixing up his boat. It may be Cap'n Will just can't bear to sell the *Leonard*. He's owned her since 1916. Keeps her up like a yacht."

Todd leaned over the rail and dumped the tobacco from his pipe into the ribbon of water and broken ice between his boat and the *Leonard*. "Cap'n Will's slipped a little these past few years—had a couple of strokes. Last summer he came home after painting on the *Leonard* all morning and had one standing at the kitchen sink. Laid him out a month.

"He's slipped a little, but I'd say of Cap'n Will he's the best man who ever dropped a drudge in the Bay. Best drudger and best sailor. He knows the bottom of the Bay like you know the palm of your hand. I'll tell you something. He could go out anywhere in the Bay and throw a brick overboard one year and pick it up the next. That's how well he knows the Bay."

The first member of Todd's five-man crew came aboard the *Anna M. Dick*, asked where the cook was, and, grumbling, went below himself to start a fire in the stove and make coffee. Todd turned back to me.

"If I was to find any argument with Cap'n Will," he said, "It would be he's always been a little stubborn about thinking he could stay out in any kind of weather. He had a little skipjack when I went with him years ago and if it commenced blowing he'd keep right on drudgin' when all the others, even the big schooners, ran for shore. He used to load that little skipjack down so low, water come in the scuppers both sides. There was one time, I remember, after I stopped going with him, when a large drudger, probably twice the size of his, capsized in a hell of a blow trying to get home. Everyone aboard of her was lost.

"Cap'n Will drudged right through the storm and didn't learn what happened till later. Him and the feller that capsized was the only ones out that day."

While Todd was talking, Cap'n Will, Les Jones, his son, who had invited me for the trip, and their cook, Tom, arrived on the bank of the creek. Cap'n Will was wearing black cotton twill work pants, a couple of thick shirts, a black leather coat, and a shapeless light-gray fedora. In the hubbub of introductions he took a minor role and my first impression was of a gentle, shy, and worn old man. His eyes were watery blue and his skin had a transparent, fragile look. His appearance surprised me, after Todd's description of his exploits.

Cap'n Will climbed aboard stiffly and shook my hand. "You're going to be with us all week, aren't you?" I told him I could only stay for the day.

"Oh. Well . . . I see . . . I thought you'd be aboard long enough for us to make a real drudger out of you." He smiled and started aft toward the cabin but stopped to stare at the boat behind us, as though trying to collect his thoughts. After a moment he turned back and asked me below for some coffee.

The cook had the wood stove going and coffee almost ready in a large enamel pot. Meanwhile the other three crew members came aboard, and they and Les Jones busied themselves on deck making preparations for departure.

"Sit down on the bench here by me anywhere," Cap'n Will said after the cook poured us each a cup of coffee. "What did you say your name was?" I told him again. "Yes. Well. Sit down and make yourself comfortable."

I asked him how long he had been dredging. Fifty or sixty years, he said. He started earning a living on the Bay in a one-man sailing log canoe when he was eighteen. In those days, he said, he enjoyed racing the other log canoes from Cambridge to the fishing grounds against a strong head wind. He spoke diffidently at first but the warmth of the cabin and the coffee seemed to thaw him out. I asked him how he liked oystering.

"Well, I found it a satisfying life. I always liked it. Liked the sailing, liked the drudgin', liked the independence. I wouldn't of traded with any man, the President or any man.

" 'Course it's different now. When I started the river was crowded with sail. Schooners going to the Indies, coasters coming in and leaving Cambridge all the time, hundreds of skipjacks, bateaus, and bugeyes working. Used to be something. Now it's nothing. Nothing now at all . . . Faded away and gone . . . Disappeared . . . Just a few old drudge boats left.

"When I started there was a thousand drudge boats on the Bay. Not a hundred now prob'ly. Prob'ly not a hundred." Shifting forward, he took a pair of wool rubber-boot liners from a locker behind him and put them on the back of the stove to get warm.

"Not many sailmakers anymore. I used to get my sails made at Sharptown. Been getting them from a feller at Deal Island recently. They all played out at Sharptown . . . All gone. Looks like the feller at Deal Island will play out soon too. He's near as old as I."

He smiled a little at this, and got up to fill his cup. "Drudgin's going to die out soon too. Just a few more years. The government will take over all the bottom, plant the whole Bay to orsters and lease it out to the big concerns. That will be the end of us fellers." He gave me a sharp look. "It's my opinion they shouldn't do that. It's always been a man could take a boat out and make a living on the Bay. Why, Lord-a-Mercy, I've drudged every orster rock from Pooles Island off of Baltimore to Honga Strait, Tangier Sound, and beyond and no one to tell me no."

He stopped, perhaps surprised by his animation. "Seems like it's coming though, the end of drudgin'," he said after a moment. "May be *right*. The young men are getting good jobs ashore now. Steady jobs. Jobs from nine to five. They're making good money.

"Well, it makes no difference to me what becomes of

drudgin'. Different things play out, I guess, when better come along."

Cap'n Will pulled the wool liners on to his feet and struggled into a pair of rubber boots. Leaning back after this exertion, he said what Charles Todd told me he had been saying for years.

"I'm selling out at the end of the season anyhow. I'm just going now, you know, because my son wants me to. If it was up to me I'd be home by the fire with the madam. That's where I'll be next year." As an afterthought he said, "I hate to see my boat go though. She's a good one. Take a tomcat to catch her."

Cap'n Will hiked himself off the bench and up the companionway ladder. A few minutes later breakfast was ready and Tom, the cook, asked me to call Cap'n Will and the crew below. We ate an enormous meal—fried eggs, bacon, pork chops, potatoes, hot biscuits, doughnuts, and coffee—then hurried on deck to get underway. Les thawed out the engine of the yawl boat, an eight-foot motorboat hung on davits over the stern of the *Leonard*. We would use the yawl boat, he told me, to push the *Leonard* out through the ice in the creek to the open water of the Choptank River, a broad estuary of the Bay. We lowered the boat into the water, snubbed its bow up tight under the stern of the *Leonard,* and moved slowly out into the creek just as the sun came up.

As the darkness disappeared I got a good view of Cambridge —small whitewashed clapboard houses crowded close together, the business district typical except for unusually narrow streets and the creek running to within a block of the municipal center. The creek varies in width from fifty to one hundred and fifty yards and is lined on both sides with wharves and bulkheads. Back lawns of some of the houses come down to the water's edge. Besides the tall-masted dredge boats, which gave the scene a nineteenth-century look, there were about fifty small motorboats used for various types of fishing and half a dozen small coastal freighters.

We passed under a drawbridge and out into the Choptank

River. The Choptank is a mile wide at Cambridge but widens to almost ten miles before it enters Chesapeake Bay fifteen miles below. Its shores are irregular—tree-lined points run out toward the channel and wide bays and smaller rivers make their way back into the land. As we left the creek the crew hoisted the sails. It took all four of them and the cook seven or eight minutes of hard work to raise the huge mainsail. The smaller sails, topsail, jib, and flying jib, were no trouble. As there was almost no wind, we continued to use the little motor yawl boat to push us downriver.

It was light enough now to see the *Leonard* clearly. Forward of the mast there were two large anchors, an ancient windlass to raise them off the bottom, the hatchway to the crew's cramped quarters in the forepeak, and the bowsprit, which extended fifteen feet out over the water. The top of the topmast was, I judged, sixty or sixty-five feet above the deck, a space of about twenty-five feet between the mast and the after cabin, was taken up by dredging gear and an open work area for sorting, or "culling," oysters. The after cabin contained the galley, table, lockers, and berths for the captain, mate, and cook. Behind this was the wheel.

Certainly no dredge boat could be kept up better. At that time of year, with her decks and topsides freshly painted and her mast and spars scraped and oiled to their gleaming natural color, she did look more like a yacht than a workboat. Her little yawl boat, with its shining bright work, looked like the launch from an admiral's flagship.

As it was perhaps a two-hour trip to the nearest oyster bed, and as there was nothing much to do, the crew gathered amidships to pass the time. Besides Les there was Sawmill, a friendly, carefree Georgian in his thirties who received a lot of good-natured ribbing about a prison term he'd served for moonshining (they called him a graduate of "Georgia State"); Robert, a husky fellow of about twenty-five; and Clarence, probably close to forty-five, a diabetic, but active and strong as an ox. They talked mostly about the various available women in Cambridge and the wild goings-on the previous weekend. Clarence did most of the talking; in fact, the conversation soon became a monologue. He told one story about a man named Shad, who appeared frequently in the Cambridge police court: "Old Shad, you should have saw him. Just as seedy-looking and still all drunked up. Judge says, 'You been here a lot of times.' Shad says, 'Yes sir!' Judge says, 'Fifty dollars and costs.' Shad says, 'Oh, I can't pay that, Judge. I can't pay that. And I'm going drudgin' Monday morning.' Judge says, 'All right then. Twenty-five dollars and costs. Next case.' Shad says, 'Oh, Judge, I can't pay that. Oh, please, Judge, I can't pay that. I feel so terrible,' he says, crying. Judge says, 'Well, then, ten dollars and never let me see you in this court again.' Old Shad pulls out a roll and asks the clerk, 'Can you change a twenty?' "

Cap'n Will, sitting on the wheelbox with one hand resting lightly on the wheel, nodded toward the crew. "Sound like an awful bunch, don't they? But they aren't half as bad as they sound. Mostly talking through their hats." He smiled mildly, looking off toward the shore. It was bright now, only a few moments, it seemed, since we had watched the sun come up as we left the creek. A few small clouds hugging the horizon and the two low shorelines were etched sharply against the pale sky. The air was thin and winter-clear.

"Beautiful, beautiful, beautiful time," Cap'n Will said, looking around and squinting up the mast for signs of a wind. "Not much good for drudgin' though . . . We get a lot of ca'm weather like this. Sometimes three days at a time. Mostly it's either blowing too hard or it's ca'm . . . Get a good day, a day just right for drudgin', only once in a while. Maybe once a month."

Cap'n Will pointed to a flock of large white birds taking off from the water near a sand bar a hundred yards away. "Look a there! Those are swans," he said in a pleased, proud tone. "Hundreds of them, thousands, come down here every winter." A dozen sea gulls came cawing up behind us looking for any scraps we might throw over. Cap'n Will turned to watch them. "They're out working all the time," he said. "They can go anywhere and it don't take 'em long. Don't take 'em long at all. Go anywhere in the world." He pointed toward the black ducks, common ducks he called them, which flew and swam in flotillas between us and the shore. Sometimes he nodded at fast little terns that buzzed the water near us.

A powerboat towing two large rowboats passed us going downstream. "That's a haul-seiner out after rockfish. He'll set his net close to shore downriver a ways and haul it in just at the edge of the night."

An oyster dredger came into view from around a point below us. Its mast was lying on deck. "Lost the mast last week," Cap'n Will told me. "Tuesday or Wednesday. It was blowing a good storm and snowing. Feller comes from Oxford. He's going up to Cambridge to see about a new mast. No telling when he'll get one."

I asked him if dismastings were frequent and he laughed. "It doesn't happen except once in a great while. I lost mine once but it was my fault and not the weather. I had a rotten mast and waited too long to replace it. Finally it just let go. Taught me, though, it don't pay to keep poor gear."

Cap'n Will had survived several disasters in his long career, I knew, and after considerable urging he told me of two of them.

"Once a waterspout hit my boat, sucked it right out of the water and slammed it down bottom side up. Drowned my crew. It was a while back. Fifty years, I guess. I was freighting orsters from Oxford to Cambridge with just the one feller for crew.

"We could see it coming—tearing the clouds all to pieces— and we got the sails down in time. It picked me right up off the deck by the wheel and dropped me in the water fifteen feet away. Done the same thing to the boat.

"I swum back. My man was hanging on to the keel yelling, 'We're going to be lost. We're going to be lost.' A sea came along and washed us both off. He didn't get back. A good swimmer too—it was enough to make you scared but a time not to be scared. A steamer picked me up a couple of hours later.

"About the worst time we've ever had in the river, recently anyway, was in a thick fog below Castle Haven. It was about 1932, I guess. Three, or it may be four, drudge boats was sunk. A lot of men drowned. I don't know how many. Twenty prob'ly. It was a Friday, and most of the boats were heading up river for home. I decided to drudge a little longer and was working off Castle Haven when the skunk hit us."

"Skunk?" I said.

"Skunk. That's what we call 'em. Squall. A squall that sneaks up on you. The fog was so thick we couldn't see it till it hit. Blew the tops'l off. We got the jib in but we couldn't get the mains'l down. The boat fell off the wind and scooted up the river. We couldn't do a thing but hang on and hope. Couldn't get the drudges in. They were jumping up and down behind us like porpoises.

"We caught up with the others when the fog cleared and I saw some of them weren't there. My oldest son Bill's boat and whole crew was lost. He wasn't aboard. It was an old boat and an old skipper. Too old, I guess. He kept sail on her too long and sailed her right under."

Les Jones had come aft and stood listening to the end of the story. "You going to drudge the lower edge?" he asked. Cap'n Will looked at him quickly, a little embarrassed, I thought, about his storytelling. "Right where we left off last Friday," he said. "Looks like the wind will come out northwest. Be just right."

Cap'n Will began peering intently at the shore and then behind him and then toward the mouth of the Choptank River. Les explained that he was lining up markers—a clump of trees on shore, the channel buoy behind us, and a lighthouse downriver a mile. When they made right angles to each other, we would be over the edge of the bed. "That's where the best orsters lay," Les said. "If you get too near the center—'up on the hill,' we call it—you get nothing but empty shells. If you get off the edge you get a drudgeful of mud."

Les pointed out the positions of six other oyster beds (or rocks, as they are called locally) between us and the mouth of the Choptank. "God know how many orster rocks in the Bay Dad's drudged altogether. For each one he's got markers, hundreds of them, maybe thousands, stored up in his mind."

Cap'n Will called out, "Les, cut the motor." Les jumped into the yawl boat astern and turned off its engine. He and the other members of the crew hoisted the yawl boat out of the water onto its davits. Les told me that Maryland law prohibits the use of engines while dredging except on certain days in certain areas and that for the rest of this day we would have to depend on the wind. The law was passed because engine-powered boats would soon strip the oyster beds, while sailing vessels are limited by the vagaries of the wind. The only mechanical power permitted where oystering is restricted to sail is a gasoline-powered winch which raises the dredges from the bottom.

The *Leonard* slowed down and, with the engine dead, the still of the early winter morning on the calm river rushed out to us broken only by individual sounds—the cry of a distant gull, the slam of a back door on shore, the report of an ax striking wood, and the soft lapping of the water against the hull. Making the boat move at all in the light wind required great care. Cap'n Will yelled forward to the crew to haul in the jib a little. Then he had the topsail reset and experimented with the mainsail until satisfied he was getting all the speed he could out of the breeze.

Meanwhile the crew was busy getting the dredging gear ready. The dredge is a triangular-shaped iron frame, four feet wide and about six feet long. The base of the triangle is a heavy iron bar with rake-like prongs along its bottom edge which loosen the oysters and throw them back into a wire mesh and twine bag as the dredge is dragged over the bottom. Two curved bars form the sides of the triangle. They join in an eye bolt from which a cable runs to the winch on deck. Two dredges are used at a time, one on each side.

When we had been sailing three or four minutes Cap'n Will called out, "Hey, looward drudge." Clarence and Sawmill threw the dredge overboard. As it sank astern the dredge cable unwound off the winch until it made approximately a forty-five degree angle in the water—which was about twenty feet deep. When the cable stopped unwinding the *Leonard* staggered slightly as the dredge dug into the bottom. Two or three minutes later Les started the winch engine to be ready when his father ordered the dredge brought aboard. Underwater, the dredge, grinding slowly along the bottom, scooped oysters, empty shells, rocks, and bits of debris into its twine bag.

After sailing for about eight minutes while the dredge filled, Cap'n Will leaned forward to the throttle lever on the cabin top and gunned the winch motor. This was Les's signal to throw the winch into gear and start hauling the dredge in. When it came to the surface and started over a roller on the rail Clarence and Sawmill grabbed it and dumped half a bushel of oysters on deck. Bits of gravelly mud clung to the gnarled black-gray oysters and a few rocks bounced onto deck. A green-shelled crab disentangled itself from the oysters and started off toward the rail before Clarence grabbed it and threw it into a bucket. "He'll go pretty good for supper," Clarence said. Most of the oysters were stuck together in clusters of three or four or five. Many of them were not oysters at all but only empty shells, because seed oysters attach themselves to old shells to grow on.

Cap'n Will left the wheel and went forward to examine the catch. He looked like a fussy housewife buying vegetables as he bent over the oysters, picked up several, turned them over, knocked them together, and threw them back on deck. He could tell by the looks of the oysters, apparently, where better might be found.

He ordered the dredge thrown overboard for a second test run and went back to the wheel. He made a dozen runs and each time the dredge came aboard he examined the catch, then lined up his marks on shore. For the most part he steered with one foot propped up against a wheel spoke while leaning over the side of the *Leonard,* his hands almost in the water, holding a fifteen-foot boat hook down against the dredge cable. The vibrations told him whether the dredge was filling with mud, good oysters, or empty shells. At the same time he was also busy tacking the boat, tending the sails, and watching the wind. Finally Cap'n Will decided he had found the right spot. The crew threw over a buoy, a five-gallon gasoline can with a piece of scrap iron for an anchor. Then they threw the second dredge over and work began in earnest. From the buoy Cap'n Will sailed toward a clump of trees on shore which marked the edge of the bed. After the dredges were hauled aboard, he brought the *Leonard* about and headed back toward the channel. Like a farmer plowing a field, he sailed back and forth along the edge of the bed between his buoy and the clump of trees on shore. It took between five and ten minutes for the dredges to fill on each run. The crew settled into the rhythm of hauling the dredges, dumping the oysters on deck, throwing the dredges overboard, culling the catch, then hauling the dredges aboard again. They worked incredibly fast, standing bent over from the hips, knocking the oysters apart with long-headed hammers, then separating the legal-sized oysters from the empty shells and small ones. They threw the good oysters into piles behind them, the trash they shoveled overboard. Usually they had two or three minutes of leisure between hauls.

By this time most of the other Cambridge dredgers had arrived on the oyster beds. They were either two-masted bugeyes or single-masted skipjacks. Both types had simpler rigs than the gaff topsail rig of the *J.T. Leonard,* which carried four sails instead of the skipjack's two or the bugeye's three. From a distance, as they tacked back and forth over the beds, the other dredge boats looked like a fleet of yachts jockeying for position at the start of a race.

The morning passed quickly, with the piles of oysters on deck behind each member of the crew growing rapidly. By nine thirty or ten the breeze had picked up enough to make the topsail and flying jib hindrances rather than a help, and we took them in. At eleven thirty, Tom, who had divided his time between preparations for dinner and helping with the catch, called us below. We ate another whopping meal, this time pork chops, boiled chicken, boiled potatoes, hot biscuits, lima beans, and coffee. I stayed below after dinner to help Tom with the dishes.

When I went back on deck the wind had freshened considerably. Rows of whitecaps ridged the river and chilly gusts of wind swept down on us every few minutes, darkening the water as they came. Bits of spray stung our faces. The air was still clear, clearer, it seemed, than it ever is in summer, but the tiny white northwest clouds that had hugged the horizon in the morning had grown large and were advancing to the center of the sky. They were big, black-lined cumulus clouds and they looked cold and ominous.

Cap'n Will seemed to have difficulty controlling the *Leonard*, and a few minutes after I came on deck he headed her up into the wind to shorten sail. The mainsail, flapping wildly with reports like cannon fire, was lowered partway down the mast. The crew tied in a double reef, reducing the sail's size by about a fourth. But even with the smaller sail area we were unable to stay on course. Squalls hit the *Leonard*, one right after the other, forcing Cap'n Will to head the boat closer and closer into the wind so as to spill some of it from the straining sails. As we headed up into the wind, we got farther and farther away from the line parallel to the edge of the bed which Cap'n Will had staked out so carefully a few hours before. Instead of the morning's orderly furrowing, the dredging became a wild hit-and-miss affair as the wind grew stronger and more variable and skittered us about in all directions. Often we sailed completely off the bed and got dredgefuls of gray-brown mud to show for it. On other runs we were forced toward the center of the bed and hauled aboard huge loads of empty shells. Sometimes a squall hit before Cap'n Will had a chance to change course to compensate, and the boat heeled over and surged ahead. When this happened the dredges would come off the bottom and spill their oysters.

Cap'n Will said that if it were only a matter of sailing, the *Leonard* was an able enough sea boat and he could have kept her running over the edge of the bed all day—by luffing her up into squalls and then falling back on course after they were over. Dredging, however, is impossible following such a zigzag path; it requires sailing in more or less a straight line. His task now was to find new grounds where the wind permitted him to dredge.

But the wind was so capricious it seemed almost as if it were making sport of the old man. He would find a good dredging spot and the wind would change direction enough to send the boat scuttling off to another part of the bed before he could make more than one run. He was busy every minute, hopping frantically from one task to the next in a desperate attempt to bring order out of the chaos the wind had made of the dredging. He seemed to be doing ten different things at once, steering much of the time with his foot while he held the boat hook over the side to feel the vibrations from one of the dredge lines, peering at the shore trying to fix his position, keeping an eye to windward for the gusts which kept coming down on the *Leonard* every few minutes. Each time the dredges came aboard he examined the haul to see whether he had caught oysters, empty shells, or mud.

Cap'n Will became less and less communicative as the wind increased. "The wind's too flawy," he said distractedly once. "The puffs force you way up where you don't want to be. I should be a couple of hundred yards downriver, but I can't head down there now. I'd float the drudges. As it is we're going too fast for the drudges half the time."

He vetoed a suggestion by his son that they sail over to the other side of the river where the rest of the fleet was working in more protected waters. But ten minutes later he told me he should have gone over there when it first breezed up. It was too late in the afternoon now, though, to make it worthwhile.

Several times Cap'n Will seemed to take his frustration out on the crew. Twice, while sailing past his marker buoy, he misjudged the distance and snagged the buoy in his dredge lines. Both times he yelled impatiently to the crew to clear the buoy and get it overboard long before they even had a chance to get it on deck and untangled. Sometimes the dredges came to the surface covered with mud and the men tried to clean them by splashing them in the water a few times before bringing them on deck. When Cap'n Will saw this he gunned the winch motor, causing the dredges to come aboard so fast the crew had to jump to avoid being hit. Tom, who was helping Les and Robert on the port dredge, shot indignant glances at the captain, but he paid no attention.

"They think they have to wash the drudges off when they come up muddy, but they don't," he said. "Five or six orsters spill off every time you drop the drudge back in the water to clean it. That's a bushel or more at the end of the day."

Once Clarence's dredge came to the surface with the wrong side next to the boat. It took two or three minutes of hard work to turn the dredge over against the pressure of the water rushing past. Cap'n Will told me he could head up into the wind a bit to ease the pressure on the dredge to make Clarence's job easier, but instead he kept right on sailing. "He won't be late again," he said. "They get to talking and joshing while the drudges are overboard and don't pay attention. I don't like to be hard on the crew. I try to be as decent as I can, but you got to keep going."

At three in the afternoon Cap'n Will ordered a third reef put in the mainsail, but even that did not make the boat more manageable. Eventually, however, we seemed to settle down into a routine again. Although the wind had not moderated it was steadier, and although we still couldn't sail along the edge of the bed Cap'n Will found new areas above it where the oysters were good. For the last couple of hours of the afternoon we consistently made good catches.

Between three thirty and four half a dozen "buy boats" started down the river from Cambridge. Big, powerful motorboats, they meet the dredgers at the end of each day and buy their catches to take back to the packing plants ashore. Two buy boats anchored in a cove behind a point called Castle Haven, about four miles away from us on the opposite shore. The other four went to a cove about six miles farther down the river.

It was so cold by now that I was spending half the time below by the stove and I marveled at Cap'n Will's stamina as I watched him through the companionway hatch. Except for a short break for dinner he had been on deck for twelve hours —directing the dredging, determining where the oysters were, sailing the boat, and in the afternoon, fighting a strong and tricky wind. In addition, of course, Cap'n Will had the responsibility for all decisions, decisions on which five other men depended for a living.

At five Cap'n Will asked me what time it was by the cabin clock. He made two more runs and then brought the boat about and headed toward Castle Haven. The crew culled the last of the catch, washed down the deck and settled themselves for the sail into the anchorage. I asked Cap'n Will how many bushels were on deck and he said about fifty. A hundred bushels was a good catch, he had told me earlier, and I realized now how much havoc the wind had caused. Cap'n Will seemed to read my thoughts. "I'm not the drudger I once was," he said shaking his head and smiling a little. "There was a couple of hours this afternoon when I couldn't do a thing. Nothing. When I was younger and I mean just five years ago the wind couldn't have got me all stirred up. I could have handled a wind like the one this afternoon."

I learned later that Cap'n Will's catch was well above the average for the day, even though the other boats were working in more protected waters and did not have as strong a wind to contend with. But for Cap'n Will there was no victory in being just above average. His old adversary had bested him and it did not have to blow exceptionally hard to do it.

But I shall always remember the sail to Castle Haven as a kind of triumphal valedictory for Cap'n Will. The sky near the western horizon was deep red shading suddenly into a clear, hard blue, as though the air was too cold for the colors to mix. The clouds which had covered half the sky in the early afternoon were retreating to the horizon again and had become as small as they were in the morning. The higher ones were white-lined, filled with black; the lower ones, reflecting the horizon, were light red. The water was so dark it was almost black and in between water and sky the low-lying land looked cold and forbidding.

Without the dredges to hamper her, the *Leonard* leapt ahead into the late afternoon breeze. We were sailing close to the wind and she heeled over sharply, the water boiling loudly under her bow and hissing past her stern. Cap'n Will, leaning against the slant of the deck with his fingers lightly on the wheel, seemed a part of the boat. There was a harmony between the two, the boat responding to his lightest touch and Cap'n Will totally absorbed in the sailing. He seemed to have forgotten our presence and the long, hard, frustrating afternoon. He was getting every ounce of speed out of his boat. A quarter of a mile ahead of us a skipjack which had dredged on the other side of the river was heading for the anchorage at Castle Haven. Gradually Cap'n Will worked the *Leonard* to windward and slowly we gained. The gap closed and we passed, close to. As we did our sails blanketed the skipjack's for a moment, long enough for her to lose headway and fall rapidly astern. No one said a word and Cap'n Will looked as he if hadn't even seen the other boat, but we were all elated.

Cap'n Will brought the *Leonard* about and headed into the anchorage. It seemed to me then that I understood why he kept coming back to the oyster beds each winter. He looked alive and alert and completely at home. Out here he wasn't just another old man waiting for the end. Out on the water he was living as fully as he had ever lived. It was as if he had to keep sailing, as if the ogre of senility and uselessness was standing behind him in the shadows waiting to claim him as soon as he left the helm of his vessel and went ashore.

The next summer, after the dredging season was over, Cap'n Will found it difficult to get about on the *Leonard* to paint and repair her, something he had always done alone. He found it impossible to hoist himself up the mast for the annual rubdown with grease that was his practice. In the fall he suffered a serious stroke, his third in four years, and at the insistence of his family sold the *Leonard*. I saw him three months later, after his release from the Cambridge hospital. He was able to walk around his house and was beginning to drive the car again. When his wife left the living room, he told me that he had talked to the new owner of the *Leonard*[2] about buying her back and would do so in time for the next dredging season unless he had another stroke. He died six months later—before the season opened.

[2] The *J.T. Leonard* went oystering for a few more years and is now preserved at the Chesapeake Bay Maritime Museum, St. Michael's, Maryland. —ED.

III

Since the days when the first boat back from the oyster beds got the best price for their catch, the spirit of competition among the watermen has been fierce. And today, if the breeze is fresh and there is another craft nearby for a test of speed, the man at the wheel of an oyster boat will drive her home, heading her up into the wind a trifle when the gusts hit, easing her off when the wind slackens, always keeping just the suggestion of a quiver in the mainsail, watching the jib to see that it is full. The helmsman becomes part of the boat. And the boat becomes part of the man.

Although it's a race whenever two boats come together on the same course, there are several formal regattas organized each year for the oyster fleet. The Deal Island Labor Day Race, started several years ago by Ben Evans and the local Lions Club, has become one of the most hotly contested races anywhere. The Solomon Island Yacht Club, with the cooperation of the Maryland Department of Tidewater Fisheries, has sponsored the Western Shore Skipjack Championship Regatta. The race that draws the most spectators is run by the Windjammers of the Chesapeake, Inc., a group of interested yachtsmen who have organized an annual Chesapeake Appreciation Day right before the start of the oyster-dredging season. The race takes place off Annapolis, just above the Bay Bridge, and in recent years more than ten thousand people have lined the shore to watch the ancient skipjacks race, while many more have watched from the thousand or so boats in the spectator fleet.

The oystermen tune up for their races much less elaborately than yachtsmen would. For the Labor Day race off Deal Island many of them, being crabbers in the summertime, are up at two in the morning on the day of the race tending their crab floats. They go home for breakfast and then set out to the race. Captain George Davis Faulkner sailed the *Mildred Lewis* some years ago with all her dredging gear aboard and a year's growth of barnacles on her bottom. Captain Faulkner, who runs a tomato-canning factory in the summer, had only one day, Sunday, to take the *Mildred Lewis* out of storage, bend on her sails, and sail her the sixty miles from Tilghman Island to Deal Island. He, his wife, his son, and eight friends finished rigging on the way.

Always an individualistic lot, the watermen race without benefit of the intricate yacht-racing rules that govern pleasure boat regattas on the Bay. In fact, the oystermen race by no rules at all except the rules of the road and they even ignore those sometimes. Often it's anybody's guess who's going to give right of way to whom. One young captain when asked the rules said "The older man and the one closest to home has the right of way."

The starts and roundings of the marks are apt to be hair-raising. One year I saw a boy on the end of the bowsprit of the boat next to us trying to fend off the stern of another boat with his feet, just after the starting gun. "Get off of there!" his father yelled, and then said to us, "No use to win the race and lose a young 'un." But the general attitude is to win the race and hang the rules.

The watermen take great pride in the speed of their boats. Several years ago in Miss Elsie's, one of the islands veteran captains began belittling the claims of another captain, Bartlett

Murphy, who was telling him, or trying to, how fast his recently purchased skipjack, the *Lena Rose,* was. The veteran captain, a domineering kind of talker, ran down the *Lena Rose* until Bart, a young fellow and not nearly his equal in argument, took out fifty dollars, put it on the bar and challenged him to a race around a buoy south of Tilghman Island the next day. The older captain declined. In the years since, Bart has almost completely rebuilt the *Lena Rose*—to make her a better dredge boat, but also so that she could hold her own or better in a race. He has lengthened her boom and added a cloth to her mainsail. He has experimented with a club at the top of the mainsail to see if it would make the sail draw better. He has raised the hounds on the mast so that he could fly a bigger jib. He has talked of putting a three-foot higher mast into her.

Bart was rigging up new lazyjacks on the *Lena Rose* at a wharf on Tilghman not long before the start of the 1966–7 dredging season when Captain John Wilson, eighty-two, walked down and came aboard. Captain John keeps threatening to retire every year but doesn't. They got talking about the race at Annapolis on October 29, the Saturday before the oyster season opened. Bart said, "That's an awful time for a race, isn't it, Cap'n John, right before the season like that."

"Oh yes, yes," Captain John said and laughed. "You could take a mast out and lose a week."

"But if I'm winning I'm not going to take any sail off her, are you, Cap'n John?"

And Cap'n John said, "Oh no, no."

During the race, Bart, after being fouled by several spectator boats, lost his chance to win. Only then, though the wind was gusting up to thirty–forty miles an hour, did he take a reef in the sail. He wasn't going to tear out his mast for any third place, he said disgustedly.

Once Bart took the *Lena Rose* out to do some crabbing. The wind came up, but he kept a whole mainsail on her until the yawl boat hanging off the stern was swamped. And later that night he said, "You'd have said she was going today if you'd seen her. Father said reef her. I said no, put it all on her, she'll take it." After the yawl boat sank, he is reported to have said, "I'll put a little tuck in now, I guess."

Captain Daniel Murphy of Tilghman talks about his boat, the *Joy Parks,* as if racing, not gathering oysters, were the chief occupation around his island home. "This is the best boat in the fleet. I bought her from Orville Parks of Cambridge, and he says himself she would beat his new boat."

Orville Parks is the racing champion and the scourge of the Bay. He has one of the newest skipjacks, the *Rosie Parks.* Her dimensions are 46.2 feet by 16.7 feet by 3.3 feet, and she was built in 1955 by his late brother, Bronza, one of the last of the great oldtime Eastern Shore builders, who was senselessly murdered several years ago by a Washingtonian in a disagreement over a small pleasure boat Bronza was building him. Unlike the America's Cup defenders, which are designed and engineered with great mathematical precision and then tank-tested in model form before construction, Bronza built the *Rosie Parks* by eye, and Captain Orville says "he could have built any boat in this world without a blueprint." When I asked about his racing he told me, "I do anything that's fair to win—I've named her after my mother and my brother built her and I'm trying to keep her record."

The *Rosie Parks* looks more like a yacht than a workboat. Captain Orville sails her without the eight or ten tons of stone ballast that most large skipjacks carry to keep them upright in a blow. "I'd rather she'd list than keep her on her feet," he told me. "They sail better over on their side. But I don't tell the others that."

Captain Orville is the man to beat, and when he sails the sixty miles down the Bay from Cambridge for the Deal Island Labor Day Race, the competition is stiffer than usual. Although he wins almost every year, his partisans claim there is an improper kind of cooperation among the boats from Deal Island.

All too often, they say, most of the skippers of the Deal Island fleet devote their talents not to winning but to harassing Captain Orville, the outlander from Cambridge. At least, that's his version of it.

One year the contest was won by Captain Ralph Ruark of Wingate, Maryland, who took a long gamble and sailed a detour on the downwind leg to avoid an adverse tide and pick up an expected wind shift first. Orville Parks claimed later that the kind of team racing indulged in by the Deal Island boats ruined any chance he had of winning. He said that the *City of Crisfield*, skippered by Captain Art Daniel, deliberately tried to slow him down. Captain Orville said that Captain Daniel yelled across to him "All's fair in love and war" after he had matched him jibe for jibe a half a dozen times in less than a mile. He could have gotten away from Captain Daniel, Captain Orville said, except that every time he tried he was blocked by another Deal Island boat, the *Robert L. Webster*. The *Webster*'s skipper, Eldon Willing, Sr., wasn't being deliberate about it, Parks said; he was just in the way.

At the baked ham and crabcake supper in the Deal Island Fire House after the race, Captain Daniel denied to me that he had any thought of slowing Orville Parks down to let another Deal Islander win. "I was out to win myself," he said. "I figured if I could stay with him off the wind, I might have him, because I believe my boat's a little better on the wind."

I am inclined to believe that that is all Captain Daniel had in mind. Thinking as he did that Orville Park's boat was the fastest in the fleet, it made sense to stick with it from the start to the first mark, to leeward, and then try to beat it going to windward. Captain Daniel said that before the race he tested the speed of Captain Ruark's *Wilma Lee* against his own boat and decided his boat was faster off the wind. What Captain Daniel did, therefore, appears to be nothing more than standard racing practice.

But, on the other hand, at the supper after the race one of the

Deal Island wives told me that the feeling on the island is that it isn't right for Captain Orville to win every year. Of course, he hasn't. That year, in fact, Captain Ruark had won for the second straight time. Parks remarked after the race, "Maybe they'll go after him next year." (Captain Ruark is a student of Orville Park's racing style, having crewed for him in previous regattas.)

And several years ago I myself heard talk on the Deal Island waterfront of a plan going to gang up on Captain Orville. In the race, five or six Deal Island boats covered the *Rosie Parks* before the start and tried to stay with her afterward. But through a bit of deft maneuvering at the start, Captain Orville got away from the local boats. He was first to cross the starting line, one second behind the gun. He sailed for several minutes at a ninety-degree angle to the race course in order to get away from the local boats that were right behind him taking his wind. The idea, a waterman said, was for these boats to keep Captain Orville covered in order to let another local one go on to win. It didn't work, and Captain Orville scored his third victory in as many years.

If these stories give the impression that the oystermen are unseemingly contentious, they are overdrawn. Captain Daniel and another Deal Islander, Captain Stanford White, of the *F.C. Lewis,* paid high tribute to Orville Parks's sailing ability. Captain White said admiringly that in the flukey airs near the end of the race, Captain Parks was a little behind him and tacked at just the right moment to catch a new wind. A few minutes later there was a quarter of a mile between them. Captain Daniel said that on the wind Captain Parks "done me just what I'd been doing to him off the wind." "I don't blame him none," he said. "It was nice." Captain Orville crossed the *City of Crisfield's* bow and tacked at exactly the right moment to give her a lethal dose of bad wind—not an easy maneuver in light, variable weather in a heavy (ten gross tons) oyster boat.

After one win at Deal Island, Captain Orville said the victory was no surprise. "I sail with them all winter during the oyster season and I beat 'em then. You race all the time—race in and race out. They're all good sailors too. There aren't any better on the Bay."

The recent revival of the Western Shore Skipjack Championship Race after a lapse of more than twenty years augurs well for the future of the skipjacks. That year a strong northwesterly kept all but six of the skipjacks scheduled to take part from sailing across the Bay for the event. Orville Parks was one of those who failed to show, and there was some derisive comment as well as jubilation aboard the other skipjacks. "It should be pointed out that Captain Orville had a fair wind from Cambridge to get here, while all out boats had to come against a head wind," Mrs. James Webster, aboard the *Geneva May,* said. The *Geneva May* and the other five skipjacks hailed from Deal Island and Winona, sixty miles by water from Captain Orville's home port.

Those that came, as always when the oystermen gather, provided colorful and intense competition. It was nip and tuck the whole way between the *Geneva May* (Captain Paul Benton, Jr.) and the *Maggie Lee* (Captain Clifton Webster). The *Geneva May* passed the *Maggie Lee* three times, sometimes so close aboard that a Pekingese could have stepped from one boat to the other. The *Geneva May*'s boom swept the deck of the *Maggie Lee* in the last encounter and very nearly bopped Captain Webster on the head.

The three times the *Geneva May* passed the *Maggie Lee* the boats were sailing on a beam reach—with sheets started. The two times the *Maggie Lee* passed the *Geneva May* they were both sailing close-hauled, on the wind. When the boats docked, under sail rather than with their motor yawl boats pushing them, which is easier, Captain Benton jumped aboard the *Maggie Lee* and yelled, "We beat you Clifton, we beat you!"

"I admit it, Paul," Webster said. "With rised sheets she always was fast."

"Yes, but on the wind, by God, I don't know what's wrong with her," Benton said.

Webster, who remembers when the *Geneva May* was built fifty-eight years ago in a little creek near his home, said that with a larger centerboard well and longer centerboard she would do much better on the wind. "The secret of a skipjack," he said, "is the centerboard and the mast. If they're right, she'll go. The *Geneva May* don't have enough well."

"She had enough well to beat you, Clifton," Benton retorted.

At the race's end Captain Benton was awarded the two hundred-dollar cash prize and a three-foot trophy put up by Governor Tawes of Maryland. "I'd rather have this cup than a thousand dollars," he said. Turning to Captain Webster he said, "By thunder, I'm going to put something on you going home tomorrow."

Captain Parks and the others have never heard, of course, of the racing theories refined by yachtsmen in the summer sun of weekend sailing centers. Captain Parks and his colleagues do their sailing in the wintertime. They are wet, cold, and tired as often as not, and they are working, not racing. Nevertheless, it seems to me that the best of them have worked out some of the same ideas as the yachtsmen. They are well aware of blanketing and backwinding, the effects of proper trim, the need to plan a start and hit the line with full way on, the advantages of proper rounding of marks, and so on.

The only disagreement a friend of mine, Fred Hecklinger, an ocean racer on Chesapeake Bay boats, and I have with the oystermen's racing style concerns their method of sailing upwind. We think they don't trim their sheets in far enough. After one race, Fred, who was sailing with Junior Benton of Deal Island, took the helm during part of the beat home. He asked if he could trim the sheets. "It'll kill her, Fred," Junior said, but he trimmed them. Fred said Junior's skipjack, the *Geneva May,* pointed perhaps ten degrees higher into the wind and that, he felt anyway, there was no loss of speed. If we are right and the oystermen are wrong, it is an understandable mistake. When working, the oystermen tow dredges back and forth across the oyster beds on a beam reach or as close to it as conditions permit. Heading too close to the wind would be fatal pulling such a load. Thus they are used to thinking instinctively in terms of maximum drive above all else. This sounds like dull sailing, but actually achieving the right speed for the bottom, using the right dredges in the right way, gauging and executing tacks, and a number of other variable factors that demand skill and judgment make dredging a satisfying and, at times, exciting kind of sailing.

And so it is that on Chesapeake Bay, as in few other places in the world, the vagrant sailing vessel ghosting home on a dying breeze has not been replaced by the efficient machines which bring the noise of the factory and the stink of the highway with them out on the sea. But in spite of the defiant gesture of Orville Parks and his brother, the late master boatbuilder Bronza Parks, who launched two skipjacks in 1955, it is unlikely that any more of these vessels will ever be built. Progress has never stood aside for beauty.

Even now the oyster fleet is dwindling. Each year a few more of the old dredge boats are sailed up to the heads of lonely creeks around the edges of the Bay, where they lie rotting in the sun. Scavengers quickly strip them of their wheels, wooden blocks, and deadeyes, and the carved and gilded trailboards that antiquarians greatly prize. Their hulls soon dry out and fall apart. When these boats and their skippers, who tell by the smell in the air and the size of that cloud to the north'ard whether it's time to kite for home before a storm or safe to stay out another night—when they are gone, much of the art of seamanship will go with them.

Part Four

The Fishermen of the Bahamas

I

The great body of knowledge that died out in New England and Nova Scotia in the 1930's remains only in diluted form as a last gasp in the dwindling Chesapeake Bay oyster fleet and is stored in the few square-rigged training ships on the world's sailing routes, but flows still in full strength in the Bahamas. The Bahamians depend entirely on the wind—while the Chesapeake Bay oystermen and the square-rigger sailors have auxiliary engines they can use when the wind is against them.

There is another distinction: each Bahamian is his own ship's carpenter, sailmaker, rigger, mastmaker. Bahamians don't just sail their boats. They go to the woods to find the trees to build them. They cut the trees, haul or float them to their building sites, and shape them into finished hulls with adzes, axes, and planes. This whole division of the arts of the sea—designing and building—which in most maritime societies is confined to a small class of specialists, is widespread among them. When you visit a seafaring community in the Bahamas, you are visiting a community of naval architects. Probably every man in it can design and build a boat and subscribes to principles and theories that the others know, may respect, and probably at least in part agree with.

The two types of craft most used in the Bahamas are a round-stemmed, heavily built, but surprisingly fast and weatherly sloop of about thirty feet, used for fishing for the Nassau market and for freighting, and an open dinghy of about twelve feet, for family fishing and running errands between cays. Both types are raced each April in the three-day Out Island Regatta at George Town in the Exumas, as well as in smaller regattas in other parts of the Bahamas.

The Bahamian craft are related to but different from those of eighteenth-century North America, from which they are descended. Their chaste Northern shapes show plainly their descent from English and Colonial wherries. In their final form these craft are close to perfect for the sea and wind conditions and for the kind of work in the Bahamas. In the evolution of what is the principal artifact of Bahamian civilization, no other community has played a greater role than Lisbon Creek, a small Out Island settlement, and no seamen in the Bahamas sail more skillfully or with more daring. The boats of Lisbon Creek are admired all over the Bahamas for their speed, weatherliness, and style.

I visited Lisbon Creek the first time for the Out Island Regatta in April 1964. I flew to Nassau and before buying a ticket on the mail boat walked along the waterfront to see if I could find a sloop bound for Lisbon Creek. By chance, I walked through a passageway between two old warehouses into a littered vacant lot, where, all alone in the scraggly shade of a single, short, bedraggled palm tree, an old man sat: khaki trousers, white shirt, wrinkled kindly face creased into friendly lines—an old man with all the time in the world, it looked, and such an air of contentment and good humor about him, shining from his face, as to make all fretting seem suddenly ridiculous. I asked if he knew of any sloops bound for Lisbon Creek.

"Why yes," he said, "I am waiting for one now." It turned out he did not expect the sloop until the next afternoon at the earliest and probably not until the day after that, and I, of course, did not have time to sit under a palm tree for two or three days. But before I left him, he told me many things about Lisbon Creek.

He said he was born there and had lived there all his life and found it a good place for living. "What showed me about this island life—I went to the States in '44, New York State, all through there. I saw no water. They had no fish. They had no conch. I was sick for home.

"We sail where we want. Catch the bonefish—a load of bone-fish right in Lisbon Creek. The ocean outside full of fish and conch. Good farm lahn up the creek a little. Good timber for boats—dogwood, madeira, two grades, cedar, no better cedar in the Bahamas, pine for planking, horseflesh for frames.

"When hurricane come, our boats safe in the creek. No hurricane get a boat in there," he said, "And always fair wind to Nassau."

"You never have to beat to windward to get to Nassau?"

"No. Never head wind. Fair wind going, fair wind coming back." He smiled and nodded.

The old man: Wellington Longley, the Reverend Wellington Longley, an elderly holy man who is also an expert sailor, who can take a vessel through a storm, handle the tiller, and by a combination of knowing a sea, a wind, a sky, the look of a squall on the water, make the vessel move at maximum efficiency; he also knows the whole art that is closed to a northern stranger, the Bahamian ability to nagivate through shoals, and for long distances out of sight of land, by the colors of his sea. Lisbon Creek has another minister, the Reverend Livingston Bethel, whom Mr. Longley mentioned affectionately. Both men are in their sixties, expert seamen, builders of fine craft, who are so easy in their use of tools that later, once when I was talking idly with Mr. Bethel in the shade of coconut palms where he was making a dinghy, I saw him absent-mindedly pick up an ax and without once looking at it, it seemed to me, sharpen a pencil to a fine point with it, the ax was so natural in his hands. He did it not by holding the ax steady and running the pencil across its blade—the only way even a somewhat experienced axman could do it—but by holding the pencil steady and slashing at it with deft strokes of the ax. What a fine thing, I thought, to have two such holy men in Lisbon Creek with such resounding names, the Reverend Wellington Longley and the Reverend Livingston Bethel—the first a Baptist, but not at all of that solemn, black-suit, straw-hat, obsequious, excessively and permanently humble kind one meets in the Bahamas enroute to conferences, bowing and smiling abnegatively and tiptoeing past one in a dither of apology, like a guilty housedog reprimanded, not of that kind at all, but a Sir Thomas Browne sort of man, curious, reflective, full of good spirits; and the second, an Anglican of the same qualities as the first, but tall, where the first is short, slow-moving and a little aloof, where the first is quick and approachable. On my first visit to Lisbon Creek both men were engaged in building churches—Mr. Longley had come to Nassau, where I met him, to buy two bags of cement for the floor of his church (a small chapel, because almost all the people of Lisbon Creek are Anglican). Mr. Bethel's church is twenty-eight by sixty-two feet, by far the largest building in Lisbon Creek or any of the settlements around it. It is built on land donated to the diocese by the people of the settlement.

Mr. Longley told me of famous sloops and schooners built in Lisbon Creek—*Water Pearl* and *Jessena, Assume, Revive, Astonish*—fast, able, and strongly built. He told me of the reputation of Lisbon Creek boats all over the Bahamas, of the demand for them, of a Lisbon Creek boat built for a man in Abaco even though Abaco is itself a well-established boat-building center; of one built for the Anglican diocese, a high honor; of how each generation in Lisbon Creek has learned from the one before and refined the earlier generation's theories and techniques.

"My grandfather, one great grand back, start it, you know. He sail to Lisbon Creek in a boat with his wife and daughters. He like the lahn and stay. He build a spacious house and scatter seeds for coconut trees, banana trees, and sour trees. He clear the ground for gardens and he begin building boats.

"James Carr his name. He very well known in those days. You see, what happen, he used to build a very good boat, very fast, nothing could beat them. He had schooners up to fifty feet on the keel, I understand from the elder folk, the ones who came behind him."

Mr. Longley told me that Carr, an emancipated slave, started out in a small sloop with his family, livestock, seeds, and tools from his home on Long Island, far to the southeast of Lisbon Creek. He lived in one or two established settlements before finding the unoccupied point of land where the ocean and Lisbon Creek meet, which must have seemed to him a most felicitous site for a community, with its long expanse of ocean beach, its comely, wide, deep, and well-protected creek, its plentitude of fish, its closeness to all the different kinds of wood needed for boat-building—wood from the interior which could be floated down to the settlement in the creek.

Carr brought apprentices to Lisbon Creek to help in his boatyard, to tend his farmland, and to sail the schooners he built to carry cargoes of produce and logwood to Nassau. Four of the apprentices married his four daughters and founded the families —Bains, Bannisters, Longleys, and Sweetings—that have, ever since, controlled the affairs of the settlement.

One of the apprentices, Joseph Bain, became the best boatbuilder in the generation after Carr. All his boats had a distinctive style—not handsome, but fast, and it was said that he never built a pretty boat or a slow one. Today Rupert Bain and his cousin Alfred Bain are among the best boatbuilders in Lisbon Creek or anywhere around it, Mr. Longley said. Another apprentice, Peter Bannister, became a famous captain of logwood schooners, an excellent farmer, and a great hymn singer—known throughout the islands for his singing. His grandson, Leroy Bannister, is one of the most skilled and daring sailors of the present generation.

Carr was a devout Anglican, known and respected by diocese officials in Nassau, and his descendants still center their cultural and social life around the church. He was influential in political affairs, as are a number of his descendants. "All people look up to him; he was a leader in this part of the islands," Mr. Longley said. "Most things he tell the government, they do." His greatest fame was as a boatbuilder, and this tradition, too, continues. No boatbuilders in the Bahamas have turned out as many champion racing sloops as Carr's descendants.

Two days later, when I was sculled ashore by the mate from the mail boat at Victoria Point (where passengers for Lisbon Creek disembark), the first person I met was Rupert Bain. He was a compact, sturdy man in his fifties, a grandfather. His face was good-natured, humorous, and strong, that of a man who finds pleasure in the moment, accepting hardship and disappointment as inevitable.

He pointed out the way to Lisbon Creek—in a grove of tall coconut palms at the end of a long crescent beach—and, after we put his dinghy in the water, he walked part of my way. Everything was new to me—the glinting sea, the shining beach, the curving palms bent inland as by a hurricane, the strange, steady sound of the trades, the harsh clicking in the palm fronds, unceasing, unvarying, overpowering, the light itself, mild as a light in fog but glaring too, clear and transparent, as if it had been polished and had substance, like the structured light in a Dali landscape or a Wyeth painting. Victoria Point struck me then as strange, romantic, picturesque, and happy, mirroring exactly old tropic movie sets I had always thought were wrong. The settlement consists of twelve houses in two meandered rows in deep shade of palm trees a hundred feet back from the ocean, the houses pastel blues, greens, and browns washed by fall rains and faded by the filtered sunlight until their chalky coral limestone walls show through their coats of paint; twelve small square houses with pointed roofs, some thatched, some shingled, surrounded by coarse dark sand and chunks of coral limestone jutting through the sand, and sparse and withered tropic weeds, and broken parts of former boats and buildings—a weathered stern post and rudder half buried, the top and one side of a door frame, the remains of a collapsed wooden porch.

Rupert Bain's house, at the edge of the settlement close to the mile-long crescent beach leading to Lisbon Creek, is twenty feet on a side and shuttered like the others. Twenty-five feet toward the ocean is his store, a smaller, oblong building with no opening except a door and almost bare of provisions, because the people of Victoria Point, like their neighbors at Lisbon Creek, buy very little and that in small quantities. (I asked Mrs. Bain for cigarettes. She suggested I try Victoria Point's other store where I might find some—if not a whole pack then part of one. The other store had nine Camels, which I bought.)

Between Rupert's store and the beach, in the rubbled lime-stone but protected from it on a makeshift cradle, half in shade, half in dappled sunlight, dazzling white, new painted, gleaming, as fragile-looking as a violin, dilapidating everything around it by its beauty and perfection, shining, drawing eyes, thoughts, feelings to itself: Rupert's *Yellow Tie*.

Rupert's *Yellow Tie*, a striving for expression, a transmitting of experience, the fierce endeavor of a grandfather, the passion of a grandfather to excel, a middle-aged man's dream which is a youthful dream and boast, a storekeeper's work of art, this is Rupert's *Yellow Tie*.

Dinghies were originally a British man-of-war's small boat. In the Bahamas they are used for visiting between settlements, fishing for home consumption, commuting to a garden or a fruit grove, and for getting ashore from a larger boat.

And although Rupert's *Yellow Tie* will be used for one or all of these chores, she was built for none of them. She was built to show her heels, to prove her owner's concepts, to vindicate his dream.

She is twelve feet long, shaped into a unity of curves named such names as entrance, run, sheer, and tumble home (names no longer current in our country since the advent of tailfins on boats and mass production), these curves tapering at both ends into a sharp bow and, at water level, an even sharper stern, the stern flaring outward from water level into the outline of a nicely balanced shallow wine glass. This wine-glass stern and the curves leading to it from the bow in general follow the character-istic style of the Bahamas dinghy, but the precise shape these curves define and the shape of the stern are entirely Rupert's own, a combining of what he has been taught and what he has learned from observing the behavior of a boat's hull in the water under varying conditions with what looks pleasing to his eye and what satisfies his feeling for proportion. She might differ from other Bahamian dinghies, which are likewise individual crea-tions, in a certain narrowing of her forward sections or a greater concaveness than is usual in the curving lines near her stern. Thus his *Yellow Tie* is entirely his secret and, if she wins, his triumph.

When I arrived she had not yet been raced at George Town, where boats from all over the Bahamas compete once a year. This was to be her first regatta there. Lifting the dinghy, which I helped to do, carrying her to the water, wading far enough out to be sure her racing keel would not strike bottom while the coral limestone cut into our bare feet, the anxiety on Rupert's face transmitted to all of us, because if one of the four of us slipped or lost his grip the others could not hold on and the certainty that then the limestone would hole her, finally, slowly lowering the dinghy into the water—our conveyance of her was complete, from her cradle to her element.

As I left Rupert Bain and started down the beach toward Lisbon Creek, two small figures zigzagged toward me, darting and stopping, sometimes holding hands, as if dancing and singing—small girls, on incredibly light feet, who when they approached me, stopped, turned as I passed, stared, laughed daringly to each other—not at me, I think, but in release from fear and in amazement they were so close (with no grownups near) to a stranger, a strange object on the beach. They ran away into a thicket behind the two rows of evenly spaces coconut palms bordering the beach. Gone, they seemed objects of fancy, part of a sequence on film.

In that strange light and the sound of wind in palm trees, and in first sight of houses—pastel, small, inconspicuous—on the edge of the settlement faintly discerned in the grove at the end of the beach, I felt an urgent curiosity, an impatience to be there, and anger at my plodding feet and body burdened with the bag on my shoulder. Near the first houses, on a path in the palm trees paralleling the beach, a group of women carried bundles of palm fronds toward the settlement, hefting their burdens in a kind of nonchalant non-attention, either on their heads so that the weight traveled straight down their trunks, or under an arm in a way that put the weight mostly on one hip and so did not tire them. A scolding hen, as brightly colored as a jungle bird, frail but full of ardor, hurried past them. At the edge of the settlement one of the four hereditary leaders of Lisbon Creek, Leroy Bannister, met me, grabbed my bag from my shoulder with a booming laugh, threw it on his shoulder, a good six feet, it looked, above the ground, and set off briskly toward his house. He was a huge, slim man, I suppose six and a half feet tall, wearing faded swimming trunks, a cotton print shirt, and sneakers, voluble and of immense energy, with a rich voice and an easily provoked, loud laugh, whose first impression on me was hustle, athleticism, and a capacity for finding life a comedy and pleasure. He was a man of about thirty-five, I judged, but as lithe and vigorous as an adolescent. I learned later that he was forty-seven. I learned, too, that he was a boat designer and builder, sailor, cement layer, dock builder, housebuilder, plasterer, stone mason, roofer, gardener, woodsman, goatherd, crawfisherman, bonefisherman, concher, sponge fisherman, turtler, rigger, electrician, and plumber (the last two skills extraneous in Lisbon Creek and which he learned to renovate a house he owns in Nassau). So he is a man with a wide variety of skills, but more, he understands and controls the man-made things in his environment (with the possible exception of his kerosene refrigerator), and is closer than we can conceive to woods and to rainfall and to the growth of plants.

We walked together under tall palms from the sea beach, across a sandy common, to the creek beach—past three or four houses facing a beach, four or five spaced around the common, and seven facing the creek beach. I noticed that the well covers of every house were built exactly like the hatch cover of a boat. This should not surprise me, I thought, in a community bordered on two sides by water and as intimately connected to seafaring as this one; when I asked Leroy how wide the creek was his answer first was in ships' cable lengths and then in fathoms—two hundred fathoms at the mouth.

Most of the settlement's activity was taking place on the creek beach and on a path that ran along it: small children swimming and sailing toy boats (made of coconut shells with palm-leaf sails), men gossiping and working on their boats, women and girls washing clothes or splitting open conch shells for stews and salads. When I remarked about this, Leroy said that in the winter the settlement does its work on the creek beach, which faces south and is never cold, and in the summer on the sea beach, which is never hot. "We build out boats here in the cold weather and over there in the summer," he said.

"A nice arrangement," I said.

"Yes. Yes. When the women want to warm the houses, they open the windows on the creek side, and to cool them they open the windows on the sea side. Some settlements bleaky in the wintertime—northeast trade blow right down on them."

He put my bag down beside his "club," a garage-sized building he had built on a small jetty in front of his house, and suggested that we drink ice-cold Coca Colas from his kerosene refrigerator—the only refrigerator in the settlement, whose people, as far as I could see, have no need to refrigerate anything. Coconuts fall down out of the trees; bananas, sours, oranges, guavas, and all kinds of herbs grow in or just outside the settlement; vegetables grow in gardens up the creek a half mile; and shoals of fish swim in the waters around it.

"So you want to go to the regatta at George Town?" he said. "That wonderful. Wonderful.

"I wish I would be able to go this year," he said. "But I has too much work. Too much work to go. I take you in my boat if I go. You bet we have some fun then. That her right there." He pointed to a sprightly looking sloop about twenty feet long leaning against another jetty he owns next to the club.

"She fast," he said. "She win three times at George Town. Every time she go to George Town, she win—except the first year. Not so good the first year. I new to racing. Didn't understand it. I had some very much bad starts," he said and laughed loudly. "Yes. We start last every time that year. All the horses saddled up and gone."

"Did you build her?"

"Alfred Bain, Burke Longley, and I build her. Maybe that why she so fast—three carpenters build her. As far as her shape—we all work it out together."

Leroy is much taken with the name of his boat, *Thunderleo,* which he pronounces musically and with gusto, Tune-d'leo, accenting the first syllable. She is, as far as he knows, the first native Bahamian vessel with thunder as part of its name. A couple of years after he built *Thunderleo,* a Nassau minister had a sponge boat built by Rupert Bain and his father, Herbert, as an investment, but also very definitely with the idea of having it make a name for itself in the sailing contests held every year at George Town, which it has. He named the boat *Thunderbird.* "I was very sorry about that," Leroy said. "I guess after he see my boat sail so fast, he think very hard about having thunder in the name."

There is usually a rationale in the names of Bahamian boats. The leo in *Thunderleo* comes from Leroy. The thunder Leroy chose after seeing an American schooner yacht named *Thunder-*

cloud. He liked the sound of the name, and, even more, its con-
notations. "The elder folk tell us thunder is the Master speaking
—He is angry with us. They think thunder is a great thing—that
you have to be in dread." When he set sail for his first regatta in
his new boat, which he already knew to be fast, he thought the
name had a fine challenging ring that might frighten his opponents.

We talked about the racing fever that gripped the men of
Lisbon Creek and the other seven settlements of Mangrove Cay.
Long before the American yachtsmen organized the Out Island
Regatta at George Town, the men of Mangrove Cay were organ-
izing and running formal races between fishing trips and freight
runs to other islands. Daxon Hepburn was a leader of this activity in the 1920's and 1930's, when the Mangrove Cay Sailing
Club organized races for all classes of vessels, some of them long-
distance races to Nassau and back. He built a clubhouse on his
land. The entire populations of the Cay settlements would watch
from his beach, and there were fine celebrations afterward,
Leroy said. The shorter races are still run every August.

Leroy told me about hurricanes and famous lesser storms,
shipwrecks, long voyages, and record passages to Nassau. He
described the exploits of many Bahamian vessels of the past and
present. Soon their names entranced me: *Eastern Wave,* and
Water Pearl; Alert, Assume, Astonish, Revive; Mrs. Maycock,
and *Lady A.; Unity* and *Charity; I'm Alone,* and *Companion*—the
first a large crayfishing boat owned and skippered by Daxon
Hepburn, the second his new boat when he went into partner-
ship; *Matchless Rose,* a name, I thought, connoting beauty, connoting pride, connoting superiority; *Lady Murial, Brothers, Virginia Nell; Jungle Queen, Headline, Ragged Gal* (from the
Ragged Islands), *Yellow Tie,* which I had seen, and *We Too Spit
Fire,* another little racing dinghy. Only boats built for Americans
to look quaintly like local craft had names such as *Ben Wood
Dick* and *George Town Mama.*

Lisbon Creek seamen have been avid racers for generations

and have worked out many theories about what makes for speed in a sailboat. The secret, Leroy said, is in the way the bow enters the water, and even more important, in the way the stern leaves it. The curves in the run—the after part of the underbody of a boat from where it begins to curve upward and inward—should be hollow, he said. "It give her a clean sweep aft, we call it. It let the water leave the boat cleanly—don't have all that dead water aft, you see."

Leroy cited Alfred Bain, Rupert's cousin and like Rupert a grandson of the greatest boatbuilder of the second generation, Joseph Bain. Leroy said Alfred is one of the best seamen and best boatbuilders in the Bahamas. Alfred and his brother-in-law, Jonathan Rolle, owned the crayfishing sloop *Unity B.* They used to race her at George Town and did very well. Then a sloop from the Ragged Islands beat not only the *Unity B.* but all the boats from Lisbon Creek. The victorious *Ragged Gal* was built specifically for the Out Island Regatta by a man who had spent several months in the United States. He said she was part six-meter yacht. This was nothing but hyperbole, as the *Ragged Gal* was a long way from the six-meter yachts (smaller versions of the twelve-meters that race for the America's Cup) that he had seen. She was, nevertheless, more yacht than workboat. Officials of the regatta feared she might start a trend away from its objective, the encouragement and development of Bahamian workboat design.

To the people of Lisbon Creek, the *Ragged Gal* challenged not only the validity of concepts evolved through five generations of boatbuilding, but also their very self-esteem and preeminence—up to then Lisbon Creek had almost monopolized top honors.

Bain, then in his forties, was, as he is today, one of the outstanding captains in the fresh-fishing fleet that supplies the Nassau market, respected by the other captains and by the six- and eight-man crews who sailed with him. His *Unity B.* was considered one of the best in the fleet.

Building a boat to beat the *Ragged Gal* would mean consecrating his energies at the peak of his career for several months, perhaps half a year, to a civic project, the retrieving of his community's reputation. It would be an artistic endeavor entirely divorced from his livelihood, because for the business of catching fish the *Unity B.* was as able and efficient a vehicle as the new one would be. Building the new boat would be expensive, time-consuming, and unjustified. Finally, it would be a gamble, because if she did not prove faster than all the other boats she met, his time, talent, and money would be wasted, and he would have placed himself as well in the inglorious position of a claimant for the accolade who failed.

Bain considered his decision during the two-day sail home from George Town in the *Unity B.*, from one end almost to the other of the chain of the beautiful Exumas and across the open ocean to Lisbon Creek, in strong breezes that pushed his boat at near top speed through moonlit seas and, in the daytime, across the incredible variety of colors of the Bahamian ocean. He was alone at the helm for the most part, his crew below sleeping or forward relaxing; guiding her home with no compass or chart or landmark, just his instinct and the Bahamian's sure guide—the colors of his sea, which tell him not only where he is but where danger lies. He was standing alone, easy and nonchalant, in the stance of the sailor from time immemorial, in seas that were higher than the sides of his small craft—furrowing, hurrying home with the light, entrancing motion, almost dancing, of a sailboat in a breeze.

He decided he could build a sloop to beat the Ragged Islands boat. He had some ideas, he said, about how to improve her speed.

It took him many months to build the new sloop. The Bahamian builder uses no blueprints or tank tests or mathematical calculations in his determination of the lines of a new boat. The process begins with a withdrawing into one's self, at first for contemplation and then to dig deeper and deeper to the best that he knows, and in outward manifestation the building of a boat is an exact parallel of an artist's applying paint to canvas. There are no power tools in Lisbon Creek, so that the keel, the stem, the stern, and all the frames are hacked out by hand from trees. The builder lays the keel, sets the stern in place and then the stem, the heavy piece of wood rising from the keel at its forward end to form the bow. Then, in Leroy's words, he backs off and takes a look. Once satisfied that the angles the stem and stern make to the keel fit the concept in his mind, he sets up the middle frame, which is one of a dozen or more curved frames, or ribs, spaced from bow to stern along the keel, as ribs on a backbone. Now the two ends and the middle of the boat are defined. How he shapes the hull between these three stations will largely determine her sailing qualities, and here his personality, prejudices, emotions, and pet theories, valid and invalid, as well as his artistic sense and the painstakingly acquired knowledge of what makes for speed and seaworthiness by, in Alfred's case, five generations of boatbuilders, play a part. The final shape of the hull he discovers in this way: he attaches thin, flexible wood strips from stem to mid-frame to stern and adjusts them until they mirror exactly the form of the boat he has evolved in his mind. Then he makes frames to fit within the strips and sets them on the keel. The skeleton complete, he planks her, decks her, launches her.

Each builder in the Bahamas has his own style, modified to some degree by a general style that predominates in his community. Alfred Bain's new boat, as it took shape, seemed to fit within the general lines of the Lisbon Creek school except for a more pronounced flaring of the bow, a greater curving of the profile from bow to stern, and a lightness and airiness around the stern.

Probably no boat ever built in the settlement attracted more interest. From the time he laid the keel, every step in her construction was watched. All the hundreds of details that go into the building of a boat, revealed as she took shape, were discussed—by the old men, sometimes with disapproval; by his contemporaries, with the interest of rivals as well as colleagues and the detached interest of students of the subject; by the women, in their gossip; by the children who played around his building site, falling over timbers and using them for games of war or hide-and-seek. When he went to the woods to find the right curved limb for a frame, people looked to see how he trimmed and fitted it. When he experimented with the slant of the transom, which is the end piece of the stern, the piece that is the silhouette of a wine glass (or in bigger boats more that of a short-stemmed glass dessert cup) and when he shaved a little from the transom to make it curve downward in a finer way, his neighbors noted what he did. Men of the other settlements of Mangrove Cay kept track. Throughout the Bahamas people knew that Alfred Bain was building a new boat to race in the next regatta, and reports of his progress were carried from island to island by trading sloops that stopped at Mangrove Cay or by fishermen who had talked recently to someone from the cay.

The name Alfred chose for her was *Mystery J*. No other name would have fitted her so well: the *J.,* carrying a short but always present reminder of Alfred's sturdy partner, Jonathan Rolle, who agreed to this venture of his more artistic colleague and who was his constant companion in all endeavors, including the racing; the *Mystery* defining Alfred's attempt. The new boat, when he sailed to George Town for her first regatta, was to be a vindication of the mysteries, perhaps sacred mysteries, of his settlement's heritage; she would excite curiosity and wonder; her abilities would be unexplained—some of them concealed on purpose, some of them unknown even by Alfred himself, these latter being the excellencies of a finished entity greater than the sum of its parts. The name of the new boat also carried a sly pride: it would be a mystery why she was so fast, but the mystery would not be completely unknown to Alfred.

The new boat turned out to be the best that Alfred had ever built and perhaps the best ever built in Lisbon Creek. She beat the *Ragged Gal* in the next regatta, which is what she was built to do, and has won more than her share of trophies. But she is flawed, flawed with a defect built into her that has made her a failure, a carrier of hopes never quite realized. The flaw is in no way Alfred's fault and has made her only a degree away from the high place she was conceived for, and is only apparent at times and in certain wind conditions. Alfred planked her with native pine, as almost everyone did in the Bahamas in the 1950's, when he built her. A few years later, however, American pine was introduced. It is much lighter, and newer boats planked with it have a great advantage in moderate winds.

"But *Mystery* beats them still. When the wind blew, she do all right. She go to windward; she take 'em all to windward," Leroy said. He said no one knows more than Alfred about building a fast boat.

"He hate to see her lose. He feel she have the speed in her— only she held back by the heavy Andros pine," he said.

"That Alfred Bain now coming from his garden," Leroy said, pointing to a small dinghy tacking down the creek toward us from the interior. "That his racing dinghy. In the dinghy races at George Town he win every time. And he win every dinghy race we have here. No one can beat him."

When Alfred landed, we helped him pull his dinghy up on the beach. Alfred, a tall, spare man in his late forties, with a thin, intellectual-looking face, reserved and unemotional, talked about boatbuilding for a few minutes. "You try to get the bailing well frame and the garboard turn as sharp as you could. If the hull a little rounder forward than aft, it go faster," he said. He said if you built boats with exactly the same shape aft and made one hollow in its forward sections and the other straight or even rounded, the one with straight or rounded forward sections would be faster.

"Well, I see you," Alfred said and picked up the two baskets of vegetables he had gathered in his garden. He stopped a few paces off. "My boat dragging," he said. He dropped the baskets and ran back to the jetty, grabbed a bucket, and began bailing out a dinghy alongside the jetty. It was half full of water. Six or eight small children, from five down to two or less, descended on him yelling they wanted fish and pointing to a fish pot tied to the jetty. Alfred, in spite of his rush, pulled it in and put it on the jetty. He went back to bailing, but stopped again when he saw they could not open it. He dumped out a dozen or so six-inch fish. The children swooped down on them like gulls and ran off with their fish. After Alfred was through bailing, he took a moment to climb onto the jetty again and gently pick up two fish that had been dropped. He threw them over. "I don't want them to die if no one will eat them," he said.

He poled himself out to the *Mystery*, which was fifty feet from shore, and let out some line on one of her two anchors. The current and the angle of the line to the other anchor pulled her in toward shore. I saw that in a minute or two she would go aground, which struck me as a bad miscalculation by Alfred. "Do you want me to try to push her off?" I shouted to him and started to wade out from the beach. Alfred, standing on the bow paying out line, shook his head. "I let her rest here a little while," he said. "So she won't disturb these other boats." The *Mystery* came in precisely, striking bottom just before she would have hit the closest one, the *Assume*. Only then did I realize that what I had thought was sloppy seamanship was, instead, a beautifully coordinated maneuver. Alfred, casual and relaxed, knowing exactly what would happen, had let the current do his work—which was to prevent his boat from colliding with the others. The only work he did was unfasten one of the two anchor lines and make it fast again at the right moment. Done on the *Mystery*, he jumped into the dinghy in such a way that it came right to shore at the jetty without his even having to pole it. He changed the dinghy's course, not with the pole or an oar, but by leaning to one side, which made the dinghy curve in to the jetty, where it stopped, inches away.

This closeness to their environment—how can I describe

that? It is an at-homeness with the land and sea, so pervasive in these Bahamians' lives that any listing of individual instances only detracts from the truth of it. It is not only that these people can cover all the thousands of square miles of trackless ocean around them without compasses and charts and cope with all the moods of the sea, not only that on the land they have discovered growing about them or with slight adjustment—the planting of coconut trees, for instance, which are not indigenous—all the necessaries for a healthful, varied, and tasty diet, and for shelter, but that they do this and have done this attractively, that they live enviable lives in which what are generally considered goods —good humor, kindliness, self-respect—are manifest. It is not only that these people can do all these things in nature, but also that nature, or their relationship to nature, in return gives their life meaning, purpose, and direction. Their life as it is lived now —and I suppose this is a last flowering and will soon disappear forever, so that what I am writing will in a decade be history of a vanquished life—contains a harmony and balance, which, it seems to me, we have long since lost.

Their at-homeness in their environment is a part of everything they do: a part of the ease with which they scull their dinghies, often for long distances, with an unconscious grace and the barest minimum of effort—an athletic adjusting and aligning of their movements, pivoting the sculling oar back and forth in its groove in the stern so that its blade meets, pushes, and then glides easily through the water at precisely the proper angles; and, on the shore, a part of every action of the women, of their grace in the daily tasks of house and garden, of washing clothes by hand, for instance, of how they heft a burden, of how they cut a cabbage from its stalk or gather palm fronds, of how they stand when gossiping, and how their movements retain beauty in middle age when many women's movements become angular, of how, even, their skin is soft and creamy at an age when that of other women is sagged, dried, and wrinkled.

And in their boats, it is a part of how the men use the seas instinctively to help them in their task, so that a man will scull or pole if the water is shallow, to a certain distance from the landing and then stand relaxed while the seas, in one, two, or three undulations, bring the boat in precisely alongside, and of the timing and immense understanding of the sea this requires, and of how the boat then lies inches from the landing, as if held there under some secret command or spell, while the seas, now breaking, pound against it and are foiled in their attempt to crush it against the landing only by the slightest and most casual adjustments of the oar or pole in the water, now and then, by the boatman, who is joking with the people on the shore or helping with one hand to unload the boat and apparently paying no attention to the seas; and of how, if the landing—as is frequently the case—is nothing more than a coral rock or jutting limestone, the slightest misjudged timing of the boatman's oar would mean a damaged boat or a sunk one.

And the same with the women, returning perhaps from a visit with relatives in Nassau aboard one of the island freight sloops, as it rises and falls in the seas, anchored a mile from shore to unload, the women standing crowded together on the deck with teenaged boys who are returning home, either in defeat after failing to find work in Nassau or victoriously on vacation, and a rounded Miami sponge merchant looking out of place so far from sidewalks. They are grandmothers and young mothers carrying babies or dry-cleaned suits and dresses in fragile polyethelene bags, holding them high, the babies and the dry cleaning, trying to keep off spray, standing between drums of kerosene, baskets of groceries, sugar and flour bags, wooden crates of soda bottles piled high in every available empty place, and empty wash tubs and five-bushel baskets that had been filled on the trip to Nassau with sours and bananas for sale in the open-air market there. The women are apprehensive and mildly scolding—the sea, after all, is part of the men's world and, therefore, also partly their fault—allowing themselves to be helped into the dinghy, which one moment is level with the deck of the sloop and the next yawing five feet down in a hollow of the sea, but only after very reluctantly giving up their babies and the dry cleaning into the hands of the men, more willing to allow the men to transfer their bulging cardboard suitcases, perhaps at first completely unwilling to give up a baby or a dry-cleaning bag but standing obstinate and afraid with the precious bundle, unable to transfer it themselves but unable to let go of it. And finally all of them are piled into the dinghy with their belongings and children (at four or five the mothers cease to be so protective of them, the children having learned by then the ways of the sea) and the dinghy's gunwhales are now a few inches only from the water, and the women are standing or sitting so that their backs shield whatever they are trying to keep dry, and as they make their way toward shore, they themselves, although they may appear to look on the sea with enmity and to be unfamiliar with it, are, too, like the men, at home and knowledgeable about it—balancing unconsciously and distributing their weight properly without being told by the men. And this at-homeness of the women is also, in part, a real enmity and hostility, because the sea can at any time drown their men, and has, and its unpredictableness runs counter to and thwarts their instinct for order and security and, in addition, has an allure for their men that makes it, in truth, a rival for their love. And this enmity, which may be universal among seamen's wives, makes them say they hope no daughter of theirs will marry a seaman and no son of theirs will become a seaman; and this enmity manifests itself in a feigned ignorance and helplessness and hides the reality of their own seamanship so that, for instance, if the men on a boat were drowned or incapacitated, the women would know what to do to bring the boat safely to shore.

And this at-homeness is seen also in the handiness and exact efficiency of the Bahamians' equipment, so that a dinghy used for shuttling between fishing and trading sloops and the shore, for family fishing, and for short trips to other settlements and cays will hold, in addition to its sail and spars, an oar for sculling and a pole for poling in shallow water, the pole perhaps fifteen feet long and not much thicker than a broomstick, looking much too light and bendy, yet of the precise weight and diameter necessary to do its job without tiring its wielder, who may have to pole the dinghy for miles; and this pole or any piece of equipment used afloat or ashore is made quickly and easily, with no false starts or wasted motion, usually from materials available close by.

I saw in the boats drawn up on the beach at Lisbon Creek bailers made of coconut shells, each shell no doubt from a coconut that had fallen from one of the trees then shading those dinghies, after it had served first to quench the thirst of some passing Lisbon Creek man, woman, boy, or girl who may have seen it fall and hacked a hole in one end for the juice and then taken it home for meat for the family larder. I saw beside the boats well-made toy catamarans for the tiny children to sail in the creek, toys that for them had a meaning no toy boat in a bathtub could have for children of a less aquatic people. I saw cement made from local limestone, shutters and doors made from local wood, and the boats, of course, made entirely of local materials except the rope, sails, nails, and a few iron fittings. (The sails were cut and sewn by hand of imported canvas.) On the trip home from the races at George Town we stopped at Rolleville and I saw instances of a simple and efficient commerce; we from Lisbon Creek, not expecting to come this way again this year bought bananas, bags of salt, and plaited mats— for curtains, rugs, and wall decorations; and while we were there, the people of Rolleville came down to the town landing to buy cuts of pork and other meats weighed out on a dinghy from a Ragged Islands trader who sculled ashore from his inter-island sloop (a big boat by Bahamian standards, forty feet long). And they could and have bought from Lisbon Creek its pre-eminent product, well-made boats.

II

The day after I arrived in Lisbon Creek the wind was blowing hard, rattling shutters, flattening bushes and grass, bending palm trees into bows and flinging their branches out ahead of them like umbrellas turned inside out, amplifying the clicking of the palm fronds into a steady roar, and flashing in across the ocean in front of Lisbon Creek in glancing squalls, the water moving fast, rushing live and white-capped, white moving like a rapids. A mile out from shore, five sloops were anchored, pitching and rearing at the ends of their anchor lines—waiting for the start of a three- or four-day journey to George Town where they would enter the Out Island Regatta.

Mangrove Cay, where Lisbon Creek is located, is one of many islands and cays making up Andros Island, the largest and westernmost island grouping in the Bahamas. George Town is on Great Exuma Island, one hundred and fifty miles southeast of Lisbon Creek. Because of the prevailing northeasterly trades and the geography of the Exuma Islands and cays, Lisbon Creek boats must sail many more miles than the straight line's distance, and a good part of it is across the open ocean. The boats from Lisbon Creek don't just sail to George Town; they race, which adds to the discomfort in rough weather, because in a race the

participants carry all the sail they dare and keep pounding ahead
no matter what conditions they meet.

The starting gun was fired; the sloops got under way in half a
gale and seas that had been building for four days—weather that
caused much larger vessels, diesel-powered inter-island tankers
and a fleet of ocean-racing yachts, for instance, to postpone departures and remain moored in Nassau.

All that day the five sloops beat dead to windward, plunging
their bows into building seas that buried their decks from end to
end in torrents of foaming water and sent spray almost masthead
high. Shivering men lay along their windward rails hour after
drenching hour. There was no way of keeping dry: if spray did
not pour down from above, sheets of water on deck seeped up
pant legs, down into shoes, between buttonholes of coats.

The five sloops separated, zigzagging across roughly fifty
miles of open ocean that lay between them and the calm waters
of the Exumas, each in its own heaving universe of sun, storm
clouds, and breaking seas until—incredibly—they joined each
other again in the last light after sundown at Green Cay, a long,
high, uninhabited island miles from any other land. On each
sloop a man who had been staring blankly for hours at endlessly
repeating waves and tumbling horizon would sight a sail ahead,
or astern, a tiny speck appearing and disappearing in his
jumbled gaze. Others, roused from their cold lethargies at the
windward rail, would look, squinting into the fading light, find
the speck, and confirm that it was indeed a sail. One with a
better seaman's eye than the rest would tell, by some peculiarity
of the cut of the mainsail even at that great distance, which
sloop it was. Then excitement would drive out their single-
minded awareness of the numbness in their feet and hands, their
clammy clothes, their chattering teeth, and they would watch
eagerly as their sloop gained slowly on the other or, it might be,
lost distance. Two more sloops might be sighted then—ahead—
close together, battling for the lead, both carrying more sail than
was prudent and leaning way over, and both now, having

achieved the smooth water in the lee of Green Cay, sailing much faster than their opponents in a brief respite from crashing head seas, small dark shadows against the lonely land that served as backdrop and eyeless witness of their duel, as a century and a half ago it may have in similar contests between pirate and victim, frigate and slaver, sloop-of-war and privateer.

The leader of the five in this mid-ocean meeting was the *Thunderbird*, a thirty-foot sloop, wide, deep, powerful, and a winner of more regattas than any other sloop in the Bahamas. Close behind her was Alfred Bain's *Mystery J.*, older, slightly smaller, built less expensively, possessor of a racing record not quite as spectacular as the *Thunderbird*'s, but fast and formidable also. Two or three miles astern, the *Headline*, a forty-foot sloop, the largest in the race, ploughed steadily along. From the distant Ragged Islands she had come to Lisbon Creek to try her speed in this race, but her smaller opponents were proving that even in a blow, when her size should give her a great advantage, they were at least her equal. The little *Alert*, Rupert Bain's twenty-three-foot sloop—against all logic, which decrees that speed is a function of length, and that in high winds and rough seas a small boat suffers incalculably more loss of drive than bigger ones—staggered along not far behind the Ragged Island sloop, close enough so that as darkness fell, the men aboard her could see all three leaders. Somehow the *Alert*, almost stopped by each of the biggest seas she met, and having rapidly fallen behind all the others near the start, had caught up and was actually several miles ahead of the fifth contestant, the thirty-foot sloop, *Lady A.*

The wind blew hard all night. Twice the men on the *Mystery* saw the *Thunderbird* in the darkness. The first time, a couple of hours after sunset, they crossed the *Thunderbird*'s wake on an opposite tack and saw her shadow in the path of the moon. The second time, near dawn, the moon came out from behind a cloud, and they saw very faintly the outline of her sail behind them. When the sun rose, she was so far back they could barely see her sail. The wind blew hard all the second day. The *Head-line* was dismasted a few miles from the Exumas and got to shore under jury rig.

The *Mystery* pounded on until sundown of the second day, when Alfred anchored because his crew told him they could not take it any longer—all that water across them. Early the next morning, Alfred started again and was in George Town before many of the tourists in the two small hotels there finished breakfast. The *Thunderbird* came in a few hours later, the *Lady A.* early that afternoon. But there was still no sign of the *Alert* by sundown, nor by sunrise the next day.

The race from Lisbon Creek to George Town is divided into two parts—first, the long, often rough, open-ocean passage to the beginning of the chain of islands that make up the Exumas; second, the passage down the chain of the Exumas to George Town, in protected waters almost the entire way. Once the bigger sloops reached calm water in the lee of the Exumas, they picked up speed, while the little *Alert* still pounded through endless stretches of open ocean—staggering up the faces of huge seas and sliding down their backs. Her crew, cold, discouraged, shivering the first day and first night, expected a landfall sometime early the next morning. When none appeared, they faced another day on the open ocean with foreboding.

The crew—John Rolle, Fred Green, King Bain, the commissioner, and I—huddled along the windward rail until the signal came to tack. Then we would crawl aft around the cabin dragging sandbags, lie down while the boom came across, drag the bags up to the high side, and heave them forward along the new windward rail where the weight of both sandbags and men was needed as ballast. Two of us would grab the stove, a wash-tub filled with sand in which a wood fire would be built when the weather moderated, and haul it across the deck to the high side. I don't know about the others, but my eyes stung terribly from salt spray incessantly dripping down my hair and forehead. I wiped them constantly, with saliva on my fingers to dilute the

A Bahamian sloop under construction at
Mangrove Cay. The keel, stem, stern, and all the
frames are hacked out by hand from native trees.

Running downwind,
dinghy sails are hoisted
as spinnakers.

Just after the starting gun.

Alfred Bain's sloop the *Mystery J.*

The wine-glass stern of Rupert Bain's dinghy *Yellow Tie* is typical of Bahamian boat design.

The *Alert,* Rupert Bain's twenty-three-foot sloop, careened for repairs to the bottom (above).

Rupert Bain of Victoria Point, Mangrove Cay (left, middle).

Alfred Bain at the helm, towing his dinghy, the *Jet,* behind.

The dinghy races, held as a side event during the
Regatta, are the consummate test of a skipper's skill.

"Get ready—gone" and *Thunderbird* makes a fast tack.

salt, but they still smarted and refused to stay open. It is almost worse than spray down the neck, I thought, but perhaps it keeps your mind off the spray. There was no relief, because all of us were needed on the windward rail to keep the little *Alert* from heeling over too far. Yet it wasn't as miserable as it sounds. There were times of joking, and I found that the body can take and become accustomed to much more than I had thought. We who never suffer hardship are infuriated by it. The men, used to it, took it in stride—or, I should say, three of us, Rupert Bain, John Rolle, and Fred Green. The other two, King Bain and Lester Turnquist, the commissioner, although natives of small Out Island communities, had become landsmen: King as the government's male nurse for Lisbon Creek and the settlements around it (a responsible job, as the nearest doctor and hospital are in Nassau); and the commissioner as the government's judicial officer in the Lisbon Creek area. They were friends, on this trip for a lark, King, about twenty, thin and short, given to half-humorous self-deprecating remarks; the commissioner, twenty-eight, suave, plump, pleasant, the picture of what one of Her Majesty's officials should look like, even in our circumstances—pith helmet, white shirt and shorts. King complained about the spray, the cold, the endlessness, in a good-humored way. "Oh lahn, where are you?" he would say, or, "I'm not feeling too sporting now, mon, I will say." The commissioner sang old English ballads to himself sometimes in a half-English, half-Bahamian accent. He said quite seriously of the race to George Town: "Oh, no, never again, never again will I go."

Rupert Bain, our skipper on the *Alert*, towed his dinghy, the *Yellow Tie*, his creation, behind him, she looking too fragile to survive the battering of the steep, sudden seas, and sometimes when an unexpected sea hit her being thrown clear so that someone on the *Alert* could look back and see daylight under the complete length of her. Once the seas were too much for *Yellow Tie*, and a section of her rail was damaged. When she was in danger of filling up with water, Rupert pulled her close to the

Alert and jumped aboard her, let her out to the end of her rope again, bailed the water out with a bucket, and then hauled himself and the dinghy hand over hand back up to the *Alert*, balanced himself on the bow of *Yellow Tie*, which was skittering about wildly, and as the two boats came together, perhaps four feet apart, jumped at the exact moment back on the *Alert*'s deck, a jump not many Americans I know who are half his age could do.

Rupert sighted land, Sandy Cay, about two o'clock in the afternoon of that second day. He said it was only a two- or three-hour sail from Sandy Cay to the protected waters of the Exumas. The commissioner and King began planning a tremendous boiled fish dinner they would eat around a bonfire on the first Exuma Cay we came to. "We'll keep the fire going all night," King said. "Yes indeed, mon, that's what I intend," the commissioner said. "If there is shore around me, I will not be on the boat." The afternoon wore on. No land appeared. Rupert sent the sharpest-eyed among us, Fred Green, aloft. Fred came down with the report, "In my opinion, no lahn there." At sundown, the commissioner, silent for a long time, aroused himself to say, "Rupee, won't you go up the mast and take a look while the sun's still up," Later, when Rupert climbed the mast, he said, "Rupee, if you see the lahn, come down. If no lahn there, don't bother."

We crouched along the windward rail, in attitude like the sandbags we had piled there, nodding uncomfortably, dozing and snapping awake, because asleep one might topple overboard, until about nine o'clock when there was a hurried call of shoal water ahead—seen by Fred Green, as usual more alert than the rest of us, from his position, the wettest on board, forward on the windward rail. We anchored hurriedly.

The next morning we sighted the Exumas after an hour's sail, and in another hour we were sailing in the smooth water in their lee. Now the *Alert* sailed on an even keel; we could leave our crouched positions on the windward rail; our clothes dried out. Basking in a luxury of warmth, sunshine, the beautiful scenery of those islands, and the immense array of colors of the sea (What you say, King, what you say? Oh fine, mon, fine), we were dry at last and picked up, one after another, the points of land that told us we were finally close to our destination. And each point of land appearing in the slight haze of the horizon was cause for new thanksgiving. Now in our ease and happiness, after sailing by many other pleasant headlands, when we first spied Barre Terre I turned to our skipper at the helm, where he had been almost continuously for two days and part of a third, not trusting less experienced helmsmen in the storm, and said, "Look at that next headland in the haze ahead, Rupert," and King, seeing it at the same time, said, "See that smoky lahn, Ru-pee," and it seemed to me that I spoke prose and he spoke poetry, softer on the ear, delighting in it, and describing exactly what "Baritari" was to us then—remote, inviting, veiled, the promised land. Smoky lahn, smoky lahn—each new headland they called smoky lahn, and the sound entranced me.

For the most part the Bahamians use the nautical terminology of all the English-speaking world, but when they depart from it the departure is usually felicitous. What we call with accuracy but no imagination a moderate breeze they call a social wind, ascribing to it affability and including in the name the ease and pleasure and relaxation of the crew at such a time—often, as on the trip to George Town, after an uncomfortably strong wind. I think their vocabulary in general is considerably smaller than the average in the United States, but they far surpass us in their ability to embody abstractions in vivid, attractive, concrete images. The Baptist minister who owns the *Thunderbird*, describing how his helmsman sailed her through the storm to George Town, said, "I thought this boy would be very good. He was wonderful. Going through those seas. He felt them. He felt those seas. He put her down like paper,"—paper, calling up exactly the placing of a vessel's bulk against a big, oncoming sea so delicately she does not pound or labor, does not stagger, but touches gently down across its roiling surface.

Fred Green, when we stopped once on the way home from George Town to hunt for iguanas on a small, uninhabited cay (he and I bearers for the hunters, Rupert Bain and another of the crew who had brought a rifle) told me of his only previous experience with an iguana, a fairly small one, "half a fathom long." "I hit him with a rock and stagnated him but when I went to cut him with my cutlass he went in a hole," Fred said, using a better verb to describe the condition of the iguana than any I had heard of. Later, I told Leroy Bannister about the new sails of the Knowles clan of Deadman's Cay (Lisbon Creek's arch-rival), which they had made of imported American cotton duck, and of how much more efficient these sails were in moderate winds than the heavy, coarse canvas sails usual in the Bahamas. He nodded. "Light cloth feel the wind quicker," he said, con-cisely pointing out the wind's way with sails, how its slightest movement billows the light sail into action, curved and full, while heavy sails hang limp, wrinkled, unsentient.

Now, gliding along the protected chain of the Exumas, Rupert sneaked us through passages close to shore, which saved us time and kept us from reentering the open water farther out.

"Green, we got to pick our way through here," Rupert said. "Okay," Green said, and went to the bow. "Look okay here."

"All right. Pick your way across this next bay."

"Yas sir."

For the next hour Fred guided the *Alert* through narrow spaces between sandbars and jagged outcroppings of coral—depending entirely on the color of the water to tell him if the *Alert* were safe or not. The water was turquoise-blue and green where it was deep and sometimes the palest green, almost white, and over shoals it was dark blue or green streaked with red or brown or black. I had heard of this kind of piloting—which enables Bahamians to sail in waters filled with shoals and ledges with an assurance that American yachtsmen, even equipped with charts, depth finders, radio direction finders, and radar, cannot equal. Fred would bring us up to a shoal so that the bow of the *Alert* might be right over it, and then guide us off from it through a narrow twisting channel that sometimes was only inches deeper than our keel. If a channel led in a direction we could not sail, right into the wind, he might tell Rupert to sail hard to the edge of the channel and then tell him to head into the wind. The *Alert*, her sails shaking, would slow down. Fred counted on her momentum to carry her through the channel and into deep water again before she stopped. Preferring chances to prudence, if he saw a short cut over a shoal he would take it. He guided us through places where the clearance was nil. "Sail a little harder," he would say. "She may touch, but I believe she jump."

Our keel would hit bottom. Then, as we waited with our hearts in our mouths to see if we were stuck fast, it would jump clear. Fred would smile in relief.

The only alternative to this kind of sailing—which depended on Fred's ability to judge depths to within inches, was a detour out to deep water and then a long, probably wet beat to windward to get back.

We came to a line of coral across our path.

"Is there blue water ahead?" Rupert called to Fred.

"Yah, just keep her taut full."

Fred peered ahead at what looked like an impenetrable line of dark coral coming almost to the surface. "Don't luff. Don't do no luffing," he shouted.

"No," Rupert said.

"I want to jump this with good speed on."

We hit the shoal and jumped clear into deep water again.

"What we do with that shoal?" Rupert said, looking ahead at the next barrier in our path.

"I would go to loo'ard of it," Fred replied. "Head her down for the blue."

"Deep water inside of that other one?"

"Yah."

"Cross it, too?"

"Yah."

Agile, quick, and easily the most valuable man Rupert had on board, Fred Green was twenty-seven, a seaman, Baptist preacher, hymn singer, lover, father of five (one illegitimate), a good and happy man; he was tall, of that easy-moving, loose-jointed, long-thighed type of African, graceful and gangling at once or, more frequently, extremely graceful in motion and awkward as a straight-limbed wooden puppet in repose; and his face contained warmth and friendliness and also a vulnerability in relation to the commissioner and King Bain, who were non-seamen and clever, sophisticated, witty; he was shy and untalkative in the first days of our coming together, very seldom offering to join in the repartee, yet understanding it and laughing at it quite often, but as an outsider, the new boy in class, the new man at the Rotary lunch. Except for two brief breaks when Rupert anchored, he sat in the forward position on the windward rail, during the fifty-five hours of the storm, when all our weight plus that of the sandbags was needed there. During the two nights of the storm, when the rest of us retreated at last to the cabin, he had stayed at his station on the windward rail, curled up in a cold ball underneath a slicker which kept off the spray that was constantly drenching the boat but was no help against the films of water running in constantly renewed sheets down his section of the deck.

Green was quicker-witted than all of us. Toward noon of our first day on the *Alert*, during the worst of the storm, the little vessel went out of control. The reason may have been that our weight was too far aft for proper balance; we may have unconsciously inched toward the stern along the windward rail to try to avoid the spray. Or perhaps Rupert's dinghy, *Yellow Tie*, was too great a burden in those seas for the *Alert*. Anyway, the *Alert* turned into the wind and lay there stopped and lifeless in spite of Rupert's efforts at the helm to get her moving and responsive again. With the *Alert* no longer pulling, the dinghy began some travels of its own. We, lying tipped over quite far on our side, were absorbed in efforts to get the *Alert* moving again; two of us were manhandling the sandbags, ready to throw them to which-ever side proved to be the high side when the *Alert* did start sail-ing; one of us was holding a handle of the unwieldly washtub ready to slide it to the high side; John was below ready to move the sandbags we had there to the high side; Rupert was desper-ately trying to get the boat to obey its rudder; and Fred was on the bow, which was now plunging below the waves and scooping green water aboard, maneuvering the jib to try to make it act as a sort of air rudder and turn our bow away from the eye of the wind. Suddenly I saw the dinghy, on the crest of a wave in front of us, heading directly for the side of the *Alert*. I yelled; someone else, the commissioner I think, took a step toward the rail of the *Alert*, and Fred sprang into the dinghy, which was the only logi-cal move. My yelling would not stop the crash, nor could the commissioner have warded it off, and he might easily have crushed a foot or hand in trying. Fred landed on the two rails of the dinghy, one foot on each, a position impossible to maintain in such seas except that he had thought out his next move. The dinghy slid from the force of his jump a few feet out from the *Alert*, close enough to the *Alert*'s boom for him to grasp that with his hands and hold himself balanced in the dinghy. The boom, more than twenty feet long, lay at about a thirty-degree angle to the boat, just above the water. Fred hauled himself and the dinghy to its outer end and then in again so that he could come back aboard the *Alert*. He had to do this to get the dinghy and its tow line behind the boom so that the dinghy would drift safely astern. There was no other practical way to do this then, and I am sure that his instant perception of the only correct alternative and his timing saved the dinghy from severe damage. We were in no position to repair the dinghy in those seas, and if it had filled with water we might have had to abandon it, not only dashing Rupert's hopes for glory in the dinghy races at George Town, but leaving us without a lifeboat in a bad storm thirty or forty miles from the nearest land.

Fred saw what the wind was going to do before the rest of us. When he took the helm, he seemed built for the job. Homeward bound, in the only calm of the eight days of our being together, the rest of the crew was fretful and irritated, groaning, feeling sorry for ourselves, sweating, angry at the heat and this delay, each scheming to himself how to take over from the man who was sitting there, the one comfortable place on board, a small corner of shade near the mast. I looked forward and saw Green at the bow in the same blazing sun as the rest of us, singing quietly to himself and watching closely for whatever he might happen to see of interest on the bottom. It no more occurred to him to feel aggrieved at this turn of events than it had in the storm to rail at the shivering cold clammy wetness which had brought the rest of us, miserable and infuriated by the hardship, close to the end of our endurance. (By the rest of the crew, I mean King Bain and the commissioner and myself. I exclude from this contrast with Green both our skipper, Rupert, and John Rolle, who on a more formal ship would be called the mate, ageless—about fifty or sixty—the ancient seaman, a part of the boat, as he effortlessly does his job; relaxed, untalkative the rest of the time, having nothing to say because nothing much matters except the boat, not that he loves that life but only that that is life—sailing. Dark, wizened, small, wiry, his exact counterparts have manned ships everywhere.)

Beyond us now in the shoal waters lay another long strip of dark water. Fred, standing on the bow and holding easily, almost carelessly, onto a shroud, watched it approach.

"Anywhere you see we could jump this bank?" Rupert called.

Fred, still undecided, did not reply.

"We could go right across?" Rupert said.

Rupert said louder: "Do you know what I said?"

"Yas, sir."

The commissioner broke in, "You better go down around it."

"Hold her full," Green cut in loudly. "Another channel is heading in."

Rupert did as Fred told him. He looked nervous. "Is all right?"

There was no reply from Fred. Finally he shouted, "All yours!"—the signal that we were through the shoal and Rupert could sail as he pleased.

Anyone who has ever raced with Bahamians notices that the skipper shares many of his decisions with the man stationed at the bow, so that it is almost accurate to say the bow man is as responsible as the skipper for the outcome. I think the origin of this practice is in their navigation of shoal waters, where the skipper depends entirely on the judgment of his look-out man in the bow and, in effect, turns command of the ship over to him. Whenever we had to tack to keep us in the channels, Fred, not Rupert, decided when. "Good full," Fred would yell and then signal the precise moment for the turn, "Gone!" Rupert would throw the tiller hard down to leeward, we would duck our heads as the boom came across, and the *Alert* would head into the wind, her canvas shaking, and then fill on the new tack.

When Fred's piloting was needed, he remained at the bow, leaning carelessly against the shrouds, humming a tune or listening with an amused smile to the repartee of King and the commissioner, a picture of the relaxed, happy Bahamian sailor.

The *Yachtsmen's Guide to the Bahamas* states that Bahamian sailors cannot use their method of piloting at night or in overcast weather. Fred was still piloting us by the color of the water three hours after sunset.

He led us through a series of narrow channels between cays in which we had to tack frequently, until it was really dark. We anchored until dawn near a settlement named Rolleville. It was a half-day's sail from there to George Town. Part of the sail was in the open ocean, on the east side of the Exumas out of their lee. Spray drenched us all again, but with our destination so close, none of us cared. After we anchored at George Town, a sixty-two-foot yawl came in, one of the ocean-racing yachts that had delayed its departure from Nassau. The owner told me he had followed us for several hours. He had only his mizzen and a staysail up—two very small sails—and had his engine going. The little *Alert,* one third his size, had full sail on.

Five boats had started and four finished. Alfred Bain in the *Mystery J.* won the race. The Reverend Elton McFee in the *Thunderbird* was second, Harcourt Hepburn in the *Lady A.* was third, and we in the *Alert* were fourth. Mr. McFee is convinced that he would have beaten the *Mystery J.* if he had not stopped to help the men on the *Headline* when she was dismasted; there is no way of telling. Our last place was natural, as the *Alert,* the smallest boat in the race, was more affected than the others by the big seas of the storm.

Rupert anchored alongside a graceful little round-stemmed sloop, on which I saw for the first time the chief rivals, men from Deadman's Cay. Most of them were young, blond, blue-eyed. The skipper, a grizzled, middle-aged man who was, Rupert said, a great seaman, nodded to Rupert. "Rough going out there!" he said.

"Yah. Long trip. Long trip from Lisbon Creek," Rupert replied.

By now the quirks of each of us had been revealed; there had been time for these to be examined by each of the others in this ship's company, to be accepted, made allowance for, with liking and respect. We respected Rupert for his competence and fairness—which is all a crew has a right to feel it can demand of its captain—but our feeling toward him included more: appreciation of a strength he had, to lead without being overbearing and at the same time to be one of us without his or our ever forgetting who he was.

III

George Town's little harbor was full of sloops. Most, like the ones from Lisbon Creek, were straight-stemmed, without bow sprits, with the typical wine-glass stern of the Bahamas and the overhanging rudders. A few had round-stemmed bows, giving them a look of miniature Grand Banks fishermen. Captains and crews were looking over each others' boats and gear; dinghies carrying laughing men and women darted here and there across the harbor; boys swam from shore to boats and back; a fishing sloop in a far state of disrepair—its mildewed sails patched a thousand times, its broken boom rudely splinted, its sides and deck almost bare of paint—was anchored in the midst of the freshly painted and yacht-like contestants, and its crew was peddling fish from boat to boat in an ancient dinghy; ashore, crowds of brightly clothed men, women, and children rambled along the harbor's edge and on the settlement's one street.

Alfred and Rupert, with most of their crews trailing behind them, strolled around George Town, stopping to talk with old friends from other settlements or to buy conch balls or other carnival delicacies from open-air vendors and restaurants on the street. A group of captains, Alfred and Rupert among them, with their crews standing back respectfully, would meet and gossip about wind and weather, past regattas, changes in rig and equipment. After our stroll from end to end of George Town, I went down to the harbor's edge, where there were two or three dozen dinghies drawn up on the shore or moored just off it. Men and boys, sometimes with wives and sisters watching, were polishing bottoms or whittling out pieces of equipment—a new cleat, perhaps, or a tiller—or examining their sails for any ravels in the seams.

I met two of the Knowles family from Deadman's Cay. They told me that there were twenty-nine men at the regatta from Long Island (where Deadman's Cay is located), and all but three of them were Knowleses. For them, the coming contest was going to be between the *Thunderbird* and a sloop built by the head of their family, Rupert Knowles. His sloop, the *Margaret L.*, beat the *Thunderbird* and won first place in both the 1962 and 1963 regattas. Besides the *Margaret L.*, the Knowleses had five other sloops entered in the regatta, the others smaller and lighter. One of them, the *Susan Chase*, was new this year, and would do well, they said.

A little distance away I found Alfred with his dinghy, the *Jet*, turned upside down on the shore. He was planing the *Jet*'s racing keel, getting ready for the afternoon dinghy race. He handled the plane with the same offhand sureness that had amazed me in Lisbon Creek when the Reverend Livingston Bethel sharpened a pencil with an ax, talking and hardly looking at the pencil. Alfred was tapering the leading and trailing edges of the racing keel so that the leading edge was rounded somewhat bluntly and the trailing edge came almost to a knife edge. This is a refinement with which the leading design theorists in such advanced racing classes as the International Fourteen Dinghy were experimenting at the same time. Their experiments were based on aerodynamics, the lift and drag formulas of wing sections; Alfred's were based, I suppose, on observation and intuition.

The next day Alfred came in first in the sloop race in the *Mystery*; in the dinghy race in the afternoon, he came in first in the *Jet*. In the second day's racing—again a sloop race in the morning and a dinghy race in the afternoon—he was second in the *Mystery*, behind the *Thunderbird*, and first again in the *Jet*.

The *Mystery* and the *Thunderbird* entered the last day of racing tied for first place. The day was clear. The wind was light—a handicap for the *Mystery*. The two sloops sailed out of the harbor well before the starting time and anchored on the line where, as in Bahamian-style racing, they would wait until the starting gun fired to set sail. Others joined them. There was some milling around: race officials made some boats, anchored too far ahead, move back; skippers of others moved of their own accord after deciding their first choice was in a disadvantageous position, too close to a bigger sloop or too far to leeward. There was much good-natured calling from boat to boat, joking, clowning; at first sight everyone seemed completely relaxed, but if you looked closer you saw signs that everyone was really tense, keyed-up, worried.

The warning gun went off. Men jumped to their places on each sloop, two men at the main halyard, one at the jib halyard, and the rest strung out in a row from the bow past the mast down the deck to the fish well, with the anchor line in their hands. The starting gun fired. Instantly all was commotion up and down the line of sloops—cries and cheers of bow men spurring on their crews; whistles of spectator boats; yells of eager crewmen packed around the masts and on the narrow, bobbing foredecks of the sloops; impatient orders from the captains; shouts of alarm or anger at a fouled halyard, an anchor overshot, a near miss or a hit by another boat, its half-raised sails filling and collapsing with puffs of wind, its anchor line coming aboard with such speed the boat itself was out of control.

On the *Mystery*, the sheaves whirred in the halyard blocks at the masthead; the shaking sails in their fast ascent whipped and cracked around the three men hoisting them; the mainsail halfway up, filled with wind and not yet clear of the deck, pressed down on the row of crewmen tugging and straining like desperados on the anchor line. It folded around two of them, nearly toppling them overboard. Jonathan Rolle, at the bow with the dripping anchor line running between his spread legs, shouted to the men behind him, "Haul her! Haul her! Haul her!" A man further down the line, gasping, croaked hoarsely, "Pull on that! Pull on that!" The *Mystery* shot ahead. Jonathan grabbed the anchor line out of the hands of the men next to him and took it outside the shrouds back to the fish well, so that the anchor came aboard not at the bow but amidships. Before it reached the deck, the *Mystery* was sailing fast, past a green boat that had been alongside her at the start, past the *Thunderbird*, past the *Margaret L.*

"Haul in the jib! Haul in the jib!" Alfred shouted. Two men slid down the deck to the jib-sheet cleat.

"Don't pull her in too much," Jonathan said. "Let her catch the air."

Alfred said: "That's right, let it catch the air. Then haul it in tight."

We crouched along the windward rail from Jonathan, at the bow, almost to the stern. The last in the line, a skinny little man, a retired fisherman and now a Baptist preacher, leaned far out to windward. "Heel out! Heel out!" he shouted.

Jonathan, prone on the bow, watched the sails with narrowed eyes. He whispered fiercely to two men behind him, "Tighten up your jib. It slacken down." Without standing, lest their shift of weight or the wind resistance of their bodies slow the *Mystery* down, they hoisted the sail taut again.

The sails were blocking the view to leeward, but to windward the only boats we saw were far behind, some still on the starting line, others jammed together so the sails of the windward boats cut off the wind from the boats to leeward of them. The *Margaret L.* had been to windward of us on the starting line. We gave her a big dose of backwind as she slid off to leeward behind us, and now, even after she was clear of our disturbed air, she sailed slower than we. We could not see the

Thunderbird, but she was anchored six or eight boats to leeward of us on the starting line—distance she would have to gain to get to the first mark. Her anchor was still down when we left the line.

The fear of a mistake, the anxiety and suspense before the starting gun, and the sixty seconds' fury and intense concentration after the gun changed to elation. If we can only keep her going, we thought—we're in the lead—we have the whole fleet behind us—the *Thunderbird*'s behind us—the race, the whole regatta, is sewed up—not quite sewed up, of course, but if we can only keep her going. Keep going, *Mystery*, we said to ourselves. The preacher said it aloud: "Keep going, keep going, *Mystery*."

Alfred was sitting poised and expectant on the deck behind the little preacher, one hand on the tiller, the other on the rail, balancing the sea, the sky, the sails, the hull, his face drawn, skin tight over the high cheekbones, eyes intent, thin lips in a single line—in attitude like a conductor in a delicate fortissimo passage, on tiptoe in his effort to balance the different sections of his orchestra and draw forth from the musicians precisely the tone, the mood, the tempo he was attempting to achieve. He eased the *Mystery*'s bow a trifle closer to the wind, keeping a slightest quiver in the mainsail near the mast until the quiver grew to the exact dimension he was aiming for. When the wind, which came in puffs, lightened, he reduced the quiver in the mainsail to almost nothing, to the merest suggestion. His face showed almost pain, but it was not pain, rather sensitivity, affectibility, susceptibility, to any change around him, in shape of waves, the sky's aspect, the motion of his vessel, the heft of the wind in the sails, as if the rudder were his fingertips, the hull his body, the sails his cheeks.

If you looked closely, you could see that Alfred held the *Mystery*'s tiller as a violinist does a bow, his wrist relaxed. He let her sail herself a little bit even now, going to windward, when a boat allowed to do as she pleases invariably tries to head up into

the wind and stop. Even so, he responded as much as he di-
rected, catching the *Mystery* up lightly, giving her her way as
much as possible.

"Heel out! Heel out! Heel out!" the little preacher shouted
again from his command post just ahead of Alfred. Jonathan
lifted a corner of the jib to look to leeward. He saw the *Thunderbird*. "Coming up! Coming up!" he shouted to Alfred in alarm.
Alfred glanced to leeward and back to the sails. Though not one
of the crew along the windward rail could see the *Thunderbird*,
nor had Jonathan said it was she, yet seeing the intense coun-
tenance of Alfred, they knew that it was and that she was threatening to steal the lead. A moment later, a flaw in the wind
righted the *Mystery* and they caught a glimpse of the *Thunderbird* in the space between the bottom of the *Mystery*'s mainsail
and her rail. She was a hundred feet away, inching ahead, sailing
faster, pointing higher. They turned resentful glances toward
Alfred, as if it were his fault.

"Watch the jib, mon! Watch the jib! Loose out!" Alfred yelled
at the jib-sheet man.

"We stopped, stopped, stopped! We ain't sailing like yesterday," Jonathan cried.

Slowly, inexorably, the *Thunderbird* worked her way from to
leeward of the *Mystery* across her bow and up to windward. The
wind lightened. Nothing we tried did any good. The *Mystery*'s
old nemesis—light air—was robbing her again. The little
preacher moved in from the rail. The rest of the crew moved in,
too; there was no longer enough wind to heel the *Mystery* over.
The excitement on the *Mystery* since the start became despair,
exaltation dashed, anger, disbelief. We watched the *Thunderbird*, heeled over in a better breeze than ours, sailing away, carrying our hopes in her wake.

"Go inshore?" Alfred called to Jonathan.

"Up to you." A moment later, Jonathan added: "In this light
air, never cotch the *Thunderbird* by following. Go some place
different, maybe find some wind."

"Yah. Okay." Alfred left the timing of the tack to Jonathan.

"Get ready!" Jonathan shouted.

"Okay."

"Come about!"

"Gone!" Alfred shouted, but instead of pushing the tiller down to bring the *Mystery* around onto the other tack, he checked himself. "No! No! *Thunderbird* tacking!"

"Yah," Jonathan said in approval of Alfred's quick change of plans. "We stay on this tack then."

Soon after the *Thunderbird*'s tack, Jonathan turned aft to call to Alfred. "We could heavy the sail."

"That's all right," Alfred said, engrossed in nursing the *Mystery* through a small puff of wind that glanced down on her. When the puff went by, he changed his mind. "You could damp the sail," he said.

A young crewman, Arlington Stuart, snatched up a bucket, dashed water on the mainsail.

"On the top. Not too much on the bottom," Jonathan said.

He and Alfred kept glancing toward shore, where the *Thunderbird* was heading and where most of the fleet was. "More wind in there?" Alfred said.

"Can't say—it dumping out here a little, I think."

"Yah, we go in," Alfred said. "Get ready. Gone!"

As he tacked toward shore, one of the Knowles sloops, the *Susan Chase,* a Class B boat that, amazingly, was staying up with the leaders of Class A, tacked out.

"That leetle boat make us tack," the preacher shouted angrily.

"I doubt it; we see," Jonathan replied, in a tone suggesting that it was up to him, not the little preacher, to decide if we would have to tack to avoid a collision. We cleared her bow by a few feet.

Near shore, we came about again. Now Jonathan could see the first mark easily, three or four hundred feet away.

"Going to fetch it?" Alfred said.

"I don't know," Jonathan said. He looked under the *Mystery*'s jib at the *Thunderbird*. "*Thunderbird* ain't," he said.

Now, with more wind again, the *Mystery* was sailing faster and pointing higher than the *Thunderbird*. If the *Thunderbird* could not fetch the mark, if she had to tack to get around it, the *Mystery* might catch her. As the *Thunderbird* neared the mark, and as it seemed certain she would have to tack to fetch it, and as the crew of the *Mystery* held their breaths, hoping, then expecting, then sure she would have to tack, she picked up a slant of wind that carried her up to the mark and, as the little preacher groaned, around it.

She sailed off before the wind down the sound in front of George Town, her immense mainsail all the way out on one side of her, her jib all the way out on the other. The *Susan Chase* followed. The *Margaret L.*, looking light and fast, sailing beautifully on the other tack with a fresher breeze she was bringing with her, crowded around just behind the *Susan Chase* and passed her. The *Mystery* was a hundred feet astern. As she went around, Alfred saw activity on the *Margaret L.*'s deck.

"*Margaret L.* getting more sail up?" he shouted.

"Yah."

Without any more words from Alfred, Arlington Stuart sprang to the mast and up it with a line to reave through a block at the masthead and slid down fast, using the lacing of the sail to the mast. He and Jonathan hauled the mainsail from Alfred's dinghy up the mast, ahead of the mast, and set it like a spinnaker —just a few seconds after the *Margaret L.*'s crew set hers. They left the boom on it, but not the mast. The sail set well. Now they planned intricate steps to lower it at the end of this leg and rig it for possible use on the next leg—a beat to windward back to the finish line—as quickly as possible. For the beat, they would use the sail as a topsail. They would have to lace it back to the dinghy mast and then hoist the mast, with the sail and boom attached, above the *Mystery*'s mast. It seemed nearly impossible to me.

The rest of the fleet followed the four leaders in bunches, three at a time, then two, then one, then a space, turning the mark, sometimes dueling at the turn, until all of them had rounded and set off down the sound before the wind. The colors of the water, shading from darkest blue to palest sandy-green, almost white, with here and there casts of reds and browns; the many different greens of the land; the shapes of the seductive palms; the newness of the clean-complexioned air—all of this added to the grandeur of the sight: thirty sails strung out in long procession down the sound—flashes of white on the blue-green coruscations of the water—an armada of windships sailing majestically past the buildings of George Town on their left and the hills, palms, and beaches of a large island on their right. A few of the American tourists at the Club Peace and Plenty walked down to the water's edge to glance briefly at the boats and then went back to their drinks at poolside on the patio.

The *Mystery* slid easily along on an even keel, her crew sprawled about on the deck amidships, her skipper, now the dinghy sail was drawing well, for once relaxed and almost easygoing, and even the little preacher, for the moment, done with exhortations.

The *Susan Chase* was between the *Margaret L.* and the *Mystery*, hidden by the *Mystery*'s mainsail. Alfred, who seemed to think of her as too small to be real, had referred to her for three days as "that little thing."

"Where that leetle thing?" he called to Jonathan.

"Down to loo'ard."

"We overtaking her?"

"Some," Jonathan said in a tone indicating no need to worry. In a moment she came out from behind the *Mystery*'s sail. The *Mystery* was gaining on her rapidly.

There were four Knowles-built boats around the *Mystery*— the *Margaret L.* and the *Susan Chase* ahead, and two other *Susan Chase*-sized sloops quite far behind.

"Them fellers good at cutting sail—eh?" Alfred said.

"Yah."

"I was looking at this leetle thing here," Alfred said, nodding toward the *Susan Chase*.

"Their boats good in this kind of wind. Light. Light built."

Alfred's eyes went back to his own boat, to her trim, to her rigging, to her sails. They stopped at the jib. The worried tone of his usual discourse with Jonathan returned.

"That sail—go up or down?"

"She can go up."

"Let her go up, then."

The *Mystery* passed the *Susan Chase*, but she was still losing steadily to the *Margaret L.* and the *Thunderbird*.

"*Thunderbird* sailing good, Jonathan."

"Better'n she ever has in moderate weather."

Their talk—idle, disappointed comment—petered out. They stared ahead.

"I start pretty good."

"Yah, she let you down good on that," a crew member from amidships said—blaming the *Mystery* for faltering after we had succeeded in getting her away from the starting line at the head of the fleet, with clear air, with nothing between her and the first mark.

Amidships the talk was desultory too, except for the little preacher, who, full of zeal for his technique, criticized Alfred—not addressing him directly, but well within his hearing—for his tactics when the *Thunderbird* passed him. "The only way I should stick with this vessel, when she go by, is if she can't do anything on you. I would of tacked and cut the *Margaret L.* and maybe beat the *Thunderbird* too." Someone pointed out to him, "Can't stop the *Thunderbird*. If she going faster, can't stop her."

We rounded the second mark two hundred yards behind the *Thunderbird* and one hundred yards behind the *Margaret L.*—too far in the short beat to the finish line to overtake either. Alfred followed them into shore. They tacked out. He kept on into a little cove, looking for a favorable breeze and because the best strategy when behind is to get away from your opponents, not follow in their tracks.

In the cove, Jonathan yelled to Alfred, "Tide lowing you."

"Yah. We go around then," Alfred said. "Gone!"

As the *Mystery* went around, Jonathan grabbed the arm of the man pulling in the jib sheet. "Don't pull her in now; let her cotch the air first."

As the *Mystery* cleared the cove, a series of headers, new wind from a new direction, glanced down on her from the sound —the first decent breeze of the race. Alfred misjudged the first one. The jib luffed, spilling some of the new wind.

"Take some of this! Take some of this!" Jonathan cried in dismay. Alfred recovered quickly. The *Mystery* heeled over; a line began drumming on the mast; the bow wave, a slow brook's lapping until now, deepened; the puffy sails hardened into parts of spheres; the deck canted over more. Her crew, forgetting the hopelessness of their position, came alive again, quickened by the freshening breeze and the *Mystery*'s new sprightliness. "Heel out! Heel out! Heel out!" the little preacher shouted happily, and Arlington Stuart's seventeen-year-old brother, Elon, who had been reserved the whole race, in consciousness of being youngest, surprised everyone with a loud "Wahoo!"

The little preacher turned to Alfred as to an old colleague. "Breeze got a good jawful now," he said. "Good jawful." Then facing back toward the bow, away from Alfred, he repeated over and over to himself, or to the *Mystery*, "Come on, come on, come on." Soon, fired by the *Mystery*'s increasing speed, he began giving Alfred directions. "All right. Hold her just like that! Hold her just like that! Don't luff her! Don't!" as if Alfred were new to sailing and he, the little preacher, were the skipper. He raised his voice to the crew, "In the puffs, heel out! In the puffs, heel out!"

Alfred made four quick tacks, each timed precisely with a wind shift. The jib would begin to luff, signaling the shift. He would shout: "Get ready—Gone!" and dash the helm hard down to leeward; the *Mystery*'s bow would shoot up into the wind, her crew would scramble to the windward rail, then he, working deliberately, would bring the tiller back amidships slowly and even a little to windward of amidships, pause a few seconds while the *Mystery* gathered headway, and, with her sheets pulled in tight, drive her slicing up to windward, pointing high, sailing fast. When the wind shifted back he shouted: "Get ready —gone!" and tacked again. The *Mystery* never lost headway in the tacks; instead, each time she swung into the wind, sails shaking, she stole a length or two up to windward before falling off on the new tack.

Alfred tacked with the headers, stayed on the tack trending closest to the finish line, tacked toward more wind when he saw it. The other two zigzagged up the sound in long tacks. The *Mystery*, lively now, almost dancing, responsive, straining ahead, gained steadily. But the *Thunderbird* was near the finish. She picked up a temporary lift, held it just long enough, and came about. "The boys tack good on that one," Jonathan said. "Going home on that."

The *Margaret L.* made a bad tack and on the *Mystery* eight pairs of eyes watched her with the beginnings of a surging hope. She was slow in gaining headway on the new tack. Rupert Knowles, glancing at the *Mystery* repeatedly, tried to make the *Margaret L.* sail close to the wind, but she couldn't do it; she began slowing down. Rupert Knowles allowed the *Margaret L.* to fall off the wind slightly to regain headway. The little preacher saw a stratagem in this. "He's reaching down on us, don't you see? He's reaching down on us," he cried.

His theory, that Rupert Knowles would maneuver into a position to give the *Mystery* a dose of bad air from his sails, proved wrong. Rupert tacked away from us. As he completed the tack, we heard a gun from the finish line and the sirens and horns of spectator boats.

"Ah yah, he get it," Alfred said, all the strain of the race in his voice. The regatta was the *Thunderbird*'s.

But even the sealing of the *Mystery*'s defeat did not dampen the excitement aboard her. The *Margaret L.* was headed for the finish line on a tack that looked as if it would carry her across. The *Mystery* was a hundred feet behind her, slightly to windward. She was sailing faster and pointing higher. If the *Margaret L.* could not reach the finish line without coming about and making one more tack, the *Mystery* had a chance. The *Margaret L.* came about. As she gathered headway on the new tack, it looked as if she had tacked too soon. She was heading almost parallel to the finish line and, on that course, would have to sail its entire length before coming about again. The *Mystery* kept gaining. Alfred sailed a couple of boat lengths past the place where the *Margaret L.* tacked before coming about. He brought the *Mystery* up into the wind, held her there a moment until her momentum carried her closer to the line, then brought her around on to the new tack. He let her fall off with her sheets slightly eased until she was sailing at top speed, then, instead of following the *Margaret L.* on a course parallel to the finish, he brought her sheets in flat, paused, and shot the *Mystery* straight up into the wind again. She headed for the finish line, sails shaking, slowing down. Her momentum carried her across.

Her crew had been excited in this maneuver and so taken up with following precise instructions from Alfred and Jonathan— who saw what Alfred was trying before it dawned on the rest of them—that they had lost track of the *Margaret L.* The last time they had looked she was somewhere down to leeward, not fetching the line, but involved in another tack to gain it. Now they saw that she had crossed ahead—but not by much. Alfred had halved the distance between them in the last few minutes of the race.

No one said much during the sail into the harbor. When the *Mystery* passed the *Margaret L.*, already anchored and her crew lounging on deck waiting for some other members of the Knowles family to come out in a dinghy to take them ashore, Alfred smiled and nodded at Rupert Knowles. "Ay, you take me today," he said. But no one was thinking of the *Margaret L.* Their minds were on the *Thunderbird.* Jonathan, now partway aft instead of in his place in the bow, shook his head. "When the breeze come up, we started to cotch him," he said. We all agreed that we had been catching the *Thunderbird* at the end of the race.

"I think I lose my nerve," Alfred said, a little later, apparently in reference to a jibe he had made that did not satisfy him. His mind went back to the *Thunderbird.* "He beat us worse than he ever did," he said, and after another pause, "But when we had a breeze in the first race, he didn't beat us."

The little Baptist preacher said an amazing thing. Filled with longing for what might have been, he said: "If we go out again, I like to have a chance. I like to have a chance on one tack," meaning he thought that he might have done what Alfred could not—sail the *Mystery* to victory in light air. Alfred smiled.

Howland Bottomley, an American yachtsman who helps run the Out Island Regatta, told me he considers Alfred the best sailor among the several hundred who gather annually at George Town. Bottomley comes from a different tradition from Alfred's, pleasure boating, but his judgment is worthy of respect. And I saw Alfred's skill, his ability to make a boat move through the water with grace and efficiency, in two races I sailed aboard the *Mystery,* but more particularly illustrated in a kind of sideshow to the races for the *Mystery*'s class of boats—the dinghy races held between the main events.

Alfred won two of the three races and led in the third until a wind shift caught him unawares and he lost the lead a few yards from the finish line. I watched that race from a judges' boat with Bottomley, about thirty feet from the first mark of the course, which Alfred came to first, sailing close hauled, with his sail all the way in and his boat tipping so that water almost came over its side. He rounded precisely, in a fairly tight U, synchronizing his turn and his letting out of the sail so that the sail stayed full and the boat moved fast during the entire rounding. A few seconds later he jibed, the most hair-raising maneuver one can make in a sailboat when the sail and boom are shifted suddenly, from all the way out on one side of the boat to all the way out on the other. He lost no time in the jibe, his sail did not flap, and there was no unsightly rocking of the boat. At the second mark, his procedure was the opposite of that at the first. He went around it in a wide arc, at the same time hauling the sail in. He positioned himself at the beginning of the rounding so that at its close he was beside the mark sailing full speed in almost the opposite direction. The others slowed down at the mark because their turns were too sudden, or else ended by sailing a boat length or two too far—which is not to say that they were clumsy sailors, but that a perfect rounding is rare. Alfred's rounding made Bottomley smile with pleasure and caused the others on his boat who knew enough to understand what they were witnessing to nod and smile back. Each of his two roundings increased his lead, I would judge, by ten seconds or more.

The boat that passed Alfred's in the final seconds of the race was Rupert's *Yellow Tie*, Rupert outfoxing the fox, his cousin Alfred. He came from perhaps a hundred and fifty feet behind at the second mark and his gaining was hidden from Alfred's view and ours by a fleet of yachts anchored beside the race course. After Alfred rounded the second mark, he tacked toward shore. Rupert followed. Alfred tacked out again toward the middle of the sound in which the race was held. Rupert didn't. He stayed in, zigzagging along the shore in several quick tacks. Alfred tacked in again to cover Rupert, but too late; on the way in he ran into a calm place that made him decide—perhaps rightly, perhaps wrongly—that he had to go back to the middle for better wind. This left Rupert in the clear. He found a wind shift close to shore that allowed him to head right for the finish and cross it just ahead of Alfred. His victory made it a Bain series from start to finish. The two times Alfred won, Rupert was second; the time Rupert won, Alfred was second; in all three races the other twenty-five competitors trailed in their wake.

Rupert and Alfred are both in their fifties, Rupert compact and sturdy, Alfred lithe and long. Alfred has an ascetic look, not thin and agonized but containing, nevertheless, a suggestion of withdrawal to a little distance away, in the eyes, in the taut, high cheekbones, in the sensitive, thin mouth, most apparent in the eyes: wisdom, perhaps also resignation, is what I saw in his eyes. Rupert is everyman—indomitable, decent, doing his work staunchly without questioning purposes or design. Alfred is poet and dreamer.

Ashore they were usually together, partaking in their moderate Anglican way of three or four beers in the carnival nights at George Town and Rolleville, Rupert completely involved in the conferences and comparisons with other captains, Alfred involved but slightly apart, so that, for instance, if someone told a joke, he laughed with the others, but in a way that made you think he saw more than the point of the joke, perhaps some folly or tragedy behind it. Usually in their travels around George Town several of their crews followed each, like a retinue, which gave their movements the air of princely strolls—in Alfred's case, particularly, because of the deliberate and elegant way he walked and talked. "He is a gentleman and a sailor," Bottomley said to me. He is.

He is also probably the greatest boatbuilder at one of the three major boatbuilding centers of the Bahamas. I, and not only I but many people, considered the *Mystery* the most beautiful boat in the races, because of the sharpness and flare of her bow and the delicate and neat proportions of her stern. It does not seem clumsy or ill-fitting to ascribe to her the quality of tragedy. I never asked Alfred, but I believe it probable that the *Mystery* contains the best that he knows and has within him, that, in other words, if he were given the opportunity to build a new fishing boat today, he could not improve on her, or at least he does not know any way of doing so now. Her flaw, then, which is in no way a flaw of concept or construction but entirely the result of the introduction of lighter woods since she was built

(*Thunderbird* and Rupert Knowles' *Margaret L.* are planked with the much lighter American pine) strikes at his mastery in his calling, mastery of the very mysteries he implied in the naming of the boat he had conquered. It strikes at his manhood because if she is his best and she is quite regularly defeated, what good is he? That he knows she is as fast as her two chief rivals, the *Thunderbird* and the *Margaret L.*, that she has proved it often when the wind has blown hard enough, as it did in the first race, to offset their advantage of lighter wood and put all three vessels on an equal footing, does not change this. Instead, it makes it worse. Every time she is defeated, Alfred's artistry—as builder, as sailor—is called into doubt. The regattas are a testing and an exhibition. They are an art show in which his concepts, inventiveness, and virtuosity cannot be judged because of this flaw—Andros pine instead of American pine—which hides his entry's true excellencies.

Alfred is not in a position to build another boat. His one great effort, the building of the *Mystery*, left him with two boats when he has need of only one. The *Mystery* was an extravagance, an investment of time and money in an abstraction, an ideal. But he is a fisherman, for whom a boat is a tool. That a boat is beautiful, that she is fast, that she is lightsome, are ornaments to his career, not necessities.

Alfred talks sometimes of stripping all the Andros pine planking off the *Mystery* and replanking her with American pine. Like the building of the *Mystery* in the first place, this would be expensive, time-consuming, and unjustified, because it would in no way make the *Mystery* a better fishing boat. Alfred has no margin of savings nor do the traditions of his profession, fishing, include an understanding and tolerance of purely artistic work. Yet I would like to see Alfred justify it to himself because I think the *Mystery* might prove to be very fast in light winds if she were free of her heavy coat of Andros pine. She is not as ponderous looking as the *Thunderbird,* and even though the Knowleses' boats are built for sailing in protected waters, not for open-ocean work as the *Mystery* was, and therefore should have the advantage in light winds, I believe Alfred put some speed in her lines that the Knowleses, good as they are, don't yet know how to do. As she is, she is as delicate and frisky as the others, or more so, in my opinion, only a bit slower in light winds because of her extra weight.

I think the sadness I see in Alfred's eyes comes in part from the failure of his masterpiece and also from the departure of his one son, who has obeyed the womanly injunction in Lisbon Creek to stay off the sea and has followed the lure of our technology; he has gone to Nassau, leaving Alfred a master of his profession, equipped with two of the finest boats in his business, and nowhere to look forward to but to a gradual failing and falling off of what he has built. In the meantime, however, there are days when the wind blows strong and the *Mystery* passes the others or gives them a hard race, or, if not racing but fishing, when she responds with a characteristic quickness to her master's hand on the tiller and, through a combining of his skill and her good sailing qualities, he and she together achieve the maximum potentialities of both, an attainment whose effect has no name but might be like the sensation a golfer feels in the moment during and immediately after making a perfect drive, and which on a sailboat is sustained and as variable in its forms as the varieties of the wind and the many different shapes of the sea. It comes in one way—a quiet exhilaration or hugging of oneself—in a light wind because you have been able through your own delicate perceptiveness to understand what the barely noticeable drafts of air around you are doing and have been able, by combining your understanding with the boat's nimbleness and sensitivity, to convert these wayward drafts of air into forward motion. It comes in another way in a storm, when your own brute force is added to your intellect as a reason for the success of the sail, and added too are fear and a feeling of outwitting the wind and the sea, which now have become enemies and threats, and a sense of awe at their magnificence in their wildness. As in a calm, the boat itself is a part of the attainment; in a storm it is her ability to stand up to high winds and heavy seas, to survive. When the boat is your creation, the feeling I have been attempting to describe, which now I think might be partially contained in the words "pride" and "delight," must, I should think, increase. So Alfred has this and will have it during the days and the years he stays in business, and I suppose he can look back on it with pleasure when he is too old to go out on the sea—and this, I believe, is more than many people ever have.

A NOTE ABOUT THE AUTHOR

WENDELL P. BRADLEY

was born in Northampton, Massachusetts, in 1927 and begin his love affair with the sea during youthful summers spent on the Maine coast. A graduate of Bowdoin, he received an M.A. in political science from the University of Chicago. From 1953 to 1964 he was a reporter for THE WASHINGTON POST, *writing feature articles and covering Maryland politics. A champion racer in his own right (in the International 14 Class) his articles on sailing have appeared in* HOLIDAY, RUD-DER, YACHTING, *and other magazines. A few years before his tragic death in 1967 in an automobile accident, he made the decision to leave the city and live with the people he had come to know and deeply admire—the oystermen of Chesapeake Bay. While writing this book, he learned the oystering trade and eventually captained his own skipjack, the* ESTHER F. *He was a leader in the effort to conserve the sailing oysterboats, the last vestige of our nation's maritime heritage, and he soon became a well-loved and respected figure along the Eastern Shore of Maryland.*

A NOTE ON THE TYPE

This book was set on the Linotype in a face called Primer, designed by Rudolph Ruzicka, who was earlier responsible for the design of Fairfield and Fairfield Medium, Linotype faces whose virtues have for some time been accorded wide recognition.

The complete range of sizes of Primer was first made available in 1954, although the pilot size of 12-point was ready as early as 1951. The design of the face makes general reference to Linotype Century—long a serviceable type, totally lacking in manner or frills of any kind—but brilliantly corrects its characterless quality.

The book was composed, printed, and bound by The Haddon Craftsmen, Inc., Scranton, Pennsylvania. Typography and binding design by Betty Anderson.